THE HISTORY OF
THE CREEDS

THE HISTORY OF
THE CREEDS

by

F. J. BADCOCK, D.D.

Fellow of St Augustine's College, Canterbury
Author of *Reviews and Studies,
Biblical and Doctrinal*

*The Pauline Epistles and the Epistle to the Hebrews
in their Historical Setting*

SECOND EDITION

Published for the Church Historical Society

LONDON
SOCIETY FOR PROMOTING
CHRISTIAN KNOWLEDGE
NEW YORK: THE MACMILLAN CO.
1938

First Edition 1930
Second Edition, largely rewritten 1938

PRINTED IN GREAT BRITAIN

CONTENTS

PART I

THE APOSTLES' CREED

CONTENTS

PART III
THE *QUICUMQUE VULT*

PART IV
THE "COMMUNION OF SAINTS" AS AN ARTICLE OF THE CREED

PREFACE TO THE SECOND EDITION

No student of the history of liturgies can afford to neglect the evidence furnished by baptismal Creeds. These were an intrinsic, though only an occasional, part of the liturgy, and in the absence of direct evidence to the contrary, evidence which is not forthcoming until the seventh century, it is a fair presumption that the type of Creed would be an index of the type of liturgy in use; and thanks to many sermons and instructions on the Creed we possess a far more detailed knowledge of the local baptismal Creed than we do of the remainder of the rite during the first five hundred years of the Christian religion.

In consequence of this I have felt myself at liberty to introduce a far larger bulk of liturgical matter and thereby to defend myself against the criticisms of the reviewer for *The Times Literary Supplement*, who thought that I had exaggerated the liturgical influence of the patriarchate of Antioch.

In this regard and for many other helpful suggestions, I am much indebted to Dr Cuthbert Atchley, to whose judgment all the new liturgical matter has been submitted.

In the former edition there were four or five major blunders besides numerous minor slips. I owe the correction of some of these to the late Dr Armitage Robinson, and, in order to keep faith with my public, as soon as I became aware of them, I wrote articles in the *Journal of Theological Studies*, the *Church Quarterly Review*, and the *Revue Bénédictine*, giving the results of my further research. I am under obligations to the respective editors of these journals and to the Delegates of the Clarendon Press for permission to reprint the substance of these articles.

I have altered the spelling of Dêr Balyzeh to Dair Balaizah, in accordance with the reports of the Egypt Exploration Fund, and of Sardica to Serdica and Petovio to Poetovio, in deference to the judgment of Professor Souter and the late Professor C. H. Turner, but I find that in the spelling Priminius instead of Pirminius I had unconsciously followed Dom Germain

Morin. Since the former edition only two new publications of manuscripts have appeared which have a bearing on the Creeds, a volume of sermons of St Augustine and the first two volumes of the works of Caesarius of Arles, both edited by Dom Morin. The former supports the *Explanatio Symboli ad Initiandos* in reading *in* with the clauses beginning *in sanctam ecclesiam* in the Creed of Milan, while as regards the latter Dom Morin has now returned to his earlier view in attributing to Caesarius a sermon falsely ascribed to St Augustine containing quotations both from the baptismal Creed of Arles and from the *Quicumque Vult.*

In accordance with the wish of certain critics I have printed more Creed forms and particularly that of the Council of Antioch in the winter of 324–325, which is not easily accessible, but as I still think it advisable to have the text before the eyes while reading the comments, I have retained the references to Lietzmann and Heurtley. To make room for the additional matter I have omitted nearly the whole of Chapter vi, the gist of which can be learnt from any ordinary book of ecclesiastical history.

Finally my thanks are due to the Rev. E. Evans, formerly Subwarden of this College, who has revised the proofs, and to my indefatigable typist Mrs Hordern.

THE AUTHOR
TO
THE THEOLOGICAL STUDENT
ON HOW TO READ
HIS BOOK

∽

*St Augustine's College,
Canterbury.*

My Dear Fellow-student,

You have got to take the History of the Creeds as part of your forthcoming examinations. I credit you with a higher desire than that of merely passing examinations with the least possible trouble. I hope at least that you desire to know and not merely to show or to pretend to the examiners that you do. The original editions of the books in English on this subject are upwards of thirty years old, and if they have been republished, the newer editions have not been brought up to date. In the last twenty years much fresh evidence has come to light. This book endeavours to take account of it; but it must, if possible, convince learned pundits. You have not the time nor the energy to become a specialist at present, and possibly you do not desire to do so. My advice to you, therefore, if you use this book, is this: Have a copy of the text of the Creeds open before you; that will save back references and the turning over of pages. Lietzmann, *Symbols of the Ancient Church*, Deighton Bell, 1s., will furnish you with nearly all that you need, and you can supplement it with Heurtley, *de Fide et Symbolo*, Parker, which you can generally get second-hand for about two shillings. Gwatkin's *Selections from Early Writers* you probably already possess. It covers less ground than Kidd's *Documents Illustrative of the History of the Church*, but gives the text as well as a translation. What is to be found in these is generally not reprinted here, but referred to under L., H., or G., with the number of the page. You have probably already been advised by your lecturers on Church

History and Liturgiology to read Brightman's Essay on *Terms of Communion and the Ministration of the Sacraments in Early Times*, and Mason's *Conceptions of the Church in Early Times* in *Essays on the Early History of the Church and the Ministry*, edited by Swete (Macmillan); both are valuable but the former is the more important of the two. Also look at the Map at the end of this book; looked at with a seeing eye it is illuminating.

With this equipment, my advice is as follows: Read the Introductory Chapter to the Apostles' Creed and Chapter II. Look at the headings of the following chapters, and see if there is anything you want in them. The concluding chapters, VIII–X, on the Creed of Rome at various dates, give you the newest things in the book.

Appendices and notes you will probably neglect, perhaps wisely. As regards the *Nicene Creed* you can if you like leave out all the criticism of Hort and of Epiphanius. The constructive work will be found in the section called "The Alternative View".

The *Quicumque Vult* was most probably composed by Ambrose. This portion is largely Heinrich Brewer, *Das Athanasische Glaubensbekenntnis* (1909), boiled down and translated, a work very little known in England.

Finally we come to the *Communion of Saints*, which contains all the Theology there is in the book. As some day you will probably have to teach the meaning of the Creed, there is something to be said for your trying to read that through.

That is my advice. God bless you.

Yours

THE AUTHOR
(1938)

PART I

THE APOSTLES' CREED

Chapter I

INTRODUCTORY

I. A Fictitious Pedigree. II. Outstanding Problems.

I. A Fictitious Pedigree

THANKS to the vast erudition of Harnack and Kattenbusch a false literary pedigree has been invented for the Old Roman Creed, that is for the baptismal Creed of the Church of Rome as it stood in the fourth and fifth centuries. These German scholars have been followed by Dr Burn and Bishop Gibson, and their theory will be stated in words drawn from Burn's *Apostles' Creed* and *Introduction to the Creeds* and Gibson's *Three Creeds*.

"The history of the Old Roman Creed is best studied backwards." It "is quoted in full by two writers of the fourth century, Marcellus and Rufinus". "This gives us a fixed point from which to work in considering this history of the Creed. We know for certain the form it took before the middle of the fourth century."

After this beginning the form is given by both writers. It consisted of twelve clauses or articles, eleven if we reckon "ascended into heaven" and "sitteth at the right hand of the Father" as one instead of two. At this time it was all but identical with our present Apostles' Creed except for the later additions: (1) Maker of heaven and earth. (2) Conceived. (3) Suffered. (4) Dead. (5) He descended into hell. (6) God...almighty. (7) Catholic. (8) The Communion of Saints. (9) The life everlasting.

"We can trace back this Old Roman Creed in the writings of...Dionysius, Bishop *c.* A.D. 259." "There is also an inter-

esting quotation in the writings of Novatian, a priest of the
Roman Church, *On the Trinity*." "At the end of the second
century Tertullian...expresses the agreement of the African
Church with the Church of Rome in matters of faith." "He
calls the creed the watchword which the African Church shares
with the Roman." "From Tertullian we learn much about the
famous Gnostic Marcion. What made opposition to Marcion
most difficult was the fact that he still held to the Roman Creed
interpreted in his own way." "The words 'holy Church' were
contained in the Roman Creed before Marcion's break with the
Church in A.D. 145. Thus we trace the Old Roman Creed up to
the earliest years of the second century." "The internal evidence
of the creed points to the early years of the century, ± 100 A.D.,
as the date of its composition."

There is one further link to add. In 1916 Dom Connolly
vindicated as the work of Hippolytus the *Apostolic Tradition*,[1]
which is one of the components of the so-called *Egyptian Church
Order*, and found in its least corrupt shape in Hauler's Verona
Fragments.

Thus our literary pedigree runs:

 Rufinus, Presbyter of Aquileia, *c.* 400.
 Marcellus, Bishop of Ancyra, *c.* 340.
 Novatian, Presbyter of Rome, *c.* 260.
 Dionysius, Bishop of Rome, *c.* 259.
 Hippolytus, Bishop of Portus (?), *c.* 220.
 Tertullian, Presbyter of Carthage, *c.* 180.
 Marcion, Bishop of some see in Pontus, *c.* 145.[2]

And it is claimed that in A.D. 100–120 the Roman baptismal
Creed had a form identical with that of the fourth century,
except that possibly in the first article it may have originally
contained the word "one", which was subsequently omitted to
counteract Sabellianism.

Unless we are overborne by the authority of the great names
of those who have fathered or sponsored this theory, our first

1 *Texts and Studies*, VIII. No. 4.
2 "He who received the tenth episcopal throne of the Apostles." Irenaeus,
6th Armenian fragment, *Pat. Orient.* X. p. 736.

feeling is one of questioning amazement. The Creeds of Marcellus and Rufinus so obviously belong to the fourth century or later, that it seems incredible that they can be survivals from the early years of the second. It is like being assured that a Norman cathedral was built in Saxon times; before ever we examine the detail it appears too spacious for its assigned period.

In the earliest days of Christianity it seems clear that the baptismal confession consisted of one clause only: "I believe in Jesus Christ, the Son of God, the Lord", or "our Lord", or of some formula even briefer than that. Later this was expanded to three clauses: "I believe in God the Father almighty; and in Jesus Christ His (only) Son our Lord; and in the Holy Ghost"; and by the middle of the first century the form was at most no fuller than this.[1] The theory, therefore, demands that in Rome in the next seventy-five years the baptismal Creed grew from three to eleven clauses, and that it then remained unaltered for upwards of two centuries and a half. Each separate portion of this hypothesis is astonishing; the rapidity of its early growth, and its subsequent period of rest or stagnation; taken together the improbability involved seems immense.

And there is nothing to account for this apparent reversal of Roman psychology. Creeds might well grow and grow rapidly in times of theological controversy. New clauses might readily be added as protests or safeguards against the assaults of pressing heresies. But heretical attacks in Rome did not begin until this time of rapid growth was over; "the creed", we are told, "was composed during a time of peace, and became a rule of faith without dispute".

Investigation only deepens our wonder. Thanks to the researches of the last thirty years we now know much more about Creeds of the last half of the second century. The publication of the *Epistola Apostolorum*, the *Dair Balaizah Papyrus*, and the *Epideixis*, or *Demonstration of Apostolic Preaching* of Irenaeus,[2] has thrown new light on this problem. In the first and second of these and in the shorter Creed of the combined Ethiopic, Coptic, and Arabic versions of the *Egyptian Church Order* there

---

1 See Chapter II.   2 See Chapters III and VI.

are five clauses only, or six if we reconstruct the orthodox Creed from the Marcosian parody given by Irenaeus. Is it really possible that some fifty years earlier in Rome, where, owing to the sort of conservatism demanded by the second half of the theory, Creeds, we should think, would tend to grow less rapidly than in the East, the baptismal Creed possessed eleven clauses?

And if we fix our attention on special members or articles of this religious fabric we seem to recognize the unmistakable pattern or moulding of a later age. In no creed-form earlier than the fourth century (except in that of Hippolytus, which shows signs of being worked over by a later hand) do we come across "of the Holy Ghost and the virgin Mary", or "under Pontius Pilate". No doubt the facts were taught; they were comprised in the common doctrine and discipline of Christendom known as the "Rule of Faith": but this "Rule of Faith", whether stated by Origen or Irenaeus or Tertullian, contained very much more matter than was ever found in the contemporary Creed; on this point Harnack is insistent.[1] This assumption that the "Rule of Faith" can be treated as equivalent to the "Symbol" or Creed is one of the main flaws in the argument, and similar to it is the assumption that the *tessera*, to which Tertullian refers, is the military *tessera* or watchword, which, no doubt, would be identical throughout the army. Tertullian is, in fact, referring not to the *tessera militaris* but to the *tessera hospitalitatis*, the coin or token divided between friends of which each had a part which fitted with the other. His metaphor, therefore, asserts identity of substance but *diversity of form*.[2] Nor does he maintain that the Church of Rome was in doctrinal agreement with the Churches of Africa specially or exclusively. "Let us see", he says, "what [the Church of Rome] has learnt, what it has taught, what are its points of agreement (*contesserarit*)[3] with the

---

1 See Chapter II, *sub fin.*

2 *de Praescr.* 20 shows the meaning to be attached to the word in 36.

3 *Contesserarit* is the reading commonly accepted, but perhaps we should read *contestetur* (see Bethune-Baker, *J.T.S.* VI. p. 625), in which case this whole argument for identity of Creed falls to the ground.

Church of Africa *also*" (i.e. as well as with the Churches of
Achaia, Macedonia, and Asia, which he has just mentioned).[1]
His Rule of Faith, therefore, would give the common belief of
Christendom and not the specific Creed of Rome. But, besides
an anachronism and a misinterpretation, the theory contains the
logical fallacy known as a *petitio principii*; it assumes the very
point to be proved, namely that the Creeds of Rufinus and Marcellus in combination give the Roman Creed, and then employs
this result as a standard; whereas it is only by knowing what was
the precise shape of the Roman Creed in the fourth century
that we can tell whether Marcellus or Rufinus is quoting it
or not.

RUFINUS[2] nowhere claims to be giving the Creed of Rome,
but that of his own Church, Aquileia. He tells us that certain
additions had been made in the Creed of Aquileia and what these
were, but he nowhere says that there were no other differences.
It follows that we are not warranted in assuming that in all other
respects the Creed of Aquileia was identical with the Creed of
Rome; we could only say this if we knew the Creed of Rome
from other sources; which is precisely the point we have to discover. As a matter of fact the assumption is proved to be false
by the evidence before us. That the Creed of Rufinus differs in
no unnamed respect from the Creed of Rome is an universal
proposition; if therefore we can show but one particular instance
to the contrary it is confuted. And Rufinus has *Unicum Filium
Ejus* instead of τὸν Υἱὸν Αὐτοῦ τὸν μονογενῆ, *Filium Ejus
unicum*, with Marcellus, which is in fact the Roman order. So
the Creed of Aquileia, apart from its additional matter, differs
from the Creed of Rome in at least one respect, and we have no
means of determining from the other authorities cited how many
more differences there may have been. Thus the authority of
Rufinus for the text of the Creed of Rome fades away.

Now let us take MARCELLUS.[3] The text of Epiphanius, in which
Marcellus's Creed occurs, rests on two bad MSS, so corruption
is possible. But (1) just so far as we suppose corruption in the
Creed of Marcellus we weaken its authority as a witness in both

1 *de Praescr.* 36.   2 See Chapter VI.   3 See Chapter IV.

directions for and against; and (2) we must not suppose corruption in a particular case unless we can justify our supposition. We cannot correct the text by the standard of what we imagine the Roman Creed to have been, and then use this corrected text as a witness to that standard, without committing the same logical fault. And if we may not assume corruption, still less may we assume inaccuracy on the part of Marcellus. Marcellus gives the Creed in a letter to Pope Julius written before he left Rome, as part of his defence against Arian accusers who failed to appear. "I thought it necessary", he says, "to deposit with you my faith in writing, having written it with all truth with my own hand, which I learnt and was taught out of the Holy Scriptures." And again: "Having received this faith from the Holy Scriptures, and been taught it by my ancestors in God, I both preach it in the Church of God, and have now written it to you, keeping a copy of this [writing] for myself".[1] His Creed, therefore, is not a mixed Roman-Ancyran form, it is either Roman or Ancyran. He does not claim to be giving the Creed of Rome; nor does he say he learnt the Creed which he gives from Pope Julius, but suggests, even if he does not definitely assert, that his Creed is that of his own diocese; nor does Julius in his letter to the Arian accusers of Marcellus ever hint that Marcellus had adopted the Roman Creed. There is therefore strong ground for holding that Marcellus's Creed is not the Creed of Rome. Nor is it. It has no word "Father" in the first clause, an omission which can be paralleled in other religious formulas in Asia Minor; it says "*whence* he cometh to judge quick and dead" and the word "whence", which in Greek cannot be confused with "thence", the Roman word, is only known to occur in Creeds in Galatia and Cappadocia; and it has "eternal life" at the end, which was not in the Roman Creed at this date, but was common in Eastern Creeds.

The whole theory, it will be noticed, hangs on these two Creeds, the one Aquileian, differing in innumerable respects from that of Rome, but no doubt having some general resemblance to it; the other almost certainly Ancyran, and certainly

1 Epiph. *adv. Haer.* lxxii.

possessing non-Roman features. And so, having no fixed point of suspension, the theory falls down.

Nevertheless, it may be worth while to look at some of the subordinate links in the chain to see if they are independently supported.

NOVATIAN[1] is quoting from the Rule of the Truth. There is no doubt that he holds the common catholic faith, but it is impossible to learn from his language the text of the Roman Creed. Thus he says: "The Rule of the Truth demands that first of all we should believe in God the Father and *Lord* almighty, that is, the most perfect *Creator of all things*". "The same Rule of the Truth teaches us to believe after the Father in the *Son of God, Christ Jesus, our Lord God*, but *Son of God*." Unless we knew beforehand the text of the Roman Creed we could not tell whether it contained in the first clause *Dominum* or *rerum omnium Conditorem* or not, or in the second *Filium Dei* or *Filium Ejus, Christum Jesum* or *Jesum Christum, Dominum Deum nostrum* or simply *Dominum nostrum*. That is, we have at most allusions to a Creed the text of which we do not know and cannot from this language discover. Nor do we know from Novatian how much the Roman Creed included; we cannot, for instance, assert that it contained the clause "born of the Holy Spirit and of the virgin Mary" merely because Novatian says: "We do not recognize that Christ of the heretics who bore within Himself nothing of our body, having received nothing from Mary, for fear lest He may not have come to us at all, in that He did not present Himself in our substance when He appeared".

The case of DIONYSIUS[1] looks more hopeful. His letter to his namesake of Alexandria says: "We ought to maintain the faith in God the Father almighty, and in Christ Jesus His Son, and in the Holy Ghost"; but this is too short to prove more than a three-clause formula, and the order εἰς τὸ Ἅγιον Πνεῦμα instead of the Roman order *in Spiritum Sanctum* prevents us laying stress on the exactness of the wording, so that we cannot say whether the Roman Creed had "Jesus Christ", or "Christ Jesus". And this is all that he gives.

1 See Chapter VIII.

HIPPOLYTUS[1] occupied so ambiguous a position that there is no certainty that he employed the same Creed as the Bishop of Rome, and his formula contains not only the clauses "who was born of the Holy Ghost and Mary the virgin", and "crucified under Pontius Pilate", which make us suspect a later recension, but *resurrexit die tertia vivus a mortuis*, where the order of the Roman Creed, when it contained the clause, was *tertia die resurrexit* without *vivus*; and *sedit*, sat down, instead of the Roman *sedet*, sitteth.

TERTULLIAN is citing the Rule of Faith, and if he quotes from the Creed at all it is from the Creed of Africa, which he does not say was identical with the Creed of Rome, but by his metaphor of the *tessera hospitalitatis* hints at the contrary; and what he says of the Gnostics is that they *claimed* to have the same *faith*, not the same *Creed*, as the orthodox. *Si subtiliter temptes* [eos], *per ambiguitates bilingues communem fidem adfirmant*,[2] "if you try them with subtle questions, by the ambiguities of their double tongue they *affirm* a community of *faith* with yourself", where the whole suggestion of the passage is that such a claim was false.

And similarly of MARCION: "[Our opponents] *say* that Marcion has not so much innovated on the Rule [of Faith] by his separation of the law and the gospel, as restored it when it has been adulterated (*non tam innovasse regulam...quam retro adulteratam recurasse*)."[3] As for the words "holy church" to which Dr Burn alludes, Zahn[4] says, "it follows...that the words 'a holy Church' were contained in Marcion's Baptismal Confession", that is, the Creed of Pontus, but not necessarily, therefore, as Zahn and Burn infer, "in the Roman Creed of A.D. 145."

But even this is too much to assert. Tertullian (*adv. Marc.* V. 4), after giving specimens of Marcion's omissions from St Paul's Epistles, says that he can be better refuted from what he has retained, and as an example quotes Gal. iv. 22–26. Though

---

1 See Appendix to Chapter x.   2 *adv. Valent.* I.

3 *adv. Marc.* 20. Cp. Irenaeus, Preface to bk. I, ὅμοια μὲν λαλοῦντας, ἀνόμοια δὲ φρονοῦντας, and III. xv. 2, the Valentinians "queruntur de nobis, quod cum similia nobiscum sentiant...et cum eadem dicant et eandem habent doctrinam, vocemus illos haereticos".

4 *Apostles' Creed*, p. 68.

work of Ambrose, as seems most probable, the identity of text with that derived from Augustine would enable us to fix the date of the Creed at *c.* 380.

Once more, in 448 Leo composed his Tome and in it he gives extracts from the Creed of Rome. Moreover, he preached a large number of sermons, and from these, as from the sermons of Augustine, we can recover other portions of his Creed. Now when we compare these four authorities together, certain rare and occasional variations cancel out, and the possible errors in the text are limited to such minute points as whether we should read *ex Maria* or *et Maria, ad* or *in, caelos* or *caelum*, and the addition of the word *mortuus.*

It seems that it is by some strange and unaccountable oversight that no single one of these four concurrent authorities figures at the head of the literary pedigree.

We will content ourselves by giving some few examples of how the standard text thus obtained justifies our previous remarks on the links in this genealogical chain.

Art. 1.

Leo: in Deum Patrem omnipotentem.
Rufinus: in Deum Patrem omnipotentem.[1]
Marcellus: εἰς Θεὸν παντοκράτορα.
Novatian: in Deum Patrem et *Dominum* omnipotentem.
Dionysius: εἰς Θεὸν Πατέρα παντοκράτορα.
Hippolytus (wanting in the Hauler Fragments).
Tertullian: in *unicum* Deum omnipotentem *mundi Conditorem (de Virg. vel.* 1);
    unum Deum *mundi Conditorem (de Praescr.* 13);
    unum Deum, *Creatorem universitatis (ib.* 36).

Neither Novatian nor Tertullian is quoting from the Creed but from the Rule of Faith, and both introduce words which formed no part of the Roman Creed.

Art. 2.

Leo: in Jesum Christum, Filium Ejus unicum, Dominum nostrum.
Rufinus: in *Christum Jesum, unicum Filium Ejus,* Dominum nostrum.[1]
Marcellus: εἰς Χριστὸν Ἰησοῦν, τὸν Υἱὸν Αὐτοῦ τὸν μονογενῆ, τὸν Κύριον ἡμῶν.

---

1 The best MSS. give ablatives, but probably the actual Creed had accusatives, see below, pp. 100, 101.

Novatian: in Filium *Dei*, *Christum Jesum*, Dominum *Deum* nostrum.
Dionysius: εἰς Χριστὸν Ἰησοῦν, τὸν Υἱὸν Αὐτοῦ.
Hippolytus: in *Christum Jesum*, Filium *Dei*.
Tertullian: Filium Ejus Jesum Christum (*de Virg. vel.* 1);
　　　　　　 Christum Jesum (*de Praescr.* 36);
　　　　　　 Filium *Dei*...Jesum Christum (*adv. Prax.* 2).

Here the preponderance of authority might seem to be in favour of the order "Christ Jesus", but Leo with his supporters is worth far more than any individual writer. The testimony of Dionysius can be discounted, as he in common with Marcellus also has the non-Roman order τὸ Ἅγιον Πνεῦμα. The phrase from Novatian which quotes a formula and not merely states the doctrine has not yet been given: it runs *Regulam veritatis per omnia custodientes, Deo gratias agere debemus per* Jesum Christum, Filium Ejus, Dominum nostrum (*de Cibis Judaicis*, c. 7, *sub fin.*). But almost as strange as the omission of Leo is the omission of Clement, who was Bishop of Rome about A.D. 90 to 99, that is to say during the period when, according to the theory, the Roman Creed was in process of formation from the threefold to the elevenfold form which it is supposed to have assumed by the beginning of the following century. Except in two extracts both reminiscent of St Paul, Clement always has throughout his epistle the order *Jesus Christus*, and this order is also preserved in the spurious homily of a later date which goes by his name, and may be also Roman.

II. Outstanding Problems

We have said enough to show in brief compass the baselessness of this fictitious genealogy; details will be given in the earlier chapters of this part, in which we shall also endeavour to provide a basis for a more logical and historical theory. There remain three outstanding problems. The first is to determine the form taken by the Roman Creed between the middle of the first century and the end of the first quarter of the third. The conservatism of the Roman temper would naturally tend to postpone development to a later date than that of the early Eastern Creeds to which we have alluded. The form must stand between the threefold formula of baptism given on pp. 17–19 and the fuller form obtained from Ambrose and Leo. It would probably need the pressure of heresy to cause so large a change in a formula sacred both by time and by religion. And the result would probably resemble the Eastern Creeds of a somewhat earlier time, at least as regards length and fullness. Even with these guides, the problem is difficult, but it will be our endeavour to show that it is not insoluble.

The second problem is, when and under what influences did this intermediate form develop into that which we find in the fourth century?

And the third is how this later form which persisted in the fifth century came to be changed into the Apostles' Creed as we know it at present. This problem, owing to the lack of evidence, cannot be precisely solved, but probability points to the early years of the seventh century, and to a district extending from Northern France to Northern Italy. These three problems will occupy the later chapters (VIII, IX and X) of this section of the book.

CHAPTER II

CREEDS AND THEIR CLASSIFICATION

I. Types of Creeds. II. The Simple Formula. III. The Triple Formula.
IV. The "Rule of Faith".

I. TYPES OF CREEDS

THERE are three main types of Creeds: (1) baptismal Creeds;
(2) conciliar Creeds; and (3) personal Creeds or professions of
faith.

(1) Baptismal Creeds are formulas of faith imposed by local
churches on candidates for baptism. An example of these would
be our own so-called Apostles' Creed; though in the Church of
England it is also used on other occasions than baptism, and with
slight variations of wording, namely, at Morning and Evening
Prayer, in the Catechism, and in the Order for the Visitation of
the Sick. Baptismal Creeds may be further divided into (a)
Declaratory, the statement of faith made by the candidate, beginning "I believe", and (b) Interrogatory, that is, the series
of questions put to him by the minister in the rite of baptism,
beginning "Dost thou believe?" In Rome in early times these
questions constituted the actual formula of baptism without any
such words as "N. is baptized", or "I baptize thee", the water
being administered after each of the three replies "I believe" to
the three questions corresponding to the Three Persons of the
Trinity.[1]

1 Brightman in Swete's *Essays*, p. 345. The evidence is derived from the
form given in the Gelasian and Gregorian Sacramentaries compared with
Hauler's Verona Fragments of the *Egyptian Church Order*, *Texts and Studies*,
VIII. 4, p. 185. The baptismal formula is also omitted in the description of
baptism in *de Sacramentis* ii. 7; in the Stowe Missal; and in a ninth-century
Sacramentary (Cod. Colbert No. 1348) published by Martène, Ordo v, vol. i,
p. 86. I have followed Dr Brightman as being an expert from whose judgement one would not willingly dissent, but I do not regard the evidence as
conclusive. Warren, *Liturgy and Ritual of the Celtic Church*, p. 216 n., suggests
that the formula was omitted because it was presumed that the minister would
know it by heart. The general argument is sufficiently strong to stand if this
support is withdrawn.

(2) Conciliar Creeds were made by councils of bishops as tests of orthodoxy, and intended to have an universal range. They were in the main drawn from baptismal Creeds, though new clauses might be added against particular heresies. Such was the Creed of the Council of Nicaea in 325, which subsequent conciliar Creeds imitated or used as a basis. When such a Creed was compiled by a single individual we may infer that it would be influenced by the Creed of his see or native place, and when the bishops of a particular district were in a large majority at a synod, the Creed would naturally reflect in some measure the local usage; and in consequence, in cases of doubt, conciliar Creeds may afford some guidance in determining the probable wording of a local baptismal Creed, while the absence of a particular phrase from a conciliar Creed would argue that it was not common at that date in the baptismal Creeds of the district from which the members of the Council were drawn.

(3) Personal professions of faith were never entirely original, but along with the compiler's own additions or enlargements embodied standardized phrases taken from one or other of the two former classes. Thus both conciliar and personal Creeds take us back to baptismal Creeds.

The Book of Common Prayer gives us no example of a personal Creed; the *Quicumque vult*, which is sometimes quoted as such, being rather a hymn, like the *Te Deum*, than a Creed.

II. The Simple Formula

From about the middle of the second century baptismal Creeds had three divisions, but it would seem that in the earliest times all that was required of the candidate was some form of profession of faith

in Jesus Christ:

Acts ii. 38, "Repent ye and be baptized...in the name of Jesus Christ...; and ye shall receive the gift of the Holy Ghost";

Acts x. 48, "He commanded them to be baptized in the name of Jesus Christ";

Cp. Acts viii. 12, "When they believed Philip preaching good tidings concerning the kingdom of God and the name of Jesus Christ";

or *in the Lord Jesus*:

Acts viii. 16, "They had been baptized into the name of the Lord Jesus";

Acts xix. 5, "They were baptized into the name of the Lord Jesus";

Cp. Acts xvi. 31, 33, "Believe on the Lord Jesus and thou shalt be saved...and he...was baptized";

1 Cor. xii. 3, "No man speaking in the Spirit of God saith Jesus is anathema; and no man can say Jesus is Lord but in the Holy Spirit (ἐν πνεύματι ἁγίῳ)";

Phil. ii. 11, "That every tongue should confess that Jesus Christ is Lord to the glory of God the Father";

or *in Jesus, the Son of God*:

Heb. iv. 14, "Having then a great high priest...Jesus the Son of God, let us hold fast our confession";

1 John iv. 15, "Whosoever shall confess that Jesus is the Son of God";

1 John v. 5, "He that believeth that Jesus is the Son of God".

St Paul's argument in 1 Cor. i. 13, "Was Paul crucified for you? or were ye baptized into the name of Paul?" seems to be based on the use of a single and not a triple formula; and ῥῆμα in Rom. x. 8, 9: "The *word* is nigh thee in thy mouth and in thy heart: that is, the *word* of faith which we preach; because if thou shalt confess with thy mouth Jesus as Lord, and shalt believe in thy heart that God raised Him from the dead, thou shalt be saved", and in Eph. v. 25, 26: "Christ loved the Church, and gave himself up for it; that he might sanctify it, having cleansed it by the washing of water with the *word*";[1] and Jas. ii. 7: "The honourable *name* which was called upon you" (in your baptism) τὸ καλὸν ὄνομα τὸ ἐπικληθὲν ἐφ᾽ ὑμᾶς point the same way.

That some confession of faith was required before baptism is seen from the early glosses upon the baptism of the eunuch (Acts viii. 37) which insert either wholly or in part: "And Philip said, If thou believest with all thy heart, thou mayest. And he answered and said, I believe that Jesus Christ is the Son of God"; and that this took the form of question and answer is suggested by 1 Pet. iii. 21: "Baptism, not the putting away of

1 See Robinson, *St Paul's Epistle to the Ephesians*, pp. 206, 207 n.; *J.T.S.* VII. pp. 193, 199.

the filth of the flesh, but the interrogation[1] of a good conscience towards God."

III. THE TRIPLE FORMULA

How widespread was the use of the simple formula, or how long it persisted, we cannot determine; but by about the middle of the second century a threefold formula appears to have been established both in the East and in the West, though individuals objected to it as late as the middle of the third century, and some refused to use it even at the end of the fourth.[2]

But we must not take it for granted that the threefold formula always and everywhere ran, "Into the name of the Father and of the Son and of the Holy Ghost", as given in Matt. xxviii. 19. It would seem more probable that at least in Rome it ran, "In God, in Jesus Christ, in the Spirit the Holy". St Matthew's Gospel was not known in Rome as early as the Gospels of St Mark and St Luke, and the threefold formula in it was intended to be rather an expanded declaration of the name and character of God than a liturgical rule.

Outside the Gospels a trinitarian formula, or something like it, occurs in the New Testament some seventy times or more, for the most part in passages of not more than three or four verses. The nearest approach to that given in St Matthew is:

1 J. iv. 13, 14, "He hath given us of his *Spirit*. And we...bear witness that the *Father* hath sent the *Son* (to be) the Saviour of the world".

But this parallel is unique. Other instances are:

Acts xx. 21–23, "Repentance toward *God* and faith toward *our Lord Jesus* (*Christ*)...the *Holy Ghost* testifieth...";
Rom. xv. 30, "I beseech you, brethren, by *our Lord Jesus Christ*, and by the love of the *Spirit*, that ye strive together with me in your prayers to *God* for me";

---

1 ἐπερώτημα=stipulatio, a promise elicited by a formal question. G. C. Richards, *J.T.S.* xxxii. p. 77.

2 Cp. Cyprian, *Ep.* lxxiii (to Jubaianus), 18; Pseudo-Cyprian, *de Rebaptismate*, 1, 6, 7; *Apostolic Canons*, 50, which commands the use of the triple formula; Ambrose, *de Spiritu Sancto*, i. 3, which defends the validity of the shorter formula.

1 Cor. ii. 2–5, "*Jesus Christ*, and him crucified...in demonstration of the *Spirit*...in the power of *God*";

1 Cor. vi. 11, "But ye were washed, but ye were sanctified, but ye were justified in the name of (our) *Lord Jesus Christ*, and in the *Spirit* of our *God*";

2 Cor. i. 21, 22, "He that stablisheth us with you into *Christ*, and anointed us, is *God*; who also sealed us, and gave (us) the earnest of the *Spirit* in our hearts";

2 Cor. iii. 3, "An epistle of *Christ*...written...with the *Spirit* of the living *God*";

2 Cor. v. 5–8, "He that wrought us for this very thing is *God*, who gave unto us the earnest of the *Spirit*...at home with the *Lord*";

2 Cor. xiii. 14, "The grace of the *Lord Jesus Christ*, and the love of *God*, and the participation in the *Holy Spirit* (ἡ κοινωνία τοῦ ἁγίου πνεύματος)";

Gal. iii. 11–14, "That no man is justified by the law in the sight of *God* is evident...the blessing of Abraham in *Christ Jesus*; that we might receive the promise of the *Spirit*";

Gal. v. 21–24, "The kingdom of *God*...the fruit of the *Spirit*... they that are of *Christ Jesus*";

Eph. ii. 20–22, "*Christ Jesus* himself being the chief corner-stone ...an habitation of *God* in the *Spirit*";

Eph. iv. 4–6, "One body, and one *Spirit*...one *Lord*, one faith, one baptism, one *God* and *Father* of all";

1 Thess. i. 2–5, "We give thanks to *God*...remembering...your ...patience of hope in our *Lord Jesus Christ*, before our *God* and *Father*; knowing...how that our gospel came...unto you...in (the) *Holy Ghost*";

1 Thess. iv. 2–8, "Ye know what charge we gave you through the *Lord Jesus*. For this is the will of *God*...he rejecteth...*God* who giveth his *Holy Spirit*";

Titus iii. 4–6, "When the kindness of *God* our Saviour...appeared ...he saved us through the washing of regeneration and renewing of (the) *Holy Ghost*, which he poured out upon us...through *Jesus Christ* our Saviour";

Heb. vi. 1–4, "The first principles of *Christ*...faith toward *God* ...made partakers of (the) *Holy Ghost*";

Heb. ix. 14, "The blood of *Christ*, who through (the) eternal *Spirit* offered Himself...unto *God*";

1 Pet. i. 2, "According to the foreknowledge of *God the Father* in sanctification of (the) *Spirit* unto obedience and sprinkling of the blood of *Jesus Christ*";

1 Pet. iv. 14, "If ye are reproached for the name of *Christ*...the *Spirit* of *God* resteth upon you";

1 J. iii. 21–24, "Confidence towards *God*...that we should believe in the name of his *Son Jesus Christ*...we know that he abideth in us, by the *Spirit* which he gave us";

1 J. iv. 2, "Hereby know ye the *Spirit* of *God*: every spirit which confesseth that *Jesus Christ* is come in the flesh is of *God*";

Jude 20, 21, "Praying in (the) *Holy Spirit*, keep yourselves in the love of *God*, looking for the mercy of our *Lord Jesus Christ*".

The repeated occurrence of the formula "God, Jesus (Christ) (our Lord), Holy Spirit" [(τὸ) πνεῦμα (τὸ) ἅγιον] together with the evidence of the priority of the simple formula "Jesus (Christ) (our Lord)" suggests that the triple is an expansion of the earlier simple formula, and outside the New Testament this formula rather than the Matthaean "Father, Son, Holy Spirit", is confirmed by

Clement, 16, "The sceptre (of the majesty) of *God*, even *our Lord Jesus Christ*...according as the *Holy Spirit* (τὸ Πνεῦμα τὸ Ἅγιον) spake";

Clement, 42, "The Apostles received the Gospel for us from *the Lord Jesus Christ*; *Jesus Christ* was sent forth from *God*...Having been fully assured through the resurrection of *our Lord Jesus Christ*, and confirmed in the word of *God*, with full assurance of the *Holy Spirit* (πνεύματος ἁγίου) they went forth" (G. p. 8);

Clement, 46, "Have we not one *God* and one *Christ* and one *Spirit* of grace?"

Clement, 58, "As *God* liveth, and the *Lord Jesus Christ* (liveth) and the *Holy Spirit* (τὸ Πνεῦμα τὸ Ἅγιον)";

Ignatius, *Eph.* ix, "Ye are stones of a temple who were prepared beforehand for a building of *God the Father*, being hoisted up to the heights by means of the crane of *Jesus Christ*, which is the Cross, and using for a rope the *Holy Spirit* (τῷ Πνεύματι τῷ Ἁγίῳ)";

Justin Martyr, *Apol.* i. 61, "In the Name of *God the Father and Lord of the universe* and of our Saviour *Jesus Christ*, and of the *Holy Spirit* (Πνεύματος Ἁγίου) do they then receive the washing in water" (G. p. 50; L. p. 3);

"There is named over him who will be regenerated...the name of *God the Father and Lord of the universe*...and in the name of *Jesus Christ* who was crucified under Pontius Pilate, and in the name of the *Holy Spirit* (Πνεύματος Ἁγίου)...he who is being illuminated is washed" (L. p. 3);

Origen, *in* 1 *Cor.* vii. 5 (*J.T.S.* IX. p. 502), "The bread...over which has been invoked the name of *God* and of *Christ* and of *the Holy Spirit*"; cp. Cyril of Jerusalem, *Catech.* iii. 3, "The water when it receives the invocation of (the) *Holy Spirit* and of *Christ* and of (the) *Father*".

Accordingly we may suppose that originally the question ran "Dost thou believe in Jesus Christ (our Lord)?" and later this was amplified into "Dost thou believe in God?" "Dost thou believe in Jesus Christ (our Lord)?" "Dost thou believe in the Holy Spirit?" And subsequently, whether by the influence of St Matthew's Gospel or for some other reason, this was further enlarged into "Dost thou believe in God the Father (almighty)?" "Dost thou believe in Jesus Christ (His Son) (only-begotten) (our Lord)?" "Dost thou believe in the Holy Spirit?"

Outside the metropolitical jurisdiction of the Roman see the threefold name of God appears to have been invoked upon the baptized in addition to the series of questions addressed to him.

Evidence of this practice is given

for *Egypt*:

Origen *in Ioan.* vi. 33, "The washing of water...is no less in itself to him who yields himself to the divine power of the *invocations of the adorable Trinity*, the beginning and source of divine gifts" (cp. *in Ioan.* iii. 5);

for *Asia Minor*:

Justin Martyr, already quoted;
Firmilian (Cyprian, *Ep.* lxxv. 9), "That, moreover, is absurd, that they do not think it is to be asked who was he who administered the baptism, on the ground that he who has been baptized could have obtained grace by the *invocation of the trinity of the names of the Father*, and of *the Son*, and of the *Holy Spirit*;"[1]

for *Lyons* and *Gaul*, the Christianity of which was derived from Asia Minor:

Irenaeus, *Frag.* xxxiii (ed. Harvey, II. p. 497), "It was not for nothing that Naaman of old, being a leper, was cleansed when he was baptized, but as an indication for us. For when we are lepers in our sins, we are cleansed from our old transgressions by the holy water and the *invocation of the Lord*";

for *Africa*:

Tertullian, *adv. Prax.* 26, "It is not once only but thrice that we are immersed into the three Persons *at each several mention of Their names*".[2]

---

1 Cp. the Creed of the Marcosians given on p. 35; *Didascalia*, III. 12, § 3; *Clem. Recogn.* III. 67; IX. 11; *Clem. Hom.* IX. 19.
2 Cp. *de Bapt.* 2, 13; Pseudo-Cyprian, *de Rebapt.* 5, 7.

IV. The Rule of Faith

Some reference must be made to the "Rule of Faith" or of "the Truth", as it has too often been assumed that the baptismal Creed of a particular place could be obtained by selecting phrases quoted by a theological writer as belonging to it:

"One great phrase, repeated with variations, resounds through all the writings of the period [i.e. the early period]....It is the Rule of Faith, the *regula veritatis*....All Christians were to be guided by the Rule. Attempts have been made to interpret the phrase in a narrow fashion. The *regula veritatis* has been held to mean the baptismal creed. Undoubtedly the baptismal formula,...and the baptismal creeds of various churches, into which that formula naturally expanded, were never far from the thoughts of the writer who used the phrase; but the baptismal creed and the *regula veritatis* are not convertible terms.... A careful study of the phrase, as found in Irenaeus, Tertullian, Hippolytus, Clement, Origen, Cyprian, Novatian, Dionysius of Rome, shews that it means the teaching of the Church as a whole."[1]

"(1) The fact that single sentences seem to be echoes of the symbol [i.e. the baptismal creed] or tally with it offers no guarantee that they themselves derive from one symbol. Before any symbol existed God was παντοκράτωρ; Jesus Christ was called 'the Only Begotten Son, our Lord'; he was proclaimed as 'born of the Holy Ghost of the Virgin Mary', as having suffered under Pontius Pilate, and as coming to judge the quick and the dead.

(2) Formula-like sentences, if not obviously a part of the baptismal formula, need not necessarily have originated in a baptismal confession, even though they be identical with the sentences of that confession. The oldest tradition gave a fixed or, as the case may be, a more fixed shape to 'The Faith', not only in the form of a baptismal confession and for the purposes of baptism, but also in (a) liturgical sentences, (b) formulas of exorcism, (c) precepts concerning faith and morals, and (d) historical summaries, and that, too, with a view to the most diverse objects (instruction, apologetics, polemics, religious worship)....

(3) In particular, the preaching of Christ, apart from the detailed form which it received in the Gospels, also underwent longer or shorter epitomisations....

(4) Out of the great number of predicates attached to God, Christ, and the Spirit, some which were in general use very soon came to the front, apart from the detailed Trinitarian confession. Those chiefly used in connexion with God are, εἷς, παντοκράτωρ, πατήρ, δεσπότης, and Creator, with additions; with Christ, ὁ υἱὸς τοῦ θεοῦ, ὁ κύριος, σωτήρ,

1 Mason, in Swete's *Essays*, p. 51.

διδάσκαλος, μονογενής, εἷς, λόγος; with the Holy Ghost, ἅγιος, προφητικός. In the same way, out of the great number of blessings which the Christian faith affords, some are named with special frequency, such as ἄφεσις ἁμαρτιῶν (with or without mention of baptism), ζωή (αἰώνιος), ἀνάστασις (with or without τῆς σαρκός), γνῶσις, ἀφθαρσία, etc. Everything thus variously produced was regarded as 'the Faith', 'the Rule of Faith', 'Kerugma' (or 'Proclamation'), 'Truth', 'Rule of Truth'....

A consideration of the facts contained in the foregoing, the truth of which no scholar will question, must make us very cautious in arguing from formula-like confessional sentences to a formulated baptismal confession in three parts."[1]

So also Ammundsen:

"*The Rule of Truth* [in Irenaeus] *primarily* is not an institution, a formula, or a book; it is Christianity itself, the genuine apostolic Christianity.... *The Truth*—which is the rule—...comprehends the whole revelation.... Its main points are: the creation—the dispensation and prophecies in the Old Testament—Christ as the second Adam, His supernatural birth, His words, His death, His resurrection and ascension—the Holy Ghost—the Church—the Christian Ethics—the Eschatology." (*J.T.S.* XIII, p. 578.)

Let us take two illustrations.

Novatian[2] writes: "The Rule of Truth demands that first of all we believe in God the Father and Lord almighty....The same Rule of Truth teaches us to believe after the Father also in the Son of God, Christ Jesus, our Lord God, but God's Son". Unless we had other sources of knowledge we might be disposed to write the Roman baptismal Creed as beginning "I believe in God the Father and Lord almighty, and in Christ Jesus, our Lord God, the Son of God", but there would be at least three if not four mistakes in our conclusion.

So a theological writer belonging to the Church of England might well say, "the Rule of Faith demands that we believe in

God the Father, who made all the world;
in God the Son, who redeemed all mankind;
and in God the Holy Ghost, who sanctifieth all the elect people of
    God;"

or that

"there is but one living and true God, the Maker, and Preserver of all

1 Harnack, *Apostles' Creed*, pp. 54–58.
2 *de Trin.* 1 and 9; L. p. 5.

things both visible and invisible. And in unity of this Godhead there be three Persons, the Father, the Son, and the Holy Ghost. The Son, begotten from everlasting of the Father, of one substance with the Father, took Man's nature in the womb of the blessed Virgin; who truly suffered, was crucified, dead and buried. So also it is to be believed that Christ went down into Hell. Christ did truly rise again from death; he ascended into Heaven, and there sitteth until he return to judge all Men at the last day. The Holy Ghost proceedeth from the Father and the Son, and is very and eternal God.

Both these are taken from authoritative documents, the former from the Catechism, and the latter from the first five Articles of Religion; but it would be impossible to construct from them the baptismal Creed of the Church of England, our Apostles' Creed, though they are contained in its Rule of Faith. In short, there is nothing in the local baptismal Creed of any Church which is not in its Rule of Faith, but the Rule of Faith as given by a theological writer is of little value, and will often prove misleading, if we attempt to construct from it the corresponding baptismal Creed.

A second characteristic is that it was claimed that the Rule of Faith was the same everywhere and always: "The rule of faith is altogether one, alone, immovable and irreformable", Tertull. *de Virg. vel.* i (L. p. 4); whereas local baptismal Creeds differed both in phraseology, and in the amount of doctrinal matter included, and, as we shall soon see,[1] in the time of Irenaeus and Tertullian the Rule of Faith was far ampler and fuller than the short baptismal Creeds.

1 Pp. 36, 37.

CHAPTER III

EARLY EASTERN CREEDS

I. *Epistola Apostolorum.* II. The Old Creed of Alexandria. III. The Shorter Creed of the *Egyptian Church Order.* IV. The Marcosian Creed. V. The Early Creed of Africa. VI. The Profession of the "Presbyters" at Smyrna. NOTES: A. Texts of the Dair Balaizah Papyrus, the Marcosian Creed, the Profession of the "Presbyters" at Smyrna; B. The Early Creeds of Africa and of Rome.

I

Epistola Apostolorum

(Faith)

In God the Father almighty;
In Jesus Christ, our Saviour;
And in the Spirit, the Holy, the
    Paraclete;
Holy Church;
Forgiveness of sins.

II

Dair Balaizah Papyrus

I believe

In God the Father almighty;
And in His only-begotten Son, our
    Lord, Jesus Christ;
And in the Spirit, the Holy,
And in resurrection of flesh;
And holy catholic Church.

III

Egyptian Church Order

I believe (*or* Dost thou believe?)
In one God the Father almighty;
And in His only Son, our Saviour,
    Jesus Christ;
And the Holy Spirit, giver of life;
In the catholic holy Church;
And life eternal.

IV

[Marcosian]

(I believe)

In God the Father of the universe;
In Jesus Christ, His Son;
In the Holy Spirit;
In one holy Church;
And forgiveness of sins;
And communion of saints.

V

Africa

I believe
In God the Father almighty, Maker of the universe;
I believe in Jesus Christ, His only Son, our Lord,
who was born,
crucified,
rose again.
I believe in the Spirit the Holy;
The forgiveness of sins,
And life eternal through the holy Church.

THE study of the history of the Creeds is a branch of archaeology, in which specimens seem to occur almost by accident; we have nothing like a complete series, and to fill the most important

gaps in our collection we must often reconstruct by analogy or
endeavour to recover an earlier form by the removal of later
growths or accretions. Hitherto we have been in the region of
little more than conjecture, but now we can obtain a solid
nucleus of fact, and round it we can group other forms more or
less hypothetical.

I. EPISTOLA APOSTOLORUM

The earliest Creed known word for word which can be dated
with reasonable certainty is contained in the so-called Letter of
the Apostles, *Epistola Apostolorum*. This is a pseudonymous
treatise originally written in Greek and now extant in full in
Ethiopic, but there is also a small portion of it in Coptic, and a
fragment in Latin.[1] It is probably to be assigned to Asia Minor
before 180, and possibly between 150 and 170,[2] less probably to
Egypt about 150.[3] The Ethiopic version contains a Creed of five
clauses, already given, compared to the five loaves of the Gospel.
This is said to be the Creed of Great Christianity, that is of the
Catholic Church in contrast to heretical sects (c. 16).

II. THE OLD CREED OF ALEXANDRIA

The Coptic and Ethiopic Creeds[4] run:

> I believe (E. "We believe")
> in one God (E. adds "the Lord")
> the Father almighty;
> And in His only-begotten Son Jesus Christ our Lord;
> And in the Spirit, the Holy, the Giver of Life;
> And the resurrection of the flesh;
> C. And in one only catholic, apostolic, holy Church of Him;
> E. And in the only holy catholic apostolic Church;
> E. *adds*, And we believe in one baptism for the remission of sins
>   unto the ages of the ages.

1 The Ethiopic version was published by Guerrier in *Pat. Orient.* IX. 3 in
1913; the whole was edited by Schmidt and published in *Texte u. U. R.* III.
Bd. 13, 1919.

2 Schmidt; Guerrier says the end of the second or beginning of the third
century, but parts may go back to the first years of the second century. He
assigns it to Egypt or perhaps to Palestine.

3 Lietzmann, *Z.N.W.* xx. 1921, pp. 173 ff.

4 Hahn³, pp. 158, 159.

It is clear that both these go back to a common original, and Coptic and Ethiopic Christianity was derived from Alexandria. The two noticeable features are the place of the "resurrection of the flesh", and the number of epithets applied to the Church, and both these are Alexandrine. Cp. the Sacramentary of Serapion 23, and the Creed of Arius and Euzoius:

> And in the Holy Spirit;
> And in the resurrection of the flesh;
> And in the life of the world to come;
> And in the kingdom of Heaven;
> And in one catholic Church of God from the world's end to the
> world's end.   (L. p. 20; H. p. 8.)

Going back before the rise of Arianism we have a letter of Alexander, Bishop of Alexandria,[1] in which he gives not the Creed but the common belief of his Church.

> We believe, as the apostolic Church teaches,
> in an only unbegotten Father....
> And in one Lord Jesus Christ, the only-begotten Son of God....
> And in addition to this pious belief respecting the Father and the
> Son, we confess as the sacred Scripture teaches one Holy
> Ghost....
> We believe in one only catholic Church, the apostolical....
> After this we know the resurrection from the dead.

Much later in date is the *Epistola Systatice* or letter sent by the Jacobite Patriarch of Alexandria to notify his election.

> We believe in one God the Father almighty,
> And in His only-begotten Son Jesus Christ, our Lord, in un-
> divided unity....
> We believe also in the Spirit the Holy,
> the resurrection of the flesh,
> and the holy catholic Church.[2]

Finally, we have the Creed found in a fragmentary liturgy at Dair Balaizah by Professor Flinders Petrie in 1907,[3] which has been given above. Possibly it is this Creed that is reflected in the writings of Dionysius of Alexandria c. 200–264 or 265: "concerning the doctrine which now arises...which is impious, and

---

1 Theodt. *H.E.* i. iv. 46; L. p. 7.
2 Renaudot, *Lit. orient. Coll.* i. p. 463.
3 *Report of the Eucharistic Congress* 1908, p. 373.

contains much blasphemy against the *almighty God and Father*
of our *Lord Jesus Christ,* and much unbelief respecting *His only-
begotten Son*...and a want of perception of the *Holy Spirit*",
ap. Eus. *H.E.* VII. 6 (L. p. 7), and "to *God the Father* and *the
Son our Lord Jesus Christ* with *the Holy Spirit*", *ap.* Basil, *de
S.S.* XXIX. 72.

The Dair Balaizah papyrus is now in the Bodleian Library: it
is of the sixth–eighth century. The liturgy as a whole cannot well
be dated earlier than the middle of the fourth century,[1] yet when
we compare these texts there can be little doubt that this Creed
underlies the other forms. Accordingly we have here the Creed
of Alexandria certainly before the Council of Nicaea, and probably as early as the second century.

III. The Shorter Creed of the *Egyptian* Church Order

The so-called *Egyptian Church Order* exists in various versions, but three of them, the Arabic, Ethiopic, and Coptic, give
two baptismal rites, one considerably abbreviated, and in them
two baptismal Creeds. The shorter Creed runs:

> I believe (A. Dost thou believe?)
> in the one *true* (E. *omits*) God, the Father Almighty;
> And in His only Son, our Lord and our Saviour, Jesus Christ;
> And the (A. His) Holy Spirit, giver of life (A. to the universe;
>   E. to all creation);
> The Trinity of the same substance,
> One Godhead (A. E. The Trinity equal in Godhead);
> One Lord (A. C. one Lordship), one kingdom, one faith, one
>   baptism.
> In the catholic (C. *adds* apostolic) holy Church,
> and life eternal.[2]

Omitting the obviously post-Nicene clause, and the quotation
which follows it and is not found in other Creeds, and in general
whatever has not the support of all three versions, we obtain the
form already given.

Dom Connolly thinks that this Creed is not a composition but

---

1 Brightman, *J.T.S.* XII. 1911, p. 311.
2 Maclean, *Ancient Church Orders,* p. 101.

was written by "some scribe or editor, probably in Egypt, who wished to find a place in this collection of apostolic documents for a short baptismal Creed with which he was familiar ".[1]

IV. THE CREED OF THE MARCOSIANS

Marcus seems to have been a slightly older contemporary of Irenaeus, and to have lived somewhere in Asia Minor. Like other Gnostics he parodied the Christian formulas and sacraments. Irenaeus writes of the Marcosians:[2]

> In baptism they say over them
> Into the name of the unknown Father of the universe;
> Into Truth, the Mother of all;
> Into Him who came down upon Jesus;
> Into union;
> And redemption;
> And communion in the powers.

The first and third clauses obviously refer to God the Father and God the Holy Ghost. "Unknown" in the first clause is a characteristically Gnostic word and may be omitted;[3] "Father of the universe" is the exact phrase we have already found in Justin Martyr, and it occurs also in his description of the Eucharist: "And he [the President of the brethren] taking them [the bread and cup of wine mixed with water] gives praise and glory to the Father of the universe, through the name of the Son, and of the Holy Ghost",[4] so "Father of the universe" would seem to be a fixed formula.

The second clause in any Christian Creed of this period must refer to Jesus Christ, and probably ran "Jesus Christ His Son" at the least. This would seem to be hinted at by the Marcosians, who, according to Irenaeus, taught "One and two and three and four when added together form ten; and this, they will have it, is Jesus. Moreover, Chreistos, he says, being a word of eight letters, indicated the first Ogdoad, and this when multiplied by ten gives birth to Jesus Christ. And Christ the Son, he says, is

---

1 *J.T.S.* xxv. p. 133. 2 *Adv. Haer.* I. xiv. 2.

3 Cp. the heresy of Cerdo: "he taught that the God who was proclaimed by the law and the prophets was not the Father of our Lord Jesus Christ, for the one was known and the other unknown." Irenaeus, *adv. Haer.* I. 24; cp. Hippolytus, *Phil.* vii. 25. 4 *Apol.* i. 65; G. p. 52.

also spoken of, that is, the Dodecad. For the name Son (ΥΙΟC) contains four letters, and Christ (ΧΡΕΙCΤΟC) eight, which, being combined, point out the greatness of the Dodecad" (viii. 13).

"The Truth" suggests "I am the Truth", John xiv. 6. Origen, *c. Cels.* viii. 63, has, "God and His only begotten Son, the Truth"; 2 Clem. 20, "To the only invisible God the Father of the Truth". "Mother of all" need not perplex us; the Gnostics always ran to female deities.

The next clause should have reference to the Church; and Marcus recognized an Aeon named "Ecclesia". "Union" may well hint at it, especially if the local Christian Creed contained "one" Church.

"Redemption" at once reminds us of Col. i. 14: "In whom we have our redemption, the forgiveness of our sins".

And "communion in the powers" points to "communion in the holies", which we translate "communion of saints", a clause which was almost certainly current in Asia Minor, since it recurs in the Creed of Niceta of Remesiana on the one side, and in an Armenian Creed[1] on the other.

But for Justin Martyr and the analogies of Creeds of much the same date, a reconstruction of this kind might be thought hazardous; but with these supports we cannot be far wrong if we write down the contemporary Christian Creed as we have given it.

The noticeable features common to all these early Creed forms are:

(1) they are quite short, consisting of five or six clauses;
(2) the first three clauses deal with the three Persons of the Trinity;
(3) they contain a clause concerning the Church, of which the standing epithet is "holy";
(4) the remaining clauses in the examples given are "forgiveness of sins", "the resurrection of the flesh", "communion of saints", "everlasting life"; but the number and order of these varies.

1 Hahn[3], p. 155.

It would seem to follow from (1) and (2) that early Creeds are expansions of the baptismal formula, but there is a considerable gap in date and structure between these early Creeds and the simple or the threefold formula of baptism, and we have no positive evidence how this gap was bridged.

V. The Early Creed of Africa

"Carthage...had a bishop of more than ordinary *auctoritas*, who could afford to disregard even a number of enemies...because he saw himself united...both to the Roman Church, in which the supremacy of an apostolic see always flourished, and to all other lands from which Africa itself received the gospel."[1]

In these words Augustine denies that Christianity came to Africa from Rome, and he asserts also that it came from the Orient, that is from the Roman province of which Antioch in Syria was the headquarters: "Pars autem Donati...non considerat...ab illa radice *orientalium ecclesiarum* se esse praecisam, unde evangelium in Africam venit."[2] These statements are borne out by the form of the early African liturgy, which, but for the position of the Pax, can be seen to belong to the Antiochene family, and by the form of the Creed itself.

The early African Creed is known to us from Tertullian, who quotes from the Rule of Faith—and thus does not give its exact wording—and makes statements indicating its length and contents; from two quotations in Cyprian, giving by no means the whole of it but merely its backbone or framework; and from later writers, of whom the most important are Augustine and Fulgentius of Ruspe (467–533), who enable us to fill up the blanks left by Cyprian in accordance with the statements made by Tertullian.

After his return from Milan Augustine, when he had become bishop, amalgamated the existing African Creed with the Milanese. He warns us that he does not quote the baptismal Creed in the precise form in which it was delivered to catechumens,[3] but in fact the differences are small, and when we

1 *Ep.* xliii. 7, to Glorius.   2 *Ep.* lii. 2, to Severinus.   3 *Retract.* i. 17.

have compared any large number of his sermons, tend to cancel
each other. Most of these sermons on the Creed give the Milanese
form of it, but two of them, *SS.* 212, 215, give the form in use
in Africa.

There are also three sermons wrongly ascribed to him, each
of them called *Sermo de Symbolo ad Catechumenos*,[1] which were
probably written in the fifth century in North Africa, and quote
the African Creed.

Cyprian writes: "But if anyone objects by saying that Novatian
holds the same law which the catholic Church holds, baptizes
with the same Creed with which we baptize, knows the same God
the Father, the same Christ the Son, the same Holy Spirit...let
him know...that there is not one law of the Creed, nor the same
interrogation common to us and the schismatics. For when they
say 'Dost thou believe in remission of sins and eternal life
through the holy Church?' they lie in the interrogation since
they have not the Church."[2] And: "But moreover the very interrogation which is put in baptism is a witness to the truth.
For when we say 'Dost thou believe in eternal life and remission
of sins through the holy Church?' we mean that remission of
sins is not granted except in the Church."[3]

Later authorities show that in this last clause the order of the
former quotation is to be preferred, as indeed is probable on
other grounds.

Thus we obtain from Cyprian:

> Credis in Deum Patrem?
> (Credis) in Christum Filium?
> (Credis) in Spiritum Sanctum;
> In remissionem peccatorum;
> Et vitam aeternam
> per sanctam ecclesiam?

But clearly Cyprian's Creed must have been fuller than this, and
we need have no hesitation in adding in the first clause *omni-*
potentem, which is given by Tertullian,[4] is a standing epithet in
nearly all the Creeds of this period known to us, and appears

---

1 Migne, *P.L.* XL. pp. 637–668.   2 *Ep.* lxix. 7, to Magnus.
3 *Ep.* lxx. 2, to Januarius; L. p. 5.   4 *de Virg. vel.* 1.

regularly in later quotations from the Creed of Africa. Tertullian also implies that there was in this clause some phrase asserting the creatorship of God,[1] but as he is explaining the Rule of Faith he does not quote the actual wording; Augustine, however, and later writers show that this was *universorum Creatorem*.

It is also highly probable that the African *declaratory* Creed repeated *Credo* at the beginning of each of the first three clauses. This seems implied in Augustine *S.* 215, the three sermons ascribed to him, and Fulgentius *Frag.* 36.

In the second clause we must place *Jesum* before *Christum*; the order in Tertullian varies,[1] but this is the regular order in Cyprian's other writings, and universal in later forms of the African Creed. We must also add *Ejus* after *Filium*, and probably also *unicum*, though this last epithet has no support in Tertullian's quotations from the Rule of Faith; and probably also *Dominum nostrum*, though this is less certain.

Tertullian also says: "Let us admit that salvation came about in times past by simple faith, before the Lord's passion and resurrection, but when faith was increased—I mean by faith the belief in His birth, passion and resurrection—there was added to the sacrament an enlargement, a ratification in baptism, the clothing, as it were, of that faith which hitherto had been naked."[2]

This language suggests that at the end of the second clause we should add *natum, passum, resurrexit*, only instead of *passum* we should probably read *crucifixum* (Tertull. *de Virg. vel.* 1; *de Praescr.* 13), which appears in the later forms of the Creed. That the first two of these words were in the past participle is thought probable by Caspari,[3] and would seem to be indicated by Augustine *S.* 215, and the three sermons ascribed to him. The abrupt change to the indicative *resurrexit* is paralleled in the Creed of Niceta of Remesiana,[4] and in both instances is probably due to the same cause, that the Creed had been imported into each district in Greek, but, as there was no past participle active

1 See above, p. 12.   2 *de Bapt.* 13.
3 *Quellen*, III. p. 91 n.
4 Cp. also the Creed in the Bobbio and Mozarabic Missals.

of *resurgo*, the translator had to render ἀναστάντα in some other way.

Anything more elaborate than this form would seem to be barred by two statements of Tertullian: "There is really nothing which so hardens the mind of men as the simplicity of divine works in their operation and the magnificence promised in their result; for example, in baptism, since with so great simplicity, without any display...a man is lowered into the water and dipped with intervals for a few words...and yet an incredible result in eternity is deemed to be assured."[1] And, "Hereupon we are thrice immersed making a somewhat fuller response (*amplius aliquid respondentes*) than the Lord appointed in the Gospel" (that is, the Matthaean formula).[2] The analogy of other early creeds tells on the same side.

But before the time of Augustine, though probably later than that of Cyprian, there was added at the end of the first clause *Regem caelorum, immortalem et invisibilem*.[3] Since Rufinus[4] tells us that the epithets "invisible" and "impassible" were added to the Creed of Aquileia as safeguards against Sabellianism, we shall probably be right in assigning the addition made to the Creed of Africa to the same cause, and Dionysius of Alexandria[5] refers to Ptolemais as a hotbed of Sabellianism about the year 260.

So we may reconstruct the African baptismal creed before the return of St Augustine as follows:

> Credo in Deum Patrem omnipotentem, universorum Creatorem, (Regem caelorum, immortalem et invisibilem);
> Credo in Jesum Christum, Filium Ejus unicum, Dominum nostrum, natum, crucifixum, resurrexit.
> Credo in Spiritum Sanctum;
> Remissionem peccatorum,
> et vitam aeternam
> per sanctam ecclesiam.

1 *de Bapt.* 2.
2 *de Cor. mil.* 3.
3 Aug. *SS.* 212, 215, Fulg. *Frag.* 36, and the three sermons of Pseudo-Augustine, though the first gives only "immortalem et invisibilem".
4 *in Symb. Apost.* 5.
5 *ap.* Euseb. *H.E.* VII. 6.

VI. The Profession of the "Presbyters" at Smyrna[1]

It may be worth while to turn aside from formal baptismal Creeds, and to deal in passing with something more akin to a personal profession of faith, probably fuller, so far as it goes, than the actual Creed of the time and place. The condemnation of Noetus can be dated within a year or two of A.D. 180. The profession of their faith by the bishops who condemned him at Smyrna is reported in slightly differing language by Hippolytus (c. Noet. 1) and Epiphanius (Haer. LVII):

H.	E.
We also know truly one God;	We ourselves also worship one God, but as we know how to worship righteously;
We know Christ, we know the Son,	And we have one Christ, but as we know Christ as Son of God,
Having suffered as He suffered,	Having suffered as He suffered,
Having died as He died,	Having died as He died,
Having risen the third day,	Having risen,
	Having ascended into the heavens,
And being on the right hand of God the Father,	Being on the right hand of the Father,
And coming to judge quick and dead.	Coming to judge quick and dead.

The third member is entirely omitted. The teaching about our Lord is far fuller than we have found hitherto, and we must not assume that all here given was contained in the Creed of Smyrna at the time. But we notice that the second member has a succession of bare, unqualified participles, "suffered, died, risen". This is an example of the way in which the events of our Lord's life on earth would be commemorated in Creeds when they were first included. So we have in the Creed of the Council of Nicaea "came down, and was incarnate, and was made man, suffered", simply, and in the Creed put forward by Eusebius of Caesarea at that Council "was incarnate, lived among men, and suffered", and in the profession of faith of Arius and Euzoius in 330 "who

[1] Routh, Reliquiae Sacrae, IV. p. 248.

came down, and was incarnate, and suffered, and rose ". This brevity of statement is similar to the corresponding clauses in the Creed of Africa as we have reconstructed it.

NOTES

A. Early Creed Forms

Dair Balaizah Papyrus

......ὁμολογεῖ τὴν πίστιν·
Πιστεύω εἰς Θεὸν Πατέρα παντοκράτορα·
Καὶ εἰς τὸν μονογενῆ Αὐτοῦ Υἱόν,
τὸν Κύριον ἡμῶν, Ἰησοῦν Χριστόν·
Καὶ εἰς τὸ Πνεῦμα τὸ Ἅγιον·
Καὶ εἰς σαρκὸς ἀνάστασιν·
Καὶ ἁγίαν καθολικὴν ἐκκλησίαν.
τ

The τ occupies a full line of the MS. and probably stands for τέλος.

Marcosian

Οἱ δὲ ἄγουσιν ἐφ᾽ ὕδωρ, καὶ βαπτίζοντες οὕτως ἐπιλέγουσιν·
Εἰς ὄνομα ἀγνώστου Πατρὸς τῶν ὅλων·
Εἰς Ἀλήθειαν μητέρα πάντων·
Εἰς τὸν κατελθόντα εἰς Ἰησοῦν·
Εἰς ἔνωσιν·
Καὶ ἀπολύτρωσιν·
Καὶ κοινωνίαν τῶν δυνάμεων.

Irenaeus, adv. Haer. I. xiv. 2, ed. Harvey.

The Profession of the 'Presbyters' at Smyrna

Hippolytus, c. Noet. 1.	Epiphanius, Haer. LVII.
Καὶ ἡμεῖς ἕνα Θεὸν οἴδαμεν ἀληθῶς·	Ἕνα Θεὸν δοξάζομεν καὶ αὐτοί, ἀλλ᾽ ὡς οἴδαμεν δικαίως δοξάζειν·
Οἴδαμεν Χριστόν,	Καὶ ἕνα Χριστὸν ἔχομεν,
οἴδαμεν τὸν Υἱόν,	ἀλλ᾽ ὡς οἴδαμεν Χριστὸν Υἱὸν Θεοῦ,
παθόντα καθὼς ἔπαθε,	παθόντα καθὼς ἔπαθεν,
ἀποθανόντα καθὼς ἀπέθανε,	ἀποθανόντα καθὼς ἀπέθανεν,
ἀναστάντα τῇ τρίτῃ ἡμέρᾳ,	ἀναστάντα,
	ἀνελθόντα εἰς τοὺς οὐρανούς,
καὶ ὄντα ἐν δεξιᾷ τοῦ Πατρός,	ὄντα ἐν δεξιᾷ τοῦ Πατρός,
καὶ ἐρχόμενον κρῖναι	ἐρχόμενον κρῖναι
ζῶντας καὶ νεκρούς.	ζῶντας καὶ νεκρούς.

B. THE EARLY CREEDS OF AFRICA AND OF ROME

In spite of the clear statement of Augustine that African Christianity came from the East, an attempt has been made to show that the
African Creed was derived from and identical with the contemporary
Creed of Rome on the ground of a supposed statement by Tertullian
that this was the case, and a second statement that the Church of Africa
recognized the *auctoritas* of the Church of Rome, as being that of its
ecclesiastical mother.

In early times the appeal in questions of doctrinal controversy was
to the Scriptures and to the common faith of the Church, which had
received a very incomplete embodiment in the slightly varying local
Creeds. This faith, it was claimed, was one and the same everywhere.

"Now with regard to this Rule of Faith—that we may at once acknowledge what it is that we defend—it is, you must know, that which
prescribes the belief that there is one only God, and that He is none
other than the Creator of the world, who produced all things out of
nothing through His own Word first of all sent down, that this Word,
called His Son, was seen under the name of God in divers manners by
the patriarchs, heard at all times in the prophets, at last brought down
by the Spirit and power of the Father into the virgin Mary, was made
flesh in her womb, and being born of her went forth as Jesus Christ;
thenceforth He preached the new law and the new promise of the
Kingdom of Heaven, worked miracles; having been crucified He rose
again the third day; being taken up into the heavens He sat on the
right hand of the Father; sent instead of Himself (*vicariam*) the power
of the Holy Ghost to lead such as believe; will come with glory to take
the saints to the enjoyment of everlasting life and of the heavenly
promises, and to condemn the wicked to everlasting fire, after the
resurrection of both together with the restoration of their flesh. Christ
delivered the faith; the Apostles spread it."[1]

"Christ Jesus...commanded the eleven to go and teach the nations
...straightway therefore the Apostles...founded in the several cities
churches from which the rest have thenceforth borrowed and daily
borrow the shoot of faith and seeds of teaching in order that they may
become churches; and it is from this fact that they too will be accounted
apostolic, as the offspring of apostolic churches. Every kind of thing
must be estimated by reference back to its origin. Therefore the
churches, whatever their size or number, form the single and primitive
Church, which comes from the Apostles, and its offspring are they all.
Thus they are all primitive and all apostolic, since they are all approved
together by their union in the common peace, the title of brotherhood,
and the interchange of hospitality (*contesseratio hospitalitatis*)—rights
which are governed by no other rule than the single tradition of the
same mystery in all."[2]

1 *de Praescr.* 13; cp. *de Virg. vel.* 1; L. pp. 4, 5.
2 *de Praescr.* 20; G. p. 120.

Tertullian is here asserting not identity of Creed but of doctrinal tradition; the same faith is held in common by all churches which are all directly or indirectly of apostolic foundation. He uses a metaphor which emphasizes the identity of the substance and the difference of form, for the *tessera hospitalitatis* was a token divided into parts, of which each friend retained one, so that if they, or their heirs, ever met in later times, the parts would be found to fit together. Against diversities of heresies he places the unity of the faith, and against their novelties of doctrine its apostolic continuity. The *tessera hospitalitatis* was held in common not only by the Churches of Africa and R⌐⌐e, but by all orthodox churches, which agreed in doctrine th⌐ ⌐u they differed in the wording of their several Creeds.

"Run over the apostolic ch⌐⌐⌐ ⌐⌐⌐ ⌐⌐⌐ wnicn the very thrones of the Apostles at this ⌐⌐⌐⌐ ⌐⌐y preside over their own places.... Is Achaia near to you? Yo⌐ ⌐ave Corinth. If you are ⌐⌐ ⌐⌐ar from Macedonia, you have Phi⌐⌐⌐p⌐, ⌐ou have th⌐ Th⌐ssalonians. If you travel into Asia, you have ⌐⌐hesus. B⌐⌐ if you are near to Italy you have Rome, and from P⌐ ⌐e (*unde⌐ ⌐⌐ns auctoritas* is at hand for us also [in Africa] . . . see w⌐⌐t she has ⌐⌐arnt, what she has taught, what agreement (*quid contesserarit⌐⌐* she has kept with the Churches of Africa as with others ⌐⌐⌐⌐⌐⌐⌐e)."

⌐⌐⌐n he proceeds to enumerate the points of agreement: "One Lord God she ac⌐nowledges, the Creator of the universe, and Christ Jesus [born] of the virgin Mary, the Son of God the Creator, and the resurrection of the flesh; the Law and the Prophets she unites with the writings of the Apostles and Evangelists, from which she drinks in her faith; this she seals with the water, feeds with the eucharist, cheers with martyrdom, and against such a discipline she admits no gainsayer."[2]

So the *tessera hospitalitatis* stands for Christian practice as well as faith. Tertullian's whole argument is geographical. If you are in Greece, you have Corinth, etc., if in Italy or Africa, Rome is your nearest source; and the *auctoritas* is, in the last resort, that of the Apostles, which you can find, as it were, concentrated in any church founded by them. "In the Lord's Apostles we possess our authorities (*Apostolos Domini habemus auctores*) for even they did not choose to introduce anything, but faithfully delivered to the nations the teaching (*disciplinam*) which they had received from Christ."[3] His claim is that of Irenaeus; the substance of the faith is one everywhere, "for the Churches which have been planted in Germany do not believe or hand down anything different, nor do those in Spain, nor those in Gaul, nor those in the East, nor those in Egypt, nor those in Libya, nor those which have been established in the central regions of the world" (probably Palestine).[4] *Auctoritas*, of course, does not imply jurisdiction, but is akin to our use of "expert authority", a powerful guarantee. The best comment on this passage of Tertullian is Augustine, *Ep.* xliii (quoted on p. 30).

1 See p. 4 n. 3.   2 *de Praescr.* 36; quoted in part, L. p. 5.
3 *de Praescr.* 6.   4 *adv. Haer.* I. 3.

CHAPTER IV

EASTERN BAPTISMAL CREEDS OF THE FOURTH CENTURY

I. INTRODUCTION

HITHERTO we have treated Creeds independently of the Liturgies, of which they nevertheless formed an intrinsic though only occasional part. However illogical such a method may be, in dealing with these early times it is inevitable, since Creeds and Liturgies were both in process of formation, and, except in regard to a very simple framework, might vary considerably even in neighbouring districts. Thus, though we have been able to produce complete specimens of Creeds dating from the second century, it is only by small fragments and scattered hints that we can conjecture the structure of Liturgies. In the fourth century, however, such a separation is indefensible, for though we have no complete liturgy untainted by the adulteration of extraneous matter—as in the pseudo-apostolical documents—yet the portions that survive are far larger and more numerous.

The three sees named in the sixth canon of the Council of Nicaea are Rome, Alexandria, and Antioch. For liturgical purposes we must add to them Caesarea and Jerusalem; and as neither Alexandria nor Palestine was in the line of tradition of the Apostles' Creed, it will be convenient to take these first of all and postpone the consideration of Antiochene or Syrian liturgies.

II. ALEXANDRIA

Until the publication of the *Sacramentary of Serapion* by Dmitriewskij we had little detailed evidence for Egyptian usage in the fourth century. Beyond a few references in writers like Athanasius and Didymus there was nothing but the so-called *Egyptian Church Order*, which is meagre and of uncertain date.

CH. IV ALEXANDRIA 39

The prayers in the Sacramentary would appear to be of a time not later than 350, though they may not all be those of Serapion himself. They are thus earlier than the Greek Liturgy of St Mark, and this has been considerably influenced by the Liturgy of St James, which itself cannot be earlier than the end of the fourth century. The Sacramentary is exclusively a celebrant's book, with no indication of the parts of the deacon or of the minor orders, and with no rubrics beyond a few notes and what is implied in the title of the prayers. The collection is ill-arranged, the elements of the several rites are scattered, and when they occur in groups it cannot be taken for granted that they represent the actual order in practice. In the Mass there is some general resemblance to the Syrian rite, but sufficient differences to show that there was already a special Egyptian type. Thus the Prayer of the kiss of peace, omitted here but noticed by Origen and Timothy of Alexandria, was perhaps borrowed from the Syrian rite, and the Prayer of the Fraction is both Syrian and Egyptian. On the other hand, in Egyptian usage there is an emphatic body of intercession by the celebrant, while in other rites there is nothing but the deacon's litany and a prayer of inclination, or in the Byzantine two prayers of the faithful.

Such being the features of the Liturgy, we shall expect to find considerable individuality in the Creed. The Alexandrian Creed of the second century has been already given, and later creeds must be in some way built upon it. Beyond this the only direct evidence we have for the form of Creed is the Profession of Arius and Euzoius (L. p. 20, H. pp. 7, 8), and the Creed of Macarius of Egypt, which, in its later clauses, is incomplete (L. p. 21).

Sozomen[1] says of the former of these: "Many considered this declaration of faith as an artful compilation, and as bearing an appearance of opposition to Arian tenets, while in reality it supported them; the terms in which it was couched being so vague that it was susceptible of diverse interpretation." Apart from matter probably added for the occasion it seems in the main to be on the general lines of Creeds of the period In the fourth century the Alexandrine Creed apparently had "one" in the first

1 *H.E.* II. 37.

clause (Arius, Macarius, *Epistola Systatice*, Coptic and Ethiopic Creeds, Egyptian Church Order); in the second member Λόγος (Arius, Macarius, Serapion, 4, 8, 10); and in the third the epithet μόνη of the Church (Letter of Alexander, Serapion 23, Liturgy of St Mark, Brightman p. 126; Coptic Jacobites, *ib.* pp. 150, 160, 161). For our purpose the Creed of Arius and Euzoius is important as showing how far Arius would go in using orthodox language while holding heretical views, and on account of the list of unqualified participles, "who came down and was incarnate and suffered and rose".

The Alexandrian Creed of the Fourth Century

Arius and Euzoius	Macarius
Πιστεύομεν εἰς ἕνα Θεὸν Πατέρα παντοκράτορα·	Πιστεύω εἰς ἕ. Θ. Π. π.
Καὶ εἰς Κύριον Ἰησοῦν Χριστόν, τὸν Υἱὸν Αὐτοῦ, τὸν ἐξ Αὐτοῦ (πρὸ πάντων τῶν αἰώνων)	Καὶ εἰς [τὸν Κ. ἡμῶν Ἰ. Χ.] τὸν [Υἱὸν] Αὐτοῦ,
γεγεννημένον (Θεὸν) Λόγον, δι᾿ οὗ τὰ πάντα ἐγένετο (τά τε ἐν τοῖς οὐρανοῖς καὶ τὰ ἐπὶ τῆς γῆς), τὸν κατελθόντα, καὶ σαρκωθέντα, καὶ παθόντα,	[τὸν μονογενῆ] Λόγον, δι᾿ οὗ ἐποίησε τοὺς αἰῶνας,
	τὸν σ. ἐκ τῆς ἁγίας παρθένου, καὶ σταυρωθέντα, καὶ ἀποθανόντα, καὶ ταφέντα,
καὶ ἀναστάντα, ἀνελθόντα εἰς τοὺς οὐρανούς,	καὶ ἀ. τῇ τρίτῃ ἡμέρᾳ, καὶ ἀ. εἰς τ. οὐ.
	καὶ {καθεζόμενον ἐν δεξιᾷ / καθίσαντα ἐκ δεξιῶν} τοῦ Π.,
καὶ πάλιν ἐρχόμενον κρῖναι ζῶντας καὶ νεκρούς· Καὶ εἰς τὸ Ἅγιον Πνεῦμα· Καὶ εἰς σαρκὸς ἀνάστασιν· Καὶ εἰς ζωὴν τοῦ μέλλοντος αἰῶνος· (καὶ εἰς βασιλείαν οὐρανῶν) Καὶ εἰς μίαν καθολικὴν ἐκκλησίαν (τοῦ Θεοῦ, τὴν ἀπὸ περάτων ἕως περάτων)	καὶ πάλιν ἐρχόμενον κρῖναι ζῶντας καὶ νεκρούς· Καὶ εἰς τὸ Ἅ. Π.· Καὶ εἰς ἀ. νεκρῶν· [Καὶ μ. ἁγίαν καὶ μόνην κ. ἐ.] [Ἄφεσιν ἁμαρτιῶν]

( ) indicate possible additions by A. and E.
[ ] indicate additions from Serapion and other sources.

III. Palestine

The Liturgy of Palestine is known to us only in part through the Catechetical Lectures of Cyril of Jerusalem, and some phrases in Jerome and Eusebius of Caesarea. *The Pilgrimage* of Etheria gives us information on the rites of Church in Jerusalem, but no details of the celebration of the Liturgy. In origin it was, of course, independent of the Liturgy of Antioch; but by the fourth century it had undoubtedly been influenced by it, as is shown by the many striking coincidences of language between the Greek and Syriac Liturgies of St James and Cyril.[1] The Creed is given in part in the letter of Eusebius to his diocese after the close of the Council of Nicaea,[2] and in Cyril's Lectures. Eusebius introduces it by saying: "As in our first catechetical instruction, and at the time of our baptism, we received from the bishops who were before us, and as we have learnt from the Holy Scriptures, and alike as presbyters and as bishops were wont to believe and teach; so we now believe and thus declare our faith." This would carry the Creed back at least to the end of the third century; but it must be remembered that Eusebius had already been condemned for his Arian views at a council held at Antioch at the end of the year 324;[3] and had presented his Creed as part of his defence, in spite of the fact that on the point at issue it was indecisive. Hence, though it obviously cannot have departed greatly from the traditional Creed of the diocese, he may have strengthened it here and there in the orthodox sense either in the transcription or in the interval between the two councils. We can check it by the Creed of Antioch and its derivatives, and by that of Cyril.

---

1 See Srawley, *Early History of the Liturgy*, p. 85. The Church of Jerusalem was reorganized by Alexander, who, before becoming Bishop of Jerusalem in 212, had been Bishop of some see in Cappadocia (Euseb. *H.E.* VI. 11). He brought his Creed to Jerusalem, and it was traceable in a MS. seen by Victorinus of Pettau in the Library at Jerusalem of which Alexander was the founder (*Liber de Computo*, Muratori, *Anecd.* III. p. 207). In matters of discipline he refers to the custom of the Churches of Asia.

2 Theodt. *H.E.* I. 12. Gwatkin, pp. 178–189.

3 See below, pp. 182–184.

Cyril's catechetical lectures were delivered in 348 when he was still a presbyter. Between "through whom all things were made" and "rose the third day" the precise wording of the Creed is unknown, and the blank has been variously filled by different editors, e.g. by Lietzmann and Heurtley; but in view of the place where the lectures were delivered, and of the claims of the Empress Helena to have discovered the true cross some twenty years before, we may feel confident that it contained the word σταυρωθέντα. About the phrase dealing with the Incarnation critics disagree, but I myself am inclined to favour γεννηθέντα ἐκ (τῆς) παρθένου καὶ (τοῦ) Ἁγίου Πνεύματος.[1]

Finally, Cyril's lectures give τὸν ἐκ τοῦ Πατρὸς γεννηθέντα Θεὸν ἀληθινόν, where we may doubt whether Θεὸν ἀληθινόν is pre-Nicene; it looks definitely dogmatic and anti-heretical. Cyril preferred not to use homoousian terminology as being unscriptural, but this phrase and that already quoted show that he was nevertheless substantially orthodox; and these words may have been introduced from the Creed of Nicaea by Macarius or Maximus.

In the Creed of Eusebius the phrases Θεὸν ἐκ Θεοῦ, φῶς ἐκ φωτός may be additions made by Eusebius himself: compare the creeds of Auxentius of Cappadocia, *Deum verum ex vero Deo Patre*, and of Eunomius, Υἱὸν ἀληθινὸν Ἀλήθειαν ἐνεργοῦσαν... φῶς, both of whom were Arians. Cyril has (*Cat*. iv. 7) πίστευε δὲ εἰς τὸν Υἱὸν τοῦ Θεοῦ, τὸν ἕνα καὶ μόνον, τὸν Κύριον ἡμῶν Ἰησοῦν Χριστόν, τὸν ἐκ φωτὸς φῶς γεννηθέντα, so the language was already familiar; but these phrases were not in Cyril's Creed; and it is far more likely that the Creed of Caesarea had (ἀνελθόντα) εἰς τοὺς οὐρανούς than πρὸς τὸν Πατέρα as Eusebius quotes it.

Ἐν ἀνθρώποις πολιτευσάμενον is also doubtful. The *Apostolic Constitutions*, which is also an Arian production, has πολιτευσάμενον ὁσίως κατὰ τοὺς νόμους τοῦ Θεοῦ καὶ Πατρὸς Αὐτοῦ, but

---

1 Cp. iv. 9 γεννηθεὶς ἐξ ἁγίας παρθένου καὶ Ἁγίου Πνεύματος: xii. 3 ἀλλ' ἐκ παρθένου καὶ Πνεύματος Ἁγίου κατὰ τὸ εὐαγγέλιον ἐνανθρωπήσαντα: xii. 4 πίστευσον ὅτι αὐτὸς ἐκεῖνος ὁ τοῦ Θεοῦ μονογενὴς Υἱὸς οὗτος ἐκ παρθένου πάλιν ἐγεννήθη.

the word was not in the Creed of Antioch as given by Cassian;
the last clauses are missing, and it is possible that Eusebius
may have left out some words in the main body.

It will be seen that neither Creed is in a state wholly satis-
factory for our purpose. I give both of them below subject to
the deductions which I have stated.

Eusebius (L. p. 14; H. p. 4)   Cyril (L. p. 15; H. pp. 12, 13)

Πιστεύομεν εἰς ἕνα Θεὸν Πατέρα   Π. εἰς ἕ. Θ. Π. π.,
  παντοκράτορα,
τὸν τῶν ὁρατῶν τε καὶ ἀοράτων   π. οὐρανοῦ καὶ γῆς,
  ποιητήν·   ὁρ. τε πάντων καὶ ἀορ.
Καὶ εἰς ἕνα Κύριον Ἰησοῦν Χριστόν,   Κ. εἰς ἕ. Κ. Ἰ. Χ.,
  τὸν Υἱὸν τοῦ Θεοῦ...Υἱὸν μονογενῆ,   τὸν Υἱ. τ. Θ. μονογενῆ,
  πρωτότοκον πάσης κτίσεως,
  πρὸ πάντων τῶν αἰώνων   τὸν ἐκ τ. Π. γεννηθέντα
  ἐκ τοῦ Πατρὸς γεγεννημένον,   προ π. τ. αἰ.,
  δι᾽ οὗ καὶ ἐγένετο τὰ πάντα,   δι᾽ οὗ τ. π. ἐγένετο,
  τὸν διὰ τὴν ἡμετέραν σωτηρίαν
  σαρκωθέντα,
καὶ παθόντα   (σταυρωθέντα)
καὶ ἀναστάντα τῇ τρίτῃ ἡμέρᾳ   καὶ ἀ. ἐκ νεκρῶν τῇ τ. ἡ.,
καὶ ἀνελθόντα...   καὶ ἀ. εἰς τοὺς οὐρανούς,
                                  καὶ καθίσαντα ἐκ δεξιῶν τ. Π.,
καὶ ἥξοντα πάλιν ἐν δόξῃ   καὶ ἐρχόμενον ἐν δ.,
κρῖναι ζῶντας καὶ νεκρούς·   κ. ζ. κ. ν.,
                                  οὗ τῆς βασιλείας οὐκ ἔσται τέλος·
Πιστεύομεν καὶ εἰς ἓν Πνεῦμα Ἅγιον   (Καὶ) εἰς ἓν Ἅ. Π., τὸν παράκλητον,
                                  τὸ λαλῆσαν ἐν τοῖς προφήταις.

                                  Καὶ εἰς ἓν βάπτισμα μετανοίας εἰς
                                    ἄφεσιν ἁμαρτιῶν·
                                  Καὶ εἰς μίαν ἁγίαν καθολικὴν ἐκκλ-
                                    ησίαν·
                                  Καὶ εἰς σαρκὸς ἀνάστασιν·
                                  Καὶ εἰς ζωὴν αἰώνιον.

Few, I think, would deny that these Creeds show signs of
Antiochene influence.

IV. ANTIOCHENE CREEDS

Until the rise of Constantinople there were only two cities of
first-class importance in the Christian East, Antioch and Alexandria. Josephus[1] calls Antioch the third city in the empire; it

1 *B.J.* III. ii. 4.

was founded by Seleucus Nicator, as a fitting central place for a rule that embraced at once Asia Minor and the region of the Euphrates, where the great roads from Mesopotamia and the river Orontes descend from the Syrian range and debouch upon the coast, and at the same time he gave to it the port of Seleucia to link it with the Mediterranean. Antioch was thus the centre of the continental eastern monarchy of the rulers of Asia, as Alexandria was the centre for the naval power and the maritime policy of the rulers of Egypt.

Once made a residency and the seat of the supreme administration of a great empire, Antioch remained in Roman times the capital of the Asiatic dominions of Rome. Here the Emperors resided when they sojourned in the East, embellishing it with buildings and adding to its prestige; it was the seat of the Legate of Syria and the base and headquarters of the legions who watched the eastern frontier of the empire. As in other great cities, the ruling class was drawn from its wealthier citizens, but these were not large landowners but traders, and the trade of Antioch was chiefly by land, since in spite of vast expenditure of money and energy, the art of the engineers contended vainly at Seleucia with the difficulties of the ground. This large overland trade gave to its inhabitants a wide outlook, and accustomed them to the idea of travel, a tone of mind stimulated by the annual visits to Jerusalem of the Jews who formed a large element in its population and probably to some extent controlled Antiochene finance.

And Antiochene Christianity had behind it a strong missionary tradition. Antioch owed its evangelization in the first instance to refugees who fled from the persecution that followed on the martyrdom of St Stephen; about the year A.D. 46 it sent a contribution to the poor of Jerusalem; it was the starting point of the first missionary journey of St Paul and St Barnabas for Cyprus, Pisidia, and Southern Galatia, and of the second journey of St Paul and Silvanus which ranged as far west as Athens and Corinth and north to Macedonia; and though the story found in Socrates (*H.E.* vi. 8), and in a different form in Theodoret (*H.E.* III. 19), which makes Antioch the teacher of the whole Christian world in antiphonal singing, is probably false (see Lightfoot, *Ap. Fathers*, Pt. 2. 1. p. 31), it nevertheless testifies to its liturgical pre-eminence. And in this respect its only possible rival was Alexandria. The Church of Jerusalem never recovered from the destruction of the city until pilgrimages gave it a new prestige; and although the history of Origen shows that there was some intimate relation between Alexandria and Palestine, yet Alexandria never exercised there an ecclesiastical dominance, while, except for the Roman province of Asia, which would naturally look to Ephesus, the seat of the Proconsul and for a long time the residence of St Paul and the reputed home of St John, Antioch could extend its liturgical influence over the whole of Asia Minor, for Ephesus was never of sufficient strength or importance to oppose more than a passive resistance to this Antiochene invasion. Moreover the various councils of bishops that met at Antioch were partly a testimony to its central position, and partly also a means of spreading its liturgical influence, for a great patriarchal church could set a standard of ceremonial usage and splendour which would impress the minds of visiting prelates, while Antioch was also the home of a distinguished theological school.

Thus in 251 a synod was held at Antioch which was attended by the bishops of Tarsus in Cilicia, Caesarea in Palestine, and Caesarea in Cappadocia (Eusebius, *H.E.* VI. 46). From 264–268 councils were held there in connexion with the case of Paul of Samosata, and these were attended by Firmilian of Cappadocia, Gregory Thaumaturgus and Athenodorus, both of Pontus, Helenus of Tarsus, Nicomas of Lycaonia and others. About the year 314, after the persecution of Galerius and Maximian, a council was held at Ancyra, presided over by the Bishop of Antioch, at which were present bishops from Palestine, Coele-Syria, Cilicia, Pamphylia, Pisidia, Lycaonia, Cappadocia, Great Armenia, Phrygia, Galatia (including Marcellus of Ancyra), Pontus and Bithynia; in short, with the exception of Roman Asia, it was a plenary council of all Asia Minor and Syria.

Duchesne says that up to the reign of Theodosius (379–395) "Antioch remained Queen of the East, the centre to which the

Greek empire and its chief ecclesiastical metropolis gravitated, the ancient Churches of Asia and the Christian communities of the diocese of Thracia being drawn into its circle of influence. Alexandria resisted its attraction." "Antioch having lost this position from the time of Theodosius the entire East looked to Constantinople. The three northern dioceses [i.e. Asia, Pontus, and Thrace] originally cut off from the ancient capital were soon seized upon by the new."[1] And Hort[2] calls Antioch the "ecclesiastical mother" of Constantinople; and so in the fourth century we may regard the Byzantine and Syrian rites as forming a single group which extended its sway at least as far north as Thrace.

Of this rite the three earliest examples are the Clementine Liturgy in the eighth book of the *Apostolic Constitutions*, and the Liturgies of St Basil and St Chrysostom. The first was composed by an Arian in the latter half of the fourth century,[3] but was never used in actual practice. Its compiler shows acquaintance with the writings of Clement of Rome, Justin Martyr, Hippolytus and Novatian; in general it is shaped on the liturgy of Antioch, and he has before him also the Anaphora of the *Egyptian Church Order*; but he has freely reshaped, reduced, and expanded his documents at pleasure, and interpolated them from other sources or out of his own head, so that his Liturgy, like his Creed, is saturated with his own style. The Liturgy of St Basil, which is earlier than that of St Chrysostom, is in large measure based upon the Anaphora of the *Apostolic Tradition* of Hippolytus. The Liturgy of St Chrysostom may be as early as his time (398–407), but there is no positive evidence of his authorship.

(a) The Creed of Antioch

But here we are confronted with a double difficulty. The Creed of Antioch is known to us by fragments given in Latin by Cassian (*cont. Nest.* VI. 3) (C) and in Greek in a treatise by Eusebius of Dorylaeum preserved in the Acts of the Council of Ephesus in 431, and in a sermon by Chrysostom, and all these authorities are late, while what we need is to get back to a form earlier than

1 *Christian Worship*, pp. 21, 25.   2 *Two Dissertations*, p. 73.
3 See Turner, *J.T.S.* XVI. pp. 54–61; XXXI. p. 129.

the end of the fourth century, after which the eyes of Asia Minor
were turned towards Constantinople.

It has been enlarged by at least one phrase taken from the
Creed of the Council of Nicaea, *et non factum, Deum verum ex
Deo vero, homousion Patri*, but when this has been removed, we
have to allow for growth in the interval, and for local peculiarities
which would not be taken over by other churches, all of which
should be eliminated. Nevertheless we can perhaps gain our end
by another route. If the Creed of Antioch affected the Creeds of
churches farther off, it would also affect the Creeds contained in
documents of Antiochene origin, such as that in the *Didascalia
Apostolorum* (D) in the third century; that in the *Apostolic Constitutions* in the fourth (A); the Creeds of the successive councils
of Antioch in 341 (1, 2, 3, 4); the Macrostich of 345 (M); and the
κατὰ μέρος πίστις, attributed to Gregory Thaumaturgus, which
Caspari claims for Apollinaris the Younger, Bishop of Laodicea
(L). We may therefore cast out from the Creed of Antioch what
has little or no support in any of these, and supply from these
the clauses on the Holy Spirit and the Church which are not
given by Cassian, Eusebius, or Chrysostom.

The resulting form, following Cassian's Latin text, is given
below. Round brackets ( ) indicate the clauses to be omitted,
and square brackets [ ] those to be supplied. The reasons are
given in the notes.

Credo in unum (et solum verum) Deum Patrem omnipotentem,
Creatorem omnium (visibilium et invisibilium creaturarum);
Et in Dominum nostrum, Jesum Christum, Filium Ejus unigenitum
(et primogenitum totius creaturae), ex Eo natum ante omnia saecula,
(et non factum, Deum verum ex Deo vero, homousion Patri,)
per quem (et saecula compaginata sunt et) omnia facta,
qui (propter nos) venit, et natus est ex Maria virgine,
et crucifixus est sub Pontio Pilato, et sepultus,
et tertia die resurrexit (secundum scripturas),
et in caelis ascendit,
et iterum veniet judicare vivos et mortuos;
[Et in Spiritum Sanctum]
[Et in unam sanctam catholicam ecclesiam]
In remissionem peccatorum;
Et carnis resurrectionem;
Et vitam aeternam.

Et solum verum in C, but omitted by 1, 2, 3, 4, M., A., D.; L. has ἀληθινόν only.

visibilium...creaturarum in L. and M., omitted by all others.

et...creaturae in C and 2, omitted by all others.

et...compaginata et sunt omitted by all.

propter nos in L. and M., omitted by all others.

secundum scripturas omitted by 4, M., A., L., D.; used of the Incarnation in 1, 2, 3.

In the clause on the Holy Spirit we should probably read
either εἰς τὸ Ἅγιον Πνεῦμα with 1, or εἰς τὸ Πνεῦμα τὸ Ἅγιον.
All others than 1 have this latter form with varying words there-
after.

On the Church, A reads ἐν τῇ ἁγίᾳ καθολικῇ καὶ ἀποστολικῇ
ἐκκλησίᾳ; 1, 2, 3 omit the clause. 4 has, in another context, ἡ καθ.
ἐκ.; L. μίαν ἁγ. ἐκ.; M., in the anathemas, ἡ ἁγ. (καὶ) καθ. ἐκ.; the
remaining clauses in the *Apostolic Constitutions* are: εἰς σαρκὸς
ἀνάστασιν καὶ εἰς ἄφεσιν ἁμαρτιῶν,...καὶ εἰς ζωὴν τοῦ μέλλοντος
αἰῶνος. 1 has πιστεύομεν περὶ σαρκὸς ἀναστάσεως καὶ ζωῆς
αἰωνίου. L. (καὶ εἰς) ἄφεσιν ἁμαρτιῶν, (καὶ εἰς) σαρκὸς ἀνάστασιν,
(καὶ εἰς) ζωὴν αἰώνιον.

Cassian states that with this Creed Nestorius was baptized, so
as it stands it cannot be later than A.D. 400, for Nestorius became
Bishop of Constantinople in 428. The enlargement was probably
made by Meletius between his coming to Antioch in 361 and his
exile in 370. Hort says "that Meletius was responsible for the
Antiochian revision, and that it took place in one of the early
years of his episcopate is likely enough".[1] We have been extremely conservative in our excisions and the resulting form is
probably too elaborate.

From Antioch the Creed would probably spread through Asia
Minor. From this region we have four Creeds; those of Auxentius
of Cappadocia, Charisius of Philadelphia, Marcellus of Ancyra,
and the Creed of the so-called *Psalter of Aethelstan*, which has
been translated into Latin in the *Codex Laudianus*. A comparison of these exported Creeds, as we may term them, with
the home Creed of Antioch will provide a method of checking
our result, and discovering its local peculiarities.

1 *Two Dissertations*, p. 128; cp. Gwatkin, *Studies in Arianism*, p. 212.

(b) The Creed of Cappadocia

The first of these is given by Auxentius, by birth a Cappadocian, ordained priest by Gregory of Cappadocia in 343, and the predecessor of Ambrose in the see of Milan (355–374), who, in writing to the Emperors Valens and Valentinian in 364 and seeking to disclaim the charge of heresy, says that he never knew Arius nor his doctrines, *sed ex infantia quemadmodum doctus sum, sicut accepi de sanctis scripturis, credidi et credo.* Then follows his Creed, which, by this statement, should be the pre-Nicene Creed of Cappadocia.

The Creed of Auxentius of Cappadocia and its Cognates

Auxentius (Hil. Pictav. T. II. p. 617, Migne)	Eunomius, *Apologeticus*
Credo in unum solum verum Deum Patrem omnipotentem, (invisibilem, impassibilem, immortalem);	πιστεύομεν εἰς τὸν ἕνα καὶ μόνον ἀληθινὸν Θεόν
Et in Filium Ejus unigenitum, Dominum nostrum, Jesum Christum,	πιστεύομεν καὶ εἰς τὸν τοῦ Θεοῦ Υἱόν. τὸν μονογενῆ Θεόν, τὸν πρωτότοκον πάσης κτίσεως
ante omnia saecula (et ante omne principium) natum ex Patre, (Deum verum Filium ex vero Deo Patre)...	Υἱὸν ἀληθινόν...πρὸ πάσης κτίσεως γενόμενον... Σοφίαν ζῶσαν, ᾿Αλήθειαν ἐνεργοῦσαν... Φῶς ἀληθινόν
Per Ipsum enim omnia facta sunt visibilia et invisibilia, qui descendit de caelis... (propter nostram salutem)	τὸν ἐπ᾽ ἐσχάτων τῶν ἡμερῶν γενόμενον ἐν σαρκί,
natus de (Spiritu Sancto et) Maria virgine...	γενόμενον ἐκ γυναικός, γενόμενον ἄνθρωπον...
et crucifixum (sub Pontio Pilato), sepultum,	τὸν γενόμενον ὑπήκοον μέχρι σταυροῦ καὶ θανάτου...
tertia die resurrexisse,	ἀναστάντα τῇ τρίτῃ τῶν ἡμερῶν, καὶ μετὰ τὴν ἀνάστασιν
ascendisse in caelis,	ἀνακεφαλαιωσάμενον τοῖς ῾Εαυτοῦ τὸ μυστήριον.
sedere ad dexteram Patris,	καὶ καθήμενον ἐν δεξιᾷ τοῦ Πατρός·
venturum judicare vivos et mortuos;	τὸν ἐρχόμενον κρῖναι ζῶντας καὶ νεκρούς.
Et in Spiritum Sanctum Paracletum...	Καὶ...πιστεύομεν εἰς τὸν Παράκλητον
Spiritum veritatis.	τὸ Πνεῦμα τῆς ἀληθείας...πιστεύομεν ...τὴν γενησομένην ἀνάστασιν...

I have put into brackets what I regard as Auxentius's own additions to the Creed of Cappadocia.

Basil (Bp. 370–379), *de Fide* (*Ascetica*, 4)	Relevant non-Nicene phrases in the Creed now used by the Armenian Church (Hort, *Two Dissertations*, pp. 146, 147)
πιστεύομεν... ἕνα μόνον ἀληθινὸν... Θεὸν	
καὶ Πατέρα παντοκράτορα,	
ἐξ οὗ τὰ πάντα...	ποιητὴν οὐρανοῦ καὶ γῆς
καὶ ἕνα τὸν μονογενῆ Αὐτοῦ Υἱόν,	
Κύριον καὶ Θεὸν ἡμῶν, Ἰησοῦν Χριστόν,	
...δι᾿ οὗ τὰ πάντα ἐγένετο,	
τά τε ὁρατὰ καὶ τὰ ἀόρατα.	ὁρατά τε καὶ ἀόρατα,
	(κατελθόντα) ἐκ τῶν οὐρανῶν,
	γεννηθέντα τελείως ἐκ Μαρίας
διὰ τῆς ἐκ παρθένου γεννήσεως...	τῆς παρθένου διὰ Πνεύματος Ἁγίου,
γενόμενος ὑπήκοος μέχρι θανάτου,	σταυρωθέντα,
θανάτου δὲ σταυροῦ.	ταφέντα.
καὶ τῇ τρίτῃ ἡμέρᾳ ἐγερθεὶς ἐκ νεκρῶν,	
...ἀνέβη εἰς τοὺς οὐρανούς,	(ἀνελθόντα εἰς τοὺς οὐρανούς)
	ἐν αὐτῷ τῷ σώματι·
καὶ κάθηται ἐν δεξιᾷ τοῦ Πατρός.	καθίσαντα ἐν δεξιᾷ τοῦ Πατρός·
ὅθεν ἔρχεται... ἀναστῆσαι πάντας	(ἐρχόμενον) ἐν αὐτῷ τῷ σώματι
ὅτε οἱ μὲν δίκαιοι προσληφθήσονται	(καὶ) ἐν τῇ δόξῃ τοῦ Πατρός·
εἰς ζωὴν αἰώνιον·	
	οὗ τῆς βασιλείας οὐκ ἔσται τέλος.
καὶ ἓν μόνον Πνεῦμα Ἅγιον τὸν Παράκλητον.	

The phrases of the Creed of Eunomius are taken from his Exposition of Faith (Mansi, iv. 645–649), which was presented to the Emperor Theodosius in 383 in vindication of the orthodoxy of his teaching. Eunomius was by birth a Cappadocian from near the border of Galatia and a pupil of Aetius. His Creed may be based only on the Creed of Antioch and the Second Formula of Antioch. This Formula seems to have been composed by the Cappadocian sophist Asterius, based upon the Creed of Lucian, a priest of Antioch who was born at Samosata. There would also seem to be some connexion between the Cappadocian Creed and the Third Formula of Antioch (L. pp. 23–25) which is ascribed to Theophronius of Tyana, also in Cappadocia.

The phrases from Basil are taken from his Sermon on the Faith, which ends "Thus we think and thus we baptize into the Trinity of one substance in accordance with the command of our Lord Himself, Jesus Christ, saying 'Go and make disciples of all nations, etc.'"

The Armenian Creed is based on the Nicene, but Christianity undoubtedly reached Armenia from Cappadocia. Only the possibly relevant phrases are given here. There is a close connexion between this Creed, the Longer Creed of Epiphanius, and the *Interpretatio in Symbolum*. Of the three the Epiphanian is undoubtedly the earliest, being composed of the Nicene, certain phrases taken from the Creed of Cyprus, and parenthetical explanations.

It is clear that Auxentius, like Eusebius of Caesarea, has omitted the concluding clauses of his Creed as dealing with matters about which there was no controversy, and that he added phrases of his own.

In the first clause I have bracketed the epithets "invisible, impassible, immortal". This phrase finds no support from our other authorities, its nearest parallels being "invisible, immortal, impassible", in the Creed of the Arian Council of Sirmium in 351, and "alone ingenerate and invisible" in the Creed of Ulphilas the Arian Bishop of the Goths. It was characteristic of the Arians to give to God the Father titles which they would deny to God the Son; cp. the Arian Fragments in Mai's *Script. vet. nova Coll.* III. 215, "Ingenerate and only begotten;...He who was seen and whom no man saw nor can see; who is impassible, and who suffered for us." The author of the *Explanatio Symboli ad Initiandos*, who was probably Ambrose, blames the Church of Aquileia for adding to its Creed "invisible and impassible", a phrase which he said was distorted by the Arians for their own purposes.

In the second clause I have bracketed "true God the Son from true God the Father"; this is also probably an Arian addition intended to throw dust in the eyes of the orthodox. Eunomius has "the only-begotten God...true Son", and Arius and Euzoius, "God, Word"; at the Council of Nicaea the Arians were asked "Will you own that the Son is God?" and replied, "We have no objection to it; if He has been so made, verily so He is."

NOTES

A. "*Born of the Holy Spirit and Mary the virgin*"

This phrase I have marked as doubtful. If we are satisfied that Auxentius makes additions to the Creed which he said he had held *ex infantia*, this may be one of them; Eunomius has "born of a woman"; Basil speaks of the "birth from a virgin". The history of the appearance of this phrase in Creeds will repay attention. Outside the Creed of Auxentius it occurs first in Eastern baptismal Creeds, in the Creed of Marcellus of Ancyra, *c.* 340, or, if that be thought to be Western, then in the Creed of Niceta of Remesiana, 370–375.

The Creeds of the *Apostolic Constitutions*, of Antioch and of Philadelphia have only "of the holy virgin Mary" with no mention of the Holy Spirit.

In Conciliar Creeds, the Council of Antioch against Paul of Samosata speaks of "the body from the virgin".

Council of Antioch, 341, First Formula, "of the (holy) virgin" (L. p. 23);
Council of Antioch, Second Formula, "of a virgin" (L. p. 23);
Council of Antioch, Third Formula, "of the virgin" (L. p. 25);
Council of Antioch, Fourth Formula, "of the holy virgin" (L. p. 26);
Council of Philippopolis, 343, "of the holy virgin";
Council of Antioch, 345, "of the holy virgin";
Council of Sirmium, 351, "of the holy virgin";
Council of Sirmium, 357, "from the womb of the virgin Mary";
Council of Sirmium, 359, "of Mary the virgin" (L. p. 27);

and the full phrase first occurs in the Creed of the Council of Nike 359, while its absence from the Creeds of Caesarea (Eusebius), Jerusalem (Cyril), and that of the Council of Nicaea would seem to show that it was rare in 325. The inference seems inevitable that it was more probably absent from the Creed of Cappadocia at the beginning of the fourth century than present in it, but that by the last quarter of the century it had become fairly common.

B. "*Under Pontius Pilate*"

This phrase has a somewhat similar history. It first appears in Conciliar Creeds in that of the Council of Ariminum in 359. It is in the Creeds of Marcellus (340), Antioch (*c.* 360), the *Apostolic Constitutions*, and Niceta, but absent from those of Arius and Euzoius, Caesarea, Jerusalem, and Philadelphia. As it has no support in the parallels to the Creed of Auxentius I have omitted it from the earlier Cappadocian Creed.

One other remark: nowhere else than in Basil have we found "whence" before our Lord's Coming to Judgement. This word therefore would appear to be an integral part of the Cappadocian Creed in Basil's day, but not as early as the "infancy" of Auxentius.

(c) The Creed of Charisius of Philadelphia

The Philadelphian Creed is preserved in the Acts of the Council of Ephesus in 431.[1] At the sixth session of that Council a certain Charisius, presbyter and steward of Philadelphia in Lydia, stated that he had been excommunicated by heretics, and produced his Creed apparently as evidence of his orthodoxy.

Πιστεύω εἰς ἕνα Θεὸν Πατέρα παντοκράτορα,
Κτίστην (? κτιστῶν) ἁπάντων ὁρατῶν τε καὶ ἀοράτων ποιητήν·
Καὶ εἰς ἕνα Κύριον Ἰησοῦν Χριστόν,
τὸν Υἱὸν Αὐτοῦ τὸν μονογενῆ,
(Θεὸν ἐκ Θεοῦ, φῶς ἐκ φωτός,
Θεὸν ἀληθινὸν ἐκ Θεοῦ ἀληθινοῦ,
ὁμοούσιον τῷ Πατρί,)
τὸν (δι' ἡμᾶς καὶ τὴν ἡμετέραν σωτηρίαν) κατελθόντα ἐκ τῶν
    οὐρανῶν,
(σαρκωθέντα,)
γεννηθέντα ἐκ τῆς ἁγίας παρθένου,
(ἐνανθρωπήσαντα,)
σταυρωθέντα ὑπὲρ ἡμῶν,
ἀποθανόντα,
ἀναστάντα τῇ τρίτῃ ἡμέρᾳ,
ἀνελθόντα εἰς τοὺς οὐρανούς,
καὶ πάλιν ἐρχόμενον κρῖναι ζῶντας καὶ νεκρούς·
Καὶ εἰς τὸ Πνεῦμα τῆς ἀληθείας, τὸ Παράκλητον,
(ὁμοούσιον Πατρὶ καὶ Υἱῷ)·
Καὶ εἰς ἁγίαν καθολικὴν ἐκκλησίαν·
Εἰς ἀνάστασιν νεκρῶν·
Εἰς ζωὴν αἰώνιον.

In the first clause κτιστῶν is Kattenbusch's very probable emendation.

The omission of the name "Mary" is paralleled in the Fourth Formula of the Council of Antioch in 341, which has "and was born of the holy virgin".

The curious phrase "the Spirit of truth, the Paraclete", may also be Antiochene, since in the Nestorian Creed, which is

1 Mansi, IV. p. 1348.

formed from the Creeds of Antioch and of the Nicene Council,
we find "And in one Spirit Holy, the Spirit of Truth", and in
the Creed of the *Apostolic Constitutions*, "In the Spirit the
Holy, that is the Paraclete"; but the phrase is probably later
than 325. Kattenbusch (*ap. Symb.* I. 361) suggests "in the
(Holy) Spirit". With these omissions, which result in a form
slightly fuller than that suggested by Kattenbusch, we get back
to the form given, which may have been in use in Philadelphia
about the year 330. This should be compared with the Creed of
Remesiana given in the following chapter.

I have bracketed expressions which are obviously post-Nicene.
Dr Hort[1] would regard many other phrases as derived from the
Creed of the Council of Nicaea, but this is a more doubtful
hypothesis, since the Creed of that Council was itself based,
except for the new anti-Arian phrases, on existing baptismal
creeds.

If we now put together the Creeds of Antioch as given by
Cassian and the other authorities, of Auxentius and of Charisius,
each after the extremely conservative excisions we have made,
and extract from them their common matter, we ought to obtain
a result approximating somewhat closely to the pre-Nicene
Creed of Antioch, and it is as follows:

> Πιστεύω εἰς ἕνα Θεὸν Πατέρα παντοκράτορα·
> Καὶ εἰς τὸν Κύριον ἡμῶν (possibly εἰς ἕνα Κύριον),
> Ἰησοῦν Χριστόν,
> τὸν Υἱὸν Αὐτοῦ τὸν μονογενῆ,
> γεννηθέντα ἐκ Μαρίας τῆς παρθένου,
> σταυρωθέντα,
> ἀναστάντα τῇ τρίτῃ ἡμέρᾳ,
> ἀνελθόντα εἰς τοὺς οὐρανούς,
> καὶ πάλιν ἐρχόμενον κρῖναι ζῶντας καὶ νεκρούς·
> Καὶ εἰς τὸ Πνεῦμα τὸ Ἅγιον·
> Καὶ εἰς ἁγίαν καθολικὴν ἐκκλησίαν·
> Ἄφεσιν ἁμαρτιῶν·
> Ἀνάστασιν νεκρῶν·
> Ζωὴν αἰώνιον.

We may be able to obtain a yet closer approximation by comparing other creeds from places within the Antiochene province,

1　*Two Dissertations*, p. 150.

but it is obvious that we have here something closely resembling a rudimentary form of our Apostles' Creed when we have omitted from it additions which we shall be able to show belong to a later and more developed type, namely *Creatorem caeli et terrae; conceptus; mortuus; descendit ad inferos;* (sedet ad dexteram) *Dei* (Patris) *omnipotentis; Credo* (in Spiritum Sanctum)*; sanctorum communionem.*

(d) The Creed of the Didascalia

The *Didascalia Apostolorum* was originally written in Greek, and probably in the first half of the third century, somewhere in Syria.[1] It now exists in a close Syriac translation and some fragments in a Latin version which has been interpolated.

Zahn[2] reconstructs from it the following creed:

> I believe in God almighty;
> And in our Lord Jesus Christ (His Son?),
> who (for us came down)
> (and) was born of (Mary the?) virgin,
> and crucified under Pontius Pilate,
> and died,
> and the third day rose from the dead,
> and ascended into heaven,
> and sitteth at the right hand of God Almighty,
> and is coming with power and glory to judge dead and quick;
> And in the Holy Spirit...
> (Holy Church?)
> Resurrection of the dead...

He calls attention to a passage following a free reproduction of Acts xv: "Since danger has arisen lest the whole Church shall fall into heresy, we twelve Apostles assembled together in Jerusalem...and we established and determined that you should pray to God the Almighty, and Jesus Christ, and the Holy Spirit, and use the Holy Scriptures, and believe in the resurrection of the dead, and enjoy all creatures with thanksgiving." So a trinitarian Creed is here traced back to a supposed apostolic council.

---

1 Achelis, *Texte u. Unter.* xxv. 2, p. 381, thinks it was written by a bishop.
2 *Neuere Beiträge zur Geschichte des apost. Symbolums,* p. 23.

NOTE

Zahn insists that in "the first article the constant use of the form Θεὸς παντοκράτωρ is characteristic.... We never read Θεὸς πατὴρ παντο-κράτωρ, for the word 'Father' on p. 102. 6 [the reference is to Lagarde] has been inserted by a second hand. The passage 1. 8 ('you who have taken the liberty of calling God the Almighty Father') does not belong here. Also there is no emphasis laid on the...Oneness of God."[1]

Zahn's contention is no doubt correct, for it is supported by ana-logies from the same district. Thus the salutation at the beginning of Polycarp's epistle runs: "Mercy and peace from *God Almighty* and Jesus Christ our Saviour be multiplied", which appears almost a deliberate alteration from that customary in the epistles of St Paul, "From *God our Father* and the Lord Jesus Christ". So at the beginning of the anaphora of the Clementine Liturgy in the *Apostolic Constitu-tions*, bk. viii, "The grace of *Almighty God* and the love of our Lord Jesus Christ and the communion of the Holy Spirit be with you all."

With this formula we can put the ascription given in Pionius's *Life of Polycarp*, ch. xxiii: "By the grace of the *Almighty God* and our Lord Jesus Christ, through whom to the invisible and incomprehensible only immortal Father in the Holy Spirit, the Paraclete, glory and honour and might both was and is and shall be for ever." Both these lines can be pursued further. Thus in Pionius, ch. xiii, we get a summary of Polycarp's teaching which naturally runs into something like a Creed:

"In his teaching he insists before all else that his hearers should know concerning God Almighty, invisible, unchangeable, incompre-hensible, and that He was pleased to send down His own Word the Son from heaven that...being made flesh He should save His own creation. Who...of a spotless virgin and Holy Spirit fulfilled the mystery of His generation. And underwent the passion for men's salvation....Whom also God raised from the dead....And being taken up into the heavens....And concerning the Holy Spirit and the gift of the Paraclete and the rest of the charismata he showed that it was impossible to have these outside the Catholic Church."

And similarly a Creed seems to lie at the back of the Clementine anaphora:

"It is meet...to hymn Thee the God who truly art...
Who hast called all things into being out of nothing through Thy only-begotten Son.
Having begotten Him before all worlds...the first-born of all creation...
through whom are all things,
For Thou, God eternal, through Him hast made all things...
For Thou art holy, and holy is Thy only-begotten Son,
our Lord and God, Jesus Christ...

1 *Apostles' Creed*, p. 98 n.

It pleased Him to become Man...
being born of a virgin...
and He was made flesh...
having lived holily...
suffered many things...
been delivered to Pilate...
He was nailed to the Cross...
and died...
and was buried...
and rose from the dead the third day...
He was taken up into the heavens...
and was seated at the right hand of Thee His God and Father."

With this we may compare Irenaeus, *adv. Haer.* IV. liii. 1:

"A full faith in God Almighty, of whom are all things,
And in the dispensations connected with Him,
through which the Son of God became man;
And a firm belief in the Spirit of God.

.   .   .   .

True knowledge consists in the teaching of the Apostles and the
ancient constitution of the Church throughout all the world."

And the beginning of the First Formula of Antioch in 341:

"To believe in one God of the universe, Maker and Designer of all
things knowable and sensible;
And in one Son of God, only begotten."

And now if we look at the Creed of the *Apostolic Constitutions*
(L. p. 19; H. p. 10):

"In one unbegotten only true God almighty,
The Father of Christ,
Creator and Maker of all things, of whom are all things;
And in the Lord Jesus Christ, His only-begotten Son, etc."

the phrase "the Father of Christ" appears to be thrust in as though it
were an interpolation by the compiler into the Creed on which his own
is based.

Finally, we can put together what looks very much like a Creed from
two homilies of Aphraates (A.D. 336–345):

"When a man shall believe
in God the Lord of all...
Who sent His Christ into the world (*Hom.* i. 19)
Jesus...
He is the first-born Son,
born of Mary...
He suffered,
lived again,

ascended into the height...
He is the judge of dead and quick,
Who shall sit upon the throne, (*Hom.* xiv. 39)

. . . . . .

Who sent His Spirit in the Prophets...
This is the faith of the Church of God.
And believe also in the mystery of Baptism.
And that a man shall believe in the resurrection of the dead."

(*Hom.* i. 19 rearranged.)

Thus a Creed, somewhat of the type reconstructed from the *Didascalia*, with no "one" or "Father" in the first clause would appear to have a wide though miscellaneous support within the Antiochene province, so that if we were to come across a Creed with these characteristics we should have no just cause to suspect textual corruption merely on this account, and should have justification in assigning it to some church within the province of Antioch.

(*e*) *The Creed of Marcellus of Ancyra*[1]

Marcellus, Bishop of Ancyra, was a zealous supporter of Athanasius at the Council of Nicaea in 325, and obtained a good report, as Pope Julius afterwards told the Eusebians, for contending earnestly for the Catholic Faith. It was at this Council that Eusebius, being under accusation as an Arian, put forward his Creed as part of his defence. Later on, in controversy with Asterius, Marcellus is said to have fallen into a heresy combining the errors of Sabellius and Paul of Samosata. This he embodied in a book in which he said that the kingdom of Christ was not perpetual and that He had been made the image of the invisible God at the conception of His body (Hilary, *C.S.L.* LXV. pp. 49, 50).[2]

Whether the accusation was true or false only now concerns us thus far, that in a letter to Pope Julius he quotes the Lucan phrase "Of whose kingdom there shall be no end" as expressing his own belief. In 336 he was condemned as a heretic in the Arian Council of Constantinople and expelled from Ancyra, but after the death of Constantine there is reason to think that he

---

1 For the text see p. 69.

2 Cp. The Letter of the Council of Serdica (H. p. 34): "He had never pretended...that the Word of God had His beginning from holy Mary, nor that His kingdom had an end; on the contrary he had written that His kingdom was both without beginning and without end." (Ath. *Ap.* § 47.)

regained his see along with the other exiled bishops (Ath. *Hist. Arian.* 10) but that disturbances again broke out (*Apol. c. Ar.* 33; cf. Soz. *H.E.* III. 2) and that he was again expelled.

The Eusebians wrote a letter to Julius denouncing Marcellus as a heretic and asking him to refuse to recognize the restoration of Athanasius, but the bearers were refuted and exposed by certain presbyters sent by Athanasius, and withdrew hurriedly after requesting Julius to summon a council in which the whole matter might be re-examined. In consequence of this letter Marcellus betook himself to Rome, travelling by land. On his way he won over Protogenes of Serdica, who had previously signed his condemnation, and, apparently, Gaudentius of Naissus, whose predecessor Cyriacus had also signed it, though this is not quite so explicitly stated (Hilary, *l.c.* pp. 49, 68).

Marcellus seems to have arrived in Rome early in 340, and there to have met Athanasius, and with him he was admitted by Julius to communion. Julius fell in with the Eusebian suggestion, and accordingly in the autumn sent a letter to the Eusebians inviting them to attend a council to be held in Rome in December of the same year. But they detained the envoys till January 341 and then sent back a defiant answer. As he had now waited fifteen months in all, and was about to leave, Marcellus, seemingly at Julius's request, wrote him a letter in his own defence and asked Julius to enclose a copy of it in his letter of summons to his suffragans. Some time later more than fifty bishops met in a council at which Athanasius was present, where they had the letter of Marcellus before them, and confirmed the action of Julius in regard to Athanasius and Marcellus, and asked him to report their decision to the Eusebians.

In his letter to Julius (Epiph. *adv. Haer.* lxxii) Marcellus first gives the reason for his presence in Rome; he wished, he said, to suggest that Julius should summon his accusers, so that he could show that their charges were false and that they still maintained their old heresies. But when they refused to come, he thought it necessary, as he was about to leave, "to deposit with you my faith in writing—having written it with all truth with my own hand—which I learned and was taught out of the

Holy Scriptures" (ἔγγραφον τὴν ἐμαυτοῦ πίστιν μετὰ πάσης
ἀληθείας τῇ ἐμαυτοῦ χειρὶ γράψας ἐπιδοῦναι, ἣν ἔμαθον, ἔκ τε
τῶν θείων γραφῶν ἐδιδάχθην). Then follows a paragraph in
which he lays bare the heresies of his accusers and gives a
doctrinal exposition of his own belief, in the course of which he
quotes the phrase "of whose kingdom there shall be no end".
At its close he resumes his original purpose and begins "I believe,
therefore" (πιστεύω οὖν), which is followed by the remainder of
the Creed. After this comes another doctrinal exposition and
finally "having received this faith (πίστις) from the Holy Scriptures and been taught it by my ancestors in God, I both preach
it in the Church of God, and have now written to you, keeping a
copy of this document by me" (τὴν ἀντίγραφον τούτου παρ'
ἐμαυτῷ κατασχών), and then he begs Julius to insert a copy in
his letter of summons.

After the Council Julius wrote to the Eusebians that Marcellus
"being requested by us to give an account of his faith, answered
in his own person with the utmost boldness, so that we were
obliged to acknowledge that he maintains nothing except the
truth. For he confessed that he held the same godly doctrine
about our Lord and Saviour Jesus Christ as the Catholic Church
holds, and he affirmed that he had not recently adopted these
opinions but had held them for a very long time; as indeed our
presbyters, who had been present at the Council of Nicaea,
testified to his orthodoxy" (Ath. *Apol. c. Ar.* 32).

In 343 Marcellus and Athanasius were at the Council of
Serdica, at which Gaudentius of Naissus was also present, and,
naturally, Protogenes of Serdica. The Council had under consideration Marcellus's book and also his letter to Julius, including the Creed. "He went up to Rome", says Athanasius,
"and there made his defence, and being required by them
(ἀπαιτούμενος παρ' αὐτῶν, as Julius said) he offered a written
declaration of his faith (δέδωκεν ἔγγραφον τὴν ἑαυτοῦ πίστιν, the
very words of Marcellus), which the Council of Serdica [subse-
quently] accepted" (*Hist. Arian.* 6).

The first point is that we have not to deal with a mixed
Romano-Ancyran form. Marcellus states that he wrote with his

own hand and with the greatest accuracy and kept a copy himself. The Creed he gives, therefore, is either Roman, the Creed of Julius, or Ancyran, the Creed of his own diocese. And secondly, while the only argument in favour of the Creed being that of Rome is its similarity to Western Creeds which become known to us at a rather later date, there is on the other side a large number of cumulative and independent probabilities.

Marcellus is giving in his letter a written defence of his orthodoxy at the time of his condemnation and subsequently.

When Eusebius produced his Creed at the Council of Nicaea, Marcellus was present and acquiesced in his acquittal. Accordingly in quoting his own Creed in circumstances somewhat similar, he would be following a successful precedent.

On his way to Rome he had won over Protogenes, if not also Gaudentius, and probably by the same method as he used in Rome; and if so, he must have employed his own Creed, and this would furnish a precedent for his use of it at Rome.

Neither Julius, nor Athanasius, nor Marcellus himself gives the least hint that he had substituted the Creed of Rome for his own, and if in his letter $\pi i \sigma \tau \iota s$ does not refer exclusively to his general dogmatic position but includes the Creed, Marcellus's language explicitly asserts that the Creed he gives is that of Ancyra.

And the words he uses in this connexion are markedly similar to those used by Eusebius, by Arius and Euzoius, and by Auxentius; and on each occasion the Creed produced is at the least based upon the Creed of their respective dioceses.

Nor would such a substitution be politic. It would not suggest that Marcellus was innocent of the heresy for which he was condemned in 336, if, in the course of his defence, he abandoned his own Creed for another, but at the best could only imply that he had changed his former dogmatic position and now adopted that of Rome: a plea for mercy, but also an implicit confession of former guilt.

And his letter was submitted to the Council of Serdica at which Protogenes and Gaudentius were present, and the whole of the proceedings would come before his own diocese into which he was to be reinstated, and where there was a party opposed to him. This must have been perfectly clear to Marcellus and was probably one of the motives which induced him to keep a copy of his letter,[1] and Marcellus's feeling with regard to his diocese may be judged by the extreme sensitiveness shown by Eusebius in his letter in somewhat similar circumstances (G. pp. 178–189).

Thus there is no argument in favour of supposing a substitution of the Roman for the Ancyran Creed in Marcellus's letter, except the likeness of the Creed he produces to other Western Creeds, and there are great probabilities against any such line of conduct.

When we examine the wording of the Creed all these probabilities receive strong support. The Creed differs in several respects from the Creed of Rome of some forty years later, and agrees equally closely with the Creed of Niceta of Remesiana, which, supported as it is by the Arian Fragments and by the Creed of Jerome, must be allowed to be Eastern. Moreover each of these differences has Eastern affinities. The omission of "Father" in the first clause has numerous parallels within the province of Antioch. The order "Christ Jesus" has analogies in the East but none in the West except in the Creeds of Hippolytus, Rufinus, and Peter Chrysologus, in each of which it is probably an Eastern feature. The omission of "suffered" agrees with Rufinus, but not with the Roman Creed as exemplified by Augustine, the *Explanatio*, most probably Leo, and by Western Creeds generally. "Whence" of the Coming to Judgement is found only here and in Basil, and Basil lived at Caesarea in Cappadocia which was connected by a high road with Ancyra, and he was associated with Basil of Ancyra in 348, and corresponded with his successor, Athanasius. We may therefore call this word a peculiarity of the district of Galatia and Cappadocia.

"The Holy Spirit", in this order, is common in Eastern Creeds, whereas the Creed of Rome had consistently "*in*

---

[1] That Marcellus's letter did become known to his diocese is both probable in itself and receives support from the fact that about the year 372 a deputation sent by the Church of Ancyra to Athanasius, finding that it was suspected of heresy, drew up a statement of faith which has many striking likenesses to the language of the letter.

Spiritum Sanctum". And "eternal life" is another common Eastern feature, but absent at this date from the Creed of Rome.

Thus the historical probabilities, the resemblance of structure to the Creed of Niceta, and the details of language combine to assure us that the Creed produced by Marcellus is that of his own diocese.

(ƒ) The Creed of the Psalter of Aethelstan and of the Codex Laudianus

The *Psalter of Aethelstan* is a document of peculiar interest, since it gives us, though in a fragmentary form, the earliest known Christian manual of private devotion. It is otherwise designated as "Brit. Mus. Galba xviii", and I shall allude to it by the letter G. The original MS. (ff. 28–119) was written on the continent in the ninth century, and probably in its earlier half. Later additions were made on the spare leaves and supplementary leaves in the tenth century. The rest of the volume (ff. 1–21, 178–200), which is our immediate concern, was written in the tenth century in England. This portion contains a litany of the saints, incomplete, the Lord's Prayer, a Creed, and the *Sanctus*, all written in Greek transliterated into Anglo-Saxon characters, with rubrics in Latin. I quote the transcription from Heurtley, *Harmonica Symbolica*, pp. 78–80, who also gives a facsimile of the Creed, but I have re-spaced the words of the Creed so as to make it more intelligible, and placed the Latin translation in the *Codex Laudianus* by its side.

Hic incipiunt Grecorum letanie: (bottom of f. 199 *b*)

     Xpe epacus ominin.
     Aie Michael euxe yperimon.
     Aie Gabriel euxe yperimon.
     Aie Raphael euxe yperimon.
     Aie Maria euxe yperimon.
     Aie Petre euxe yperimon.
     Aie Paule euxe yperimon, et rl.
     Pantas yaies euxaste yperimon.
     Ileos genuce fise ymas cyrie.
     Ileos genuce lutrose ymas cyrie.
     Apopantes cacu lutrose ymas cyrie.
     Diatus taurusu lustrose ymas cyrie.

Amarthuluse paraca lumen epacus ominin.
Inagrinin dosisse paraca lumen epacus ominin.
Ygie tutheuse paraca lumen epacus ominin.
Ao amnos tutheu oerronan tin amartias tu cosmu eleison imas.

Hinc incipit Pater noster in lingua Grecorum.
Pater imon...apatu poniru.

Credo gr.[1]	*Codex Laudianus*
Pistheu is theu patera panto-cratero ce is criston ihū yon autu ton monogen	Credo in dm̄ patrem omnipotem et in xpō Ihū Filium eIs unicum
ton quirion imon	dominum nostrum.
ton genegenta ec pneumatus agiu	qui natus est de spū scō
ce maria tis parthenu	et maria uirgine
ton epi pontio pilatu staurothente	qui sub pontio pilato crucifixus est
ce tafinta	et sepultus
te trite imera anastanta eg nicron	tertia die resurrexit a mortuis
anaunta is tos uranos	ascendit In caelis,
catimeron in dexia tu patros	sedet ad dextera patris
oten erchete crine zontas ce nicros	unde uenturus est Iudicare uiuos et mortuos
ce is preuma agion	et In spū scō
agri ———	scā ecclesia
afisin amartion	remissione peccatorum
sarcos anasta. amen.	carnis resurrectionis
scs	scs	scs

agios agios agios cyrus otheos sabaoth plyris urano cegastisdoxis.

The next leaf, which gave the conclusion of the *Sanctus*, is missing.

The *Codex Laudianus* is a Graeco-Latin uncial MS. of the first half of the seventh century apparently written outside Italy as is shown by the minuscule *b* in an otherwise uncial Latin alphabet. It is best known as Codex E of the Acts, and it was used by Bede (673–735) in his commentary. It was probably brought to England by Abbot Adrian, who lived in a monastery near Naples[2] and accompanied Archbishop Theodore in 638. In the eighth century it was at Hornbach in the Rhenish Palatinate.[3] Its subsequent history is unknown until it was given by Archbishop Laud to the British Museum.

1 For the Greek text see p. 69.
2 Bede, *H.E.* IV. 1; Morin, *Liber Comicus*, p. 426.
3 R. L. Poole, *J.T.S.* XXIX. p. 400.

But G does not stand alone. Cotton MS. Titus D. xviii (T), also in the British Museum, of about the twelfth century, has on the eighth line of f. 12 b a title: *Ymnus Grecorum ante canonem* followed by the complete *Sanctus*:

Agios. Agios. Agios. Kyrrius. otheos sabaoth. plyris urano. ke getis doxis autu. Osanna entis ipsistis; Eulogumenos o erchanos en ono mati kyri^u. Osanna entis ypsistis.

Then comes: "Incipit letania Grecorum" and the first eleven suffrages of the G Litany, occupying the rest of the page; f. 13 is blank. This is not a copy of G, as is shown by the variations in the transliteration, e.g.:

> (3) Agie Gabriel euche yper imon
> (8) Pantes agies euchiste yper ymon
> (9) Ileos genuse; phise ymas Kyrie.

But there is also in the British Museum a Latin MS. Royal 2 A xx (R) which has been printed as an appendix to the Book of Cerne, ed. Kuypers, pp. 199 ff. This was written in England probably in the first quarter of the eighth century. It contains on f. 26a a complete litany based on that in G and T; the *Hymnus Angelicus* or *Gloria in excelsis* on f. 28 a; the Lord's Prayer and the Creed on ff. 11 b, 12 a. The Creed is an independent translation of that given in G and nearer to the current creed of the day than that given in the Codex Laudianus.

Next the Stowe Missal (S) written in an Irish Monastery in the first decade of the ninth century. Here the Litany forms part of the Preparation of the Priest, and, after several intervening prayers, is followed by the *Gloria in excelsis* on ff. 13 b, 14 a, and the *Sanctus* on f. 23 b.

Then a Fulda MS. (F) printed by G. Witzel in his *Exercitamenta sincerae pietatis*, 1559, sign P, which has now been lost. This MS. "was evidently another copy of the Old Irish Missal of which the only copy now extant is *Stowe*; and though, as appears from so much as Witzel prints, the names of the saints invoked in the litany of the 'Praeparatio' differed, the 'framework' is identical with that of the litanies in *Stowe* and 2 A xx".[1]

1 Bishop, *Liturgica Historica*, p. 140.

Finally, the order of St Amand (A), printed in Duchesne's *Christian Worship*, pp. 456–480. This "is one of the most corrupt, as it is the most deceptive and audacious of the Gallican perversions that pass under the name of 'Roman Ordos'. It may date from any time in the ninth century after probably 850".[1]

Each of these MSS. is independent of the others, but all go back to a common Greek original (O). G and T are independent transcriptions of O. The Codex Laudianus (E) is earlier than any of the others, and so cannot be based on any of them; G is not based on R, for R has no *Sanctus*; nor R, S, or F. on G or T, for they contain fuller litanies; nor R on E, since its creed form differs.

So we obtain the following diagram:

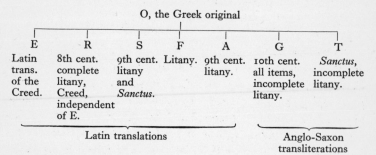

			O, the Greek original			
E	R	S	F	A	G	T
Latin trans. of the Creed.	8th cent. complete litany, Creed, independent of E.	9th cent. litany and *Sanctus*.	Litany.	9th cent. litany.	10th cent. all items, incomplete litany.	*Sanctus*, incomplete litany.

Latin translations   Anglo-Saxon transliterations

If we now look at the list of the saints, we find that there are two lists in the Stowe Missal, one in the litany, f. 12 a, and a second in the diptychs, f. 32 a. Of these the former is based upon the latter, and both are all but identical with those in the Great Intercession of the Greek Liturgy of St James and in *Royal*, and with the incomplete lists in *Galba* and *Titus*. It follows that all these must ultimately go back to some form of liturgy which is the common source of O and St James, and therefore that O has Antiochene affinities.

"Barnabas" in *Royal* is probably taken from the prayer *Nobis quoque peccatoribus* in the Roman canon, which, however, gives a list of saints in a different order John, Stephen, Matthias, Barnabas. The *Kyrie eleison* is an addition by the compiler of the Stowe Litany.

1 Bishop, *Liturgica Historica*, p. 160.

G and T	R	S. Litany	S. Dipt.	St James
Xpe epacus	Christe	Christe audi	Old Testament	
onimin	audi nos	nos (3 times)	Saints	
Michael	Michael	Kyrie eleison		
Gabriel	Gabriel			
Raphael	Raphael			
—	John	—	John Baptist	Mary
Mary	Mary	Mary	Mary	John Baptist
Peter	Peter	Peter	Peter	Peter
Paul	Paul	Paul	Paul	Paul
et rl	Andrew	Andrew	Andrew	Andrew
(T omits	James	James	James	James
et rl)	John	—	John	John
	Philip	—	Philip	Philip
	Bartholomew	Bartholomew	Bartholomew	Bartholomew
	Thomas	Thomas	Thomas	Thomas
	Matthew	Matthew	Matthew	Thaddaeus
	James	James	James	Matthew
	Simon	—	Simon	James
	Thaddaeus	Thaddaeus	Thaddaeus	Simon
	Matthias	Matthias	Matthias	Jude
	Barnabas	—	—	Matthias
	Mark	Mark	Mark	Mark
	Luke	Luke	Luke	Luke[1]

The Last Suffrage

G.	R., S.
Ὁ ἀμνὸς τοῦ Θεοῦ ὁ αἴρων τὴν ἁμαρτίας τοῦ κόσμου, ἐλέησον ἡμᾶς	Agnus (Stowe, *Agne*) Dei qui tollis peccata mundi, miserere nobis.

This comes from the *Gloria in excelsis*, a morning hymn found complete in the Alexandrine MS. of the New Testament of the fifth century; in part in a form interpolated by the writer known as Pseudo-Ignatius in the *Apostolic Constitutions*, VII. 46, a collection made at Antioch in the fourth century; in part in the *de Virginitate*, written in Egypt in the fourth century and possibly by Athanasius to whom it is ascribed in all the MSS. The first record of the use of the *Agnus Dei* in Rome occurs in the time of Pope Sergius (687–701), and Sergius, though born at Palermo, was a Syrian from the region of Antioch. It is not in the Gelasian Sacramentary.

In the Stowe diptychs the names of New Testament saints are preceded by: Abel, Seth, Enoch, Noah, Melchizedek, Abraham,

1 See also Brightman, *L.E.W.* p. 230, Liturgy of the Abyssinian Jacobites.

Isaac, Jacob, Joseph; Job, Moses, Samuel, David, Elijah, Isaiah and so on in the Vulgate order to Malachi, except that Esther is inserted between Daniel and Hosea; then Tobit, the Three Holy Children, the Maccabees, the Holy Innocents. Any list of Old Testament saints is rare in the Liturgy, but the East Syrian rite (Brightman, p. 276) gives: Adam, Abel, Seth, Enoch, Noah, Shem, Abraham, Isaac, Jacob, Joseph, Melchizedek, Aaron, Zechariah and all priests; Moses, Saul, David, Nathan and all prophets; and a somewhat similar list is found in the *Apostolic Constitutions*, VII. 37.

It is probable also that there was a similar list in the Moesian rite to which Niceta alludes in *de Symbolo*, 10: "Ab exordio saeculi sive patriarchae, Abraham et Isaac et Jacob, sive prophetae; sive apostoli, sive martyres, sive ceteri justi...una ecclesia sunt...etiam angeli...in hac una confoederantur ecclesia."

With this we may compare the following specimens from the prayer called *Post nomina* of the Mozarabic rite (the references are to Férotin, *Liber Sacramentorum*).

"Sanctorum tuorum Domine communicantes memorie. Patriarcharum Prophetarumque tuorum (non) sumus immemores...immemoramus etiam Apostolos tuos...Facimus quoque et tuorum Martyrum sanctorum mentionem" (col. 19).

"Inter Patriarcharum inclite memorie titulos, Prophetarumque sublimes vaticinio fasces, atque martyrum...triumphos" (col. 114).

"Beatorum quoque Angelorum, Patriarcharum, Prophetarum, Apostolorum, Martyrum omniumque sanctorum qui de Ecclesie corpore gloriosa Christi membra facti sunt suffragiis" (col. 142).

"Advocamus...Patriarchas...Prophetas...Martyres...Apostolos" (col. 255).

W. C. Bishop asserts that "the form given in the Missal contained originally the names of the patriarchs and prophets".[1]

The Sanctus

The special form of the *Sanctus*, *Lord* God *of Sabaoth*, does not occur either in the Hebrew or in the Septuagint version of Isaiah, vi. 3, nor in the Greek Liturgies, but it occurs in Origen (Rufinus) *Hom.* I *in Vis. Isaiae*, 3, in the East Syrian Liturgy of

1 *Mozarabic and Ambrosian Rites*, p. 33 n.

Addai and Mari (Brightman, p. 284), in the Liturgy of the
Syrian Jacobites (p. 86), and the Second Prayer of Cyprian of
Antioch (Migne, *P.L.* IV, p. 908) which belongs to Asia Minor.
Then it occurs in the *Te Deum*, composed by Niceta of Reme-
siana; in Ambrose *de Spiritu Sancto*, II. xvi. 112; in the Ambrosian
Liturgy; and in Spain, in the Mozarabic Missal (Migne, *P.L.*
LXXXV, pp. 116, 484, 549), the *Liber Ordinum*, coll. 20, 237 and
in the *Liber Sacramentorum*, col. 210.

Hence we have three links between our original Greek MS.,
O, and the Syrian Liturgy, and an indication that Syrian phrases
travelled to Spain by way of Moesia and Northern Italy.

And now we come to the Creed, and I put in parallel columns
the Creeds of *Galba* and Marcellus.

Galba	Marcellus
Πιστεύω εἰς Θεὸν Πατέρα παντο-κράτορα·	Πιστεύω εἰς Θεὸν παντοκράτορα·
Καὶ εἰς Χριστὸν Ἰησοῦν,	Καὶ εἰς Χριστὸν Ἰησοῦν,
Υἱὸν Αὐτοῦ τὸν μονογενῆ,	τὸν Υἱὸν Αὐτοῦ τὸν μονογενῆ,
τὸν Κύριον ἡμῶν,	τὸν Κύριον ἡμῶν,
τὸν γεννηθέντα ἐκ Πνεύματος Ἁγίου	τὸν γεννηθέντα ἐκ Πνεύματος Ἁγίου
καὶ Μαρίας τῆς παρθένου,	καὶ Μαρίας τῆς παρθένου,
τὸν ἐπὶ Ποντίου Πιλάτου σταυρω-θέντα,	τὸν ἐπὶ Ποντίου Πιλάτου σταυρω-θέντα,
καὶ ταφέντα,	καὶ ταφέντα,
τῇ τρίτῃ ἡμέρᾳ ἀναστάντα ἐκ νεκρῶν,	καὶ τῇ τρίτῃ ἡμέρᾳ ἀναστάντα ἐκ τῶν νεκρῶν,
ἀναβάντα εἰς τοὺς οὐρανούς,	ἀναβάντα εἰς τοὺς οὐρανούς,
καθήμενον ἐν δεξιᾷ τοῦ Πατρός,	καὶ καθήμενον ἐν δεξιᾷ τοῦ Πατρός,
ὅθεν ἔρχεται κρῖναι ζῶντας καὶ νεκρούς·	ὅθεν ἔρχεται κρίνειν ζῶντας καὶ νεκρούς·
Καὶ εἰς Πνεῦμα Ἅγιον·	Καὶ εἰς τὸ Ἅγιον Πνεῦμα·
Ἁγίαν ἐκκλησίαν·	Ἁγίαν ἐκκλησίαν·
Ἄφεσιν ἁμαρτιῶν·	Ἄφεσιν ἁμαρτιῶν·
Σαρκὸς ἀνάστασιν.	Σαρκὸς ἀνάστασιν·
	Ζωὴν αἰώνιον.

There are sufficient differences between them to show that
neither is a copy of the other, but their resemblances are so close
that they must have come from the same neighbourhood, and
may be nearly contemporary. But the original Greek manual
from which G and T are transcripts has been shown to belong

to the Antiochene sphere of influence; hence the Creed of Marcellus is genuinely Ancyran, and these two Creeds may be taken to represent the Creed of Antioch at an earlier stage than we have hitherto been able to reach, without its later and local enlargements.

Before going on to consider the Creeds of Moesia, Northern Italy, Gaul and Spain, let us sum up the results we have so far reached. The Creed of the *Psalter of Aethelstan, Galba,* occurs in what may be called in a wide sense a Syrian document; its affinities are with Antioch and Syrian Liturgies, and the Creed of the *Codex Laudianus* is a translation of it; but both these are quoted by Burn as authorities for the Old Roman Creed.[1] The Creed of Marcellus is shown by its resemblance to these to be the Creed of his own diocese, as was probable on other grounds; but Burn gives this Creed also as an example of the Old Roman Creed.[2] Kattenbusch[3] thought that Niceta's Creed was due to a back wave of influence from Gaul, but was well answered by Sanday that at this time the wave of the liturgical influence was precisely in the opposite direction.[4]

In short, all three Creeds, which were once claimed as typically Western, have turned out to be Eastern, and the distinction between Eastern and Western Creeds has broken down. Eastern Creeds, it is said, begin with "We believe", Western with "I believe". The truth is that conciliar Creeds and Creeds emanating from a body of persons naturally employ the plural number, baptismal Creeds *as used* equally naturally begin with the singular, but *as quoted* as the Creed of a diocese the plural might be used, and sometimes the plural is merely "editorial", as in the Letter of Eusebius, "as in *our* first catechetical instruction, and at the time of *our* baptism, *we* received...". But even so he begins his (Eastern) Creed with the singular "I believe". Again, many Eastern Creeds have "one God" in the first clause, but by no means all, and "one Lord" in the second is comparatively rare in Eastern *baptismal* Creeds. So it was said that Eastern Creeds are controversial and antiheretical while Western

---

1 *Introduction,* p. 199.   2 *Op. cit.* p. 45.

3 *Das apostolische Symbol,* II. p. 979.   4 *J.T.S.* III. p. 14.

Creeds are expository, but we shall see that the expository clause "of the Holy Ghost and Mary the Virgin" was added to the Creed of the Council of Nicaea with a controversial interest, and *natum et passum* in the Creed of the Gelasian Sacramentary is a protest against Gnosticism.

Our next point is this; structurally, the Creed of the *Psalter of Aethelstan* and the Creed of Marcellus, which he learnt from his "ancestors in God", are typical specimens of a Creed of Antiochene extraction somewhere about the year 300. The Creed of Marcellus leaves out "Father" in the first clause, and adds "eternal life" at the end; that of the *Psalter of Aethelstan* includes the word "Father" but has no "eternal life"; the other differences are very minute and in fact negligible. The Creed of Niceta has one "personal addition", as it may be called, "resurrexit *vivus*", and several natural developments, "caeli et terrae Creatorem", "mortuum", "communionem sanctorum". It is a typical specimen of Antiochene Creeds of the latter half of the fourth century. The Creed of Antioch, as given by Cassian (*c.* 429), and that of Charisius of Philadelphia (431) represent this Creed in the Eastern exuberance of the fifth century, but if we prune away the new shoots, all can be seen to belong to the same family tree.

Finally, it is obvious that the former group are our Apostles' Creed in an earlier stage, which in the West grew into the *Textus Receptus*, and in the East into the Creeds of Antioch and Philadelphia. To speak of any of them as the "Old Roman Creed" is an entire misnomer, though in the fourth century, as we shall see in the sequel, the Roman Church grafted Eastern branches on to its own ancestral stem. The only connexion of the Church of Rome with our Apostles' Creed is that, having adopted successive importations, in the days of its power it spread its rite, including its Creed, over the whole of the West.

Chapter V

THE CREEDS OF NICETA OF REMESIANA AND JEROME

I. The Creed of Niceta and Mai's Arian Fragments. II. The Creed of Jerome.

The Creed of Niceta of Remesiana (Burn, *Niceta*, p. lxxxiv)	Mai's Arian Fragments (*Scriptorum veterum nova Collectio*, T. III, Romae, 1828)
	VII. *Ipsi praeponunt Patrem Filio in Symbolo, dum dicunt*:
Credo in Deum Patrem omnipotentem,	Credis in Deum Patrem omnipotentem,
caeli et terrae Creatorem;	Creatorem caeli et terrae?
Et in Filium ejus Jesum Christum, (Dominum nostrum?)	Credis et in Jesu Christo, Filio ejus?
natum ex Spiritu Sancto et ex virgine Maria,	XV. templum suum quod sumpsit ex Maria virgine,
	de Maria natus est
passum sub Pontio Pilato,	IV. qui pro nobis passus est;
crucifixum, mortuum,	XVII. et mortem crucis et tertia die resurrectionem
tertia die resurrexit vivus a mortuis,	IV. qui resurrexit a mortuis...
ascendit in caelos,	qui ascendit super caelos...
	XVII. per...ascensionem in caelis
sedet ad dexteram Patris	IV. qui sedet in dextera Dei...[1]
	XVII. Filius ejus ad dexteram suam sedeat;
	XIV. recipiens ad dexteram sedem suam;
inde venturus judicare vivos et mortuos;	IV. qui judicaturus est...
	XIV. venturus inde...judicare vivos et mortuos.
Et in Spiritum Sanctum;	XV. Spiritum Sanctum, *quem tertio loco a Patre post Filium in symbolo...tradimus.*
Sanctam ecclesiam catholicam;	VIII. Nos ecclesia Dei sancta.
Communionem sanctorum;	XVII. quos etiam ecclesia cognovisset
Remissionem peccatorum;	VII. (Pater) remisit nobis peccata per Filium....
Carnis resurrectionem; Et vitam aeternam.	*Daturus est Deus Pater justis* vitam aeternam.

1 Cf. "Quia jussus *sedet ad dexteram Patris*, non nostro argumento docemus, sed divinis scripturis quantum valet exiguitas nostra, Domino adjuvante docemus" (from a sermon of the Arian bishop Maximian, who came with the Gothic soldiers into Africa in 427, or 428. *J.T.S.* XIII. p. 23; XXIV. p. 77).

NICETA preached in Latin because his congregation consisted largely of the Roman garrison and their descendants. But the Creed reached Remesiana from the East and in Greek, and he gives a translation. This is shown by the Creed; by the general spread of Christianity in the district south of the Danube; and by personal details respecting Niceta himself.

Gallican and Italian Creeds have uniformly, in the second member, *qui* with the indicative, whereas Niceta has past participles; this shows that the Creed did not reach Remesiana from the West. Moreover, no Western Creed at this date had a phrase in the first article corresponding to *caeli et terrae Creatorem*, whereas this was a common feature in Eastern Creeds. Similarly, there is good reason to believe that the phrase *communionem sanctorum* first occurred in Creeds in Asia Minor (cp. the Marcosian Creed), and like *caeli et terrae Creatorem* it is of much later occurrence in Western Creeds, and the same is true of the epithet *catholica* as applied to the Church; and finally the concluding clause is of early date in the East, but is not in Italian or Gallican Creeds before the fifth century. Moreover, if we extract peculiarities such as *ex Spiritu Sancto, vivus, inde, communionem sanctorum*, the general structure of the remainder bears a very close resemblance to Antiochene Creeds of the fourth century.

That the spread of Christianity over this region was from Asia Minor can best be visualized by looking at the map.

In the second half of the third century the Goths from the north of the Danube laid waste Moesia, and then crossed into Cappadocia and Galatia, and carried back a vast number of captives, including many Christian ecclesiastics, into Dacia. "These pious captives, by their intercourse with the barbarians, brought over large numbers to the true faith, and persuaded them to embrace Christianity" (Philostorgius, *H.E.* II. 5). In Dalmatia to the west, in Macedonia and Thrace to the south and east were Christian settlements in early times owing nothing to Rome or Italy. The first notice we have of Christianity to the north of them is in the *Acts of the Martyrs*, namely, that very many years (*plurimi anni*) had elapsed since Bishop Eusebius suffered

martyrdom, during the Valerian or Diocletian persecution, at
Cibalae, in the south-east of Pannonia between the Danube and
the Save. Eusebius the historian writes that at the dedication of
the church at Jerusalem in 335 the Moesians and Pannonians
were represented by "the fairest bloom of God's youthful stock
among them",[1] thus putting back the evangelization of these
districts at least to the early years of the fourth century. At the
Council of Nicaea in 325 there were present a Pannonian bishop
called Domus, Protogenes, a Greek from Serdica, Pistus from
Marcianopolis in Lower or Eastern Moesia; and about the year
337 Marcellus was entertained by a bishop at Naissus on his
journey to Rome. The dioceses of Valens at Mursa to the north-
west of Cibalae and Sirmium, and of Ursacius at Singidunum
(Belgrade) at the confluence of the Danube and the Drave to the
south-east of Sirmium, were without doubt ante-Nicene, and so
was also the diocese of Victorinus at Poetovio on the Drave at
the extreme west of Pannonia, on the confines of Noricum. The
Acts of the Martyrs also attests the presence of Christian communities at Scarabantia near Lake Pelso (Lake Balaton in
Hungary); Sabaria (the birthplace of Martin of Tours), both west
of Poetovio; Siscia and Sirmium in Pannonia; at Tomi on the
Black Sea and at Axiopolis and Durostorum on the Danube in
Lower Moesia.

Christianity made its way up the Danube with its tributaries
the Drave and Save, but it was helped also, and that mightily, by
the great imperial road which ran from Constantinople through
Adrianople, Philippopolis, Serdica, Remesiana, Naissus, Singidunum, Sirmium, Mursa, and Siscia, to Aquileia, and across the
plains of Lombardy to Vienne and Lyons. Thus before the Council of Nicaea we find Christian communities each presided over
by its bishop at a line of points near the western edge of Pannonia, Scarabantia, Sabaria, Poetovio, Siscia, and Stridon, all
deriving their Christianity from Asia Minor, either by way of the
Black Sea and up the Danube, or by road.

The existence of Christianity in Remesiana as early as the
beginning of the fourth century is sufficiently shown by its mere

1 *Vita Constantini*, IV. 48.

position on the road between Serdica and Sirmium, but it is
corroborated also by the fact that Niceta, while still remaining its
bishop, worked among the Bessi in the mountain range of Thrace
which divides Thrace from Macedonia, a task which he would
not have undertaken if his own diocese had been still unsettled.[1]

Niceta was himself apparently Greek, as his name shows, but
ecclesiastically would seem to have looked towards Rome and
accepted the fact that his diocese was within the Western Empire—and therefore beyond the limits of Eastern ecclesiastical
jurisdiction—with a hearty acquiescence. But this casts no doubt
on the fact that Remesiana derived its Christianity from the
East. Niceta's list of canticles is Eastern rather than Western,[2]
his introduction of antiphonal singing goes back to Basil of
Caesarea,[3] he translates from the Septuagint,[4] and, as we have
said, *Creatorem caeli et terrae* and *vitam aeternam* in his Creed
are Eastern touches.[5]

Next, by comparison with the Arian Fragments[6] from the
region of the Danube, we notice that this type of Creed was not
confined to Remesiana, but stretched over a larger district.[7] In
this connexion we should notice the occurrence in both of
Creatorem caeli et terrae, and *inde* before *venturus*. *Inde* (ἐκεῖθεν)
is not found to the east of this district, and when it occurs in
Creeds in the West, they are of a later date.

II. The Creed of Jerome

(Dom Morin, *Anecdota Maredsolana*, III. 3. pp. 199, 200)

Credo in unum Deum Patrem omnipotentem,
visibilium et invisibilium Factorem;
Credo in unum Dominum, Jesum Christum,
Filium Dei, natum de Deo, Deum de Deo,
lumen de lumine, (omnipotentem de omnipotente),
Deum verum de Deo vero,
natum ante saecula, non factum,

---

1 The Irish *Liber Hymnorum* (*H.B.S.* I. p. 59) says that the predecessor of
Niceta was named Peter.

2 Burn, *Niceta*, p. xciv.   3 *Ibid.* p. xc.   4 *Ibid.* pp. 20, 32.

5 Cp. *Introduction*, p. 261.   6 Burn, *J.T.S.* III. p. 500.

7 On these see Mercati, *Studi e Testi* 7, who incidentally shows their
"Gallican" affinities.

per quem facta sunt omnia in caelo et in terra,
qui propter nostram salutem descendit de caelo,
conceptus est de Spiritu Sancto, natus ex Maria virgine,
passus est (passione) sub Pontio Pilato (sub Herode rege),
crucifixus, sepultus,
descendit ad inferna, (calcavit aculeum mortis,)
tertia die resurrexit, (apparuit apostolis,)
(post haec) ascendit ad caelos,
sedet ad dexteram Dei Patris,
inde venturus judicare vivos et mortuos;
Credo et in Spiritum Sanctum (Deum non ingenitum neque
   genitum,
non creatum, neque factum, sed Patri et Filio coaeternum);
Credo remissionem peccatorum
in sancta ecclesia catholica;
Sanctorum communionem;
Carnis resurrectionem
ad vitam aeternam.

I have bracketed certain expressions which appear to be
Jerome's own additions, and do not occur in any official Creed
known to us. Jerome was born at Stridon in Pannonia, a town
not far from Aquileia, about the year 346. His parents were
orthodox Christians, but he was baptized in Rome under
Liberius between 363 and 366, when he was from seventeen
to twenty years of age. He spent the years of 370 and 373 between his home at Stridon and Aquileia.

The earlier portion of his profession of faith is obviously based
on the Creed of the Council of Nicaea (L. p. 22; H. pp. 5, 6)—
naturally enough, seeing that Jerome was a Catholic and nearly
all the bishops of Pannonia were Arians—and but for a few
alterations is identical with it. Jerome omits "all" before
"things visible and invisible" and "of one substance with the
Father", and compresses "begotten of the Father, only-begotten,
that is of one substance with the Father" into "begotten of
God", and he expands "begotten not made" by adding "before
the worlds"—a characteristically Eastern phrase—and for "who
for us men and our salvation descended", writes "who for our
salvation (omitting 'for us men') descended from heaven". Then
he continues "conceived of the Holy Ghost, born of Mary the
virgin". The nearest analogues to this phrase are in the Creed of

Niceta, and in that of Auxentius of Milan, where it appears to be his own addition to his native Creed of Cappadocia.

With the later clauses we may compare: *Qui passus es sub Pontio Pilato bonam confessionem, qui crucifixus descendisti, et conculcasti aculeum mortis....Tu resurrexisti et apparuisti apostolis tuis: sedes ad dexteram Patris, qui venturus es judicare vivos et mortuos* in the Second Prayer of Cyprian of Antioch (Migne, *P.L.* IV. p. 908). *Calcavit aculeum mortis* appears in the *Te Deum* in the form *Tu devicto mortis aculeo*, and this is now ascribed to Niceta; the Missal of Bobbio (*H.B.S.* p. 81) has *aculeus mortis obtritus*; the Gothic Missal (*H.B.S.* p. 17) *aculeo mortis extincto*, and (p. 107) *mortis vicit aculeum*; Gaudentius of Brescia, *S.* XIX *calcato mortis aculeo, victor caelos ascendens* (Migne, *P.L.* xx. p. 990). *Descendit ad inferna* is in the Creed of Aquileia. *Inde* before *venturus* occurs in Niceta's Creed and the Arian Fragments. *Sanctorum communionem* is in Niceta's Creed: and the epithet "catholic" and the phrase "eternal life" are both in Niceta's Creed and both as we have seen are characteristically Eastern. These affinities make it clear that Jerome is drawing on the Creed of his native place, and that Stridon derived its Christianity from the East.

CHAPTER VI

WESTERN EUROPEAN CREEDS

I. INTRODUCTION

(a) *Eastern Liturgical Influences*

WE have already produced evidence of the extension of Antiochene liturgical influence throughout Asia Minor, in the neighbourhood of the Danube, and in part also in Palestine, and further investigation will confirm our conclusions, for in fact it stretched even as far as Spain.

Edmund Bishop has called attention to the "curious similarity, I might say almost identity, of devotional spirit" in the Syrian, the Spanish, and the Irish books, and as examples of these last he instances the Stowe Missal, the Book of Cerne and *Royal*, that is MS. Reg. 2 A xx in the British Museum. "This Syrian religious influence", he says, "began to make itself felt in Western piety in Spain." "It is specifically the kind of piety that prevailed among the Semitic Syrians, whether they be from the neighbourhood of Antioch, Edessa, or Nisibis, that is recalled so unmistakeably to us in the documents of the Hispano-Visigothic and Irish churches and peoples...and it was the Spanish Church that inoculated the Irish." "G. H. Forbes pointed out how Spanish forms lay behind the most interesting and characteristic features of the Bobbio Missal."[1]

Even though these statements assert no more than a Syrian liturgical influence at work in Spain subsequently to the Visigothic invasion, it is in the first place clear that Spain possessed a non-Roman rite in earlier times, and if this rite was not in origin Syrian, we shall have to ask ourselves how the Visigoths themselves became imbued with Syrian influence.

[1] *Liturgica Historica*, pp. 161–163.

We are not, indeed, without some evidence that the Antiochene influence had already penetrated into Spain by the fourth century, and it is probable that Spanish Christianity, if we disregard St Paul's intended visit, came from those "oriental churches" to which Augustine attributed the evangelization of Roman Africa; but if so, the form of Creed, with which we shall deal hereafter, would seem to indicate that it came not mediately through the African Church, but by sea from the East. In the fourth century, however, the Priscillianist troubles show an intimate connexion between Spain and Gaul, and Eastern influence seems to have travelled by the land route through the Balkans.

Intermediate between Spain and Antioch lay the province of Moesia, and we have already traced the transportation of the *Sanctus* along this line. Further evidence is furnished by the fact that Martin of Bracara in the sixth century used the same form of baptismal renunciation as was employed by Niceta of Remesiana in the latter half of the fourth: "Quotiens inimicus mentem tuam...titillaverit, responde:...Et abrenuntiavi et abrenuntiabo *tibi, operibus* pariter, *et angelis tuis*" (Niceta, *de Symbolo*, 14). "Non enim ante ad confessionem venitur, nisi prius *diabolo* fuerit renunciatum....Deinde abrenuntiat et *operibus ejus malignis*" (Niceta, *in libro quinto ad competentes*);[1] "Promisistis vos abrenuntiare *diabolo et angelis suis et omnibus operibus ejus malis*" (Martin, *de Correctione Rusticorum*).

On the other side we have another link between Niceta and Asia Minor beyond those already given in connexion with the *Sanctus* and his Creed. Niceta writes: "Sicut in mysteriis ore dicimus, ita conscientiam teneamus: Unus sanctus, utique Spiritus, unus Dominus Jesus Christus in gloria Dei Patris, Amen" (*de Spiritu Sancto*, 22), and this, but for the explanatory interpolation *utique Spiritus*, is the response to the *Sancta sanctis* in the *Apostolic Constitutions*, the Liturgy of St James, John of Damascus and Cyril of Jerusalem. Possibly also we have another importation in the fifth chapter of the same treatise: "Hunc Spiritum novimus...fontem sanctificationis", with which com-

1 Burn, *Niceta of Remesiana*, pp. 52–54.

pare τὸ Πνεῦμα τὸ Ἅγιον...ἡ πηγὴ τοῦ ἁγιασμοῦ in the Anaphora of the Liturgy of St Basil in the Byzantine rite.[1]

Further evidence of the intermediate liturgical position of the
neighbourhood of the Danube between Spain and Antioch is
furnished by the Preface. Cardinal Mai[2] gives portions of two
prefaces from this region of which the first begins: "Dignum et
justum est nos Tibi *hic et ubique* gratias agere." *Hic* does not
occur in any Roman Preface, but in the Mozarabic rite we have:
"Dignum quidem et justum est, Domine, nos Tibi semper *hic et
ubique gratias agere*" (*Liber Ordinum*, 263) and: "Dignum et justum est, vere equum et salutare est, nos Tibi (semper 477, 582)
hic et ubique gratias agere" (*Liber Sacramentorum*, 204, 477, 582)
in the Mozarabic Missal (Migne, *P.L.* LXXXV. pp. 375, 642, 967),
the Gothic Missal (*H.B.S.* pp. 55, 79, 82, 105, 120, 138, 140),
and in the Stowe Missal: "Vere dignum et justum est, equum
et salutare, nos Tibi *hic* semper *et ubique* gratias agere".[3]

The second Preface begins "Dignum et justum est, aequum
et justum est nos Tibi super omnia gratias agere", which recalls
Ἄξιον ὡς ἀληθῶς καὶ δίκαιον πρὸ πάντων ἀνυμνεῖν Σε in the
Clementine rite.

Next let us take the verse which in the *Te Deum* precedes the
Sanctus: *Tibi cherubim et seraphim incessabili voce proclamant.*
In this also Niceta would seem to be quoting from the local
liturgy. In Christian literature we meet with the phrase "the
cherubim of glory" in reference to the Jewish Temple in Heb.
ix. 3, but nowhere in the Bible do we find the two classes
mentioned together. Origen speaks of each order separately, the
Cherubim in his commentary on Rom. iii. 8, and the Seraphim
in *de Principiis*, I. iii. 4. In the Anaphora of the Sacramentary
of Serapion, the seraphim alone are mentioned, the language
used here being taken from Isaiah vi. 2, 3 combined with Eph. i.
21; Daniel vii. 10; Col. i. 16; and Heb. xii. 22, a collection of texts
which in slightly different form meets us in other rites; but the
first collocation of the two is in the *Epideixis* or *Demonstration of
Apostolic Preaching* by Irenaeus, "the powers of these [the Word

---

1 Brightman, *L.E.W.* p. 323.   2 *Script. vet. nova coll.* III. p. 223.
3 *H.B.S.* p. 9.

and the Holy Spirit]...which are called cherubim and seraphim, with unceasing voices glorify God". This points to an Anatolian source, and the form of words is precisely that of Niceta. Next *qui sedes super ch. et s.* in the Second Prayer of Cyprian of Antioch (Migne, *P.L.* IV. pp. 907–908); then in the Clementine Liturgy (*Apost. Const.* viii. 12) we have "the cherubim and six winged seraphim...say...incessantly with constant and loud voices...Holy, Holy, Holy, Lord of Hosts, etc.", and this, or something very like it is common in the Greek Liturgies. Then we have it in the Ambrosian Liturgy, in the form "Quem ch. et s. socia exultatione concelebrant"; in the Gallican Missal (Mone, *Lateinische und griechische Messe*, M. II. p. 17, III. p. 20); in the Gothic Missal "cui merito omnes angeli et archangeli ch. quoque et s. sine intermissione proclamant" (*H.B.S.* p. 41); "ch. quoque et s. qui gloriam Tuam non cessant clamare" (p. 126); in the Mozarabic *Liber Sacramentorum* "Te Dominum cum ch. ac s. sine cessatione conlaudat" (p. 70); "cum ch. et s. sine cessatione proclamant" (p. 82); "cum ch. ac s. sine cessatione sic dicunt" (p. 250); "cum ch. ac s. sine fine conlaudant" (p. 387); "cum ch. ac s....incessabiliter conlaudare mereamur" (p. 434); "cum ch. et s. eterno solio conlaudans atque sine cessatione proclamans" (p. 596); "ch. quoque ac s. incessabili voce proclamant" (p. 622).

Then we come to the Irish books. The Bobbio Missal "cyrobin quoque ac serafin" (*H.B.S.* p. 122); "quem cyrobin et serafin aurigam sedentem pauida subieccione mirantur" (p. 149); "ch. atque s. intercedite pro me" (*Royal*, f. 18 b). The collocation does not occur in any Preface of the Roman rite before the tenth century.

Duchesne writes: "We have no documentary evidence for the uses followed in Aquileia, in the Danubian provinces, and in Dalmatia. It is probable that the use observed in Aquileia and the Danubian provinces resembled rather the Milan than the Roman Liturgy."[1]

Then in regard to the *Post Sanctus* he says: "The agreement of the Mozarabic and Ambrosian Liturgies with each other, and

1 *Christian Worship*, p. 88.

with the Eastern Liturgies in a detail of this importance is a remarkable coincidence."[1]

Next the *Diaconal Litany.* "The Prayer of the Faithful [in the Gallican Mass] begins with a diaconal litany....A prayer in the form of a litany...occurs in the Mozarabic Liturgy for the Sundays in Lent between the Prophecy and the Epistle. The Ambrosian Liturgy also preserves a trace of the Litany after the Gospel in the threefold *Kyrie eleison*....The Litany itself is still in use in Milan in the Masses for the Sundays in Lent, but it is placed at the beginning of the Mass."[2] Duchesne then gives the text from the Sacramentary of Biasca, and continues: "In the Stowe Missal, representing the Irish use, there is a very similar litany between the Epistle and the Gospel....By comparing this litany with those found in the Oriental liturgies, from that of the Apostolic Constitutions onwards, we shall see that they are all absolutely of the same type. We may go even further and say that the examples given are nothing more than translations from a Greek text....We may say the same of the form of the response.... As for the petitions...they are arranged in the same order and drawn up in the same manner as the Greek. There is less difference between the Latin Litany and those contained in the Greek liturgies of St James, St Chrysostom, etc., than there is between the latter and those of the Apostolic Constitutions."

"The Litany was followed by a prayer said by the bishop. This was the *Collectio post precem*....This collect corresponds with the prayer Κύριε παντοκράτορ in the Liturgy of the Apostolic Constitutions, and with the shorter formulary...in the Liturgy of Constantinople."[3]

So again, with regard to the *Gloria Patri.* In the Greek Church this had, and has, the form Δόξα Πατρὶ καὶ Υἱῷ καὶ Ἁγίῳ Πνεύματι καὶ νῦν καὶ ἀεὶ κ.τ.λ. with no *sicut in principio.* The addition penetrated into Gaul and was accepted at the Council of Vaison in 529. The Spanish books[4] retain the form *Gloria et*

---

1 Duchesne, *Christian Worship*, p. 217.   2 *Op. cit.* p. 198.

3 *Op. cit.* pp. 199–201. Cp. Honorius of Autun, *Gemma Animae*, xix, "Populus per *Kyrie eleison*, clerus autem per *Credo in unum Deum* se spondet cuncta servaturum."

4 Mozarabic *Missal*, Migne, *P.L.* LXXXV. p. 109; *Breviary*, LXXXVI. pp. 47 ff.

honor Patri et Filio et Spiritui Sancto in saecula saeculorum, without any *sicut erat in principio*, and this form is commended as customary and enjoined by the 13th and 15th canons of the Fourth Council of Toledo in 633, and is found also in the Ambrosian and Irish MSS.

We will now take a single example from the *Lectionary*. The Gospel for the Saturday before Palm Sunday in the Byzantine rite is John xi. 1–45, and for the Sunday itself John xii. 1–18. In the Ambrosian rite the former passage is the Gospel for the fifth Sunday in Lent, and in the Mozarabic for the Third. The Gospel for Palm Sunday in the Ambrosian rite is John xi. 55–xii. 11, and in the Mozarabic John xi. 55–xii. 13. The Ambrosian omits the last two verses and so stops just short of the Triumphal Entry, because it belongs properly to the Vigil on the previous night, on which the *traditio symboli* takes place, and this has been pushed back to an earlier hour. Thus the emphasis falls on the story of the Anointing of our Lord which was regarded as being parallel to the baptismal unction. Here, then, we have a further link between the Byzantine, the Ambrosian, and the Spanish usages. But further, John xii. 1 ff. is also the Gospel for Palm Sunday in the lectionary of Naples of the seventh century.

We may sum up the apparent conclusion so far in three quotations: The author of the *Te Deum* "moved naturally and easily in the circle of phrases and expressions found in the fragments that remain to us of the Gallican Liturgy, but *not* found in that of the Church of Rome; and...the source on which he drew must have been the Eucharistic service of his Church."[1]

"The Mozarabic Illations are very various in character, but the oldest of them shew a close resemblance to the Eastern type....It seems quite possible that the original type of the Western illations resembled the Eastern type even more closely than is indicated by any extant Masses."[2]

1 Gibson, *Church Quarterly Review*, XVIII. p. 19.
2 *Church Quarterly Review*, LXIII. p. 316; for the baptismal preparation in the Mozarabic rite and its analogues in the Ambrosian and Byzantine rites see *op. cit.* pp. 118–121.

"There is no difficulty...in the identification of the liturgy of the Churches of Spain, or Mozarabic Liturgy...with that which was followed by the churches of Gaul before Charlemagne ...This is not all. It is well known by everyone that the Gallican Liturgy, in the features which distinguish it from the Roman use, betrays all the characteristics of the Eastern liturgies... some of its formularies are to be found word for word in the Greek texts which were in use in the Churches of the Syro-Byzantine rite either in the fourth century, or somewhat later. This close resemblance, this essential identity, implies an importation. The Gallican Liturgy is an Oriental liturgy introduced into the West."[1]

We have now reached certain provisional conclusions and raised certain questions. We have traced the transmission of liturgical phrases and influence from the Antiochene, or Oriental, province, along the land route by way of Constantinople, the Danubian province, Northern Italy and Gaul; but the only dates which we have obtained before the invasions of the barbarians are those of the *Apostolic Constitutions* and Niceta, both of which belong to the latter half of the fourth century. Whence, in the first place, did Spain derive its Christianity and by what route? Did this Antiochene influence which is manifest in the Mozarabic Liturgy reach it before the Visigothic invasion? How far do the forms of Creed support the conclusions at which we have arrived?

(b) The Church of Rome

The first outstanding fact in this period which demands recognition is the smallness of the area within the liturgical influence of the great Church of Rome.

This is so contrary to our natural expectations that we shall be obliged to dwell upon it at some length. Thus Dr Brightman says that in 416, when Pope Innocent I wrote to Decentius, Bishop

---

1 Duchesne, *Christian Worship*, pp. 88, 93, cp. H. Leclercq, *Dict. d'Arch. Chr.* t. VI. pp. 474, 475, "La liturgie gallicane est un type d'inspiration et de forme orientales....Cet usage...s'étendait sur une aire considérable: Italie du nord (et peut-être aussi la province d'Aquilie et la région Danubienne...), la Gaule, l'Espagne, la Bretagne, l'Irlande."

of Eugubium[1] (Gubbio) within a hundred miles of Rome, and therefore within the Pope's metropolitical jurisdiction, "Gubbio, in the fifth century, was not Roman, but Gallican; and the lectionaries of Naples...and of Capua[2] show that Campania was not Roman in the seventh century. And, in fact, it is at least possible that 'Gallican' means simply Western"; and he speaks of the Roman rite as "forming, as it were, an island in a Gallican sea, upon which it gradually, but only gradually, encroached by expansion."[3]

As explaining what he here means by "Western", in reviewing E. G. P. Wyatt's book, *The Eucharistic Prayer* (Alcuin Club Prayer Book Revision Pamphlets, v (1914)), Dr Brightman says that Mr Wyatt brings out that the survival in the Milanese form of the Roman Canon of a *Vere sanctus* in place of the *Te igitur—Quam oblationem* on Easter Even, and the direct passage from *Post Pridie* to *Per quem* on Maundy Thursday, suggest that the Ambrosian [rite] was originally identified with the Gallican and the Mozarabic.[4]

W. C. Bishop uses even stronger language:

"In the Western portion of the Church...we find two rites in the early centuries—the Roman, then a purely local rite, used only (so far as evidence shews) in the city of Rome and perhaps also in the immediate neighbourhood; and the other, called Gallican, Gothic, Mozarabic, Celtic, in different localities, but really one and the same rite, and used over the whole West, with the exception of Rome, so that it might fitly be called the Western or European rite. There is no evidence that the Roman liturgy was used outside the immediate neighbourhood of Rome before St Augustine's arrival in England....On the contrary the evidence of liturgical allusions (so far as they are conclusive) agrees with the 'Gallican' rite as against the Roman for Spain, France, the Celtic Church, and also in North Italy. In Africa the same may be said, except that the Pax had apparently the Roman position."[5]

1 *Ep.* 25.   2 Morin, *Liber Comicus*, pp. 426 ff., 436 ff.
3 *J.T.S.* i. pp. 449, 450.   4 *J.T.S.* xvii. p. 317.
5 *Church Quarterly Review*, lxvi. p. 393.

So also Dr Fortescue: "In the first period it [the Roman rite] was the local rite of the city of Rome only. It was not used in North Italy; even the Southern dioceses of the peninsula had their own liturgical use. Nor does the old rite of Africa appear to have been Roman, though it had Roman features. Since about the VIIIth century this local Roman rite gradually spread all over the West, displacing the others."[1]

Nor, except when in later times the two rites have overlapped, is confusion between them possible. Edmund Bishop writes that "there is no possibility of mistaking a Gallican or Gothic for a Roman book, and *vice versa*; and that, not for any recondite reason that may appeal only to the professed scholar, not for any ritual peculiarity on which the rubrician would be called in to decide, but for a reason plain on the face of the books themselves —viz. a style, a run of thought, and a mode of expression, so clearly different as to declare the two things to be the product of the mind, spirit, and genius of two different peoples." "These early Gallican and Spanish books...evince a tone of mind, and are the product of a spirit alien to that which we have now become accustomed to regard as most befitting the Divine worship, tutored as we have so long been in the sobriety of Roman forms."[2]

Confining ourselves to the fourth century, which is a time as late as our immediate purpose needs, we next ask how this state of things came about, and the negative answer is, because in no countries north of the Apennines was Rome exercising any effective jurisdiction. The sixth canon of the Council of Nicaea in 325 runs: "Let the ancient customs prevail, namely those in Egypt, Libya, and Pentapolis; that the Bishop of Alexandria have jurisdiction over all these, since the same is customary for the Bishop of Rome"; but Rufinus of Aquileia writing in 402 or 403 glosses it: "*Et apud Alexandriam et in urbe Roma vetusta consuetudo servetur ut vel ille Aegypti, vel hic, suburbicariarum ecclesiarum sollicitudinem gerat.*" The "suburbicarian" churches would be those of the civil province governed by the Vicarius Urbis, as distinct from the region of Northern Italy which was subject to the Vicarius Italiae. There was, therefore, a tradition

1 *The Mass*, pp. 97, 98.   2 *Liturgia Historica*, pp. 13, 14, 55.

at Aquileia that up to the end of the fourth century the Church
of Rome had exercised no jurisdiction in that district. It is, however, possible that Rufinus was adopting a version current in
Africa: *Quoniam et urbis Romae episcopo similis mos est, ut in*
suburbicaria *loca sollicitudinem gerat.* This version has been
attributed to Caecilian, Bishop of Carthage, who was himself
present at the Council, but in any event the mention of "suburbicarian" churches or places is a gloss, as may be seen by
reference to the Greek, and shows that neither Northern Italy
nor Africa regarded itself at this period as under the effective
jurisdiction of Rome. So Duchesne writes: "We must not...
ignore the peculiar position which Milan held, towards the close
of the fourth century, as a centre of influence, which was felt
more in Gaul than elsewhere. For a short but important period
it would thus appear that the Western episcopate recognised a
twofold hegemony—that of the Pope and that of the Bishop of
Milan. This divided authority became first apparent in the time
of St Ambrose.... The influence of Ambrose made itself felt in
the Eastern Church—at Antioch, at Caesarea, at Constantinople,
and at Thessalonica.... At Aquileia he presided over a council
at which the last difficulties connected with the Arian crisis in
the Lower Danubian provinces were disposed of. It is, however,
particularly in Gaul and Spain that the ecclesiastical authority
of Milan seems to have been accepted as a natural and superior
tribunal."[1]

In 390, when Gaul was still without a full metropolitical
system, the Gallican bishops found themselves in need of help
and counsel. By that time Milan had become the metropolitical
see of Northern Italy, so they applied to Ambrose and to Pope
Siricius. Eight years later the Gallican bishops applied to the
successor of Ambrose, Simplicianus, and to him only. A council
of the bishops of the province was held at Turin in 398, and its
sixth canon refers to the letters of Ambrose and of the Bishop
of the Roman Church, in this order.

As regards Gaul, Duchesne writes that it was not until the
time of Zosimus that the Pope "took the effective direction of

[1] *Christian Worship*, pp. 32, 33.

the episcopate of the Gallic provinces, over which, up till that time, he had not been able to exercise more than a feeble and intermittent influence".[1] And he did so by the intermediation of Patroclus, Bishop of Arles, whom he made his "Vicar" in 407; but when he summoned Proculus, Bishop of Marseilles, to Rome, Proculus disregarded the summons, and persevered in this attitude after the death of Zosimus in the following year, and was left in peace by his successor Boniface I.

And if it was not before the fifth century at the earliest that Rome exercised any effective jurisdiction over Northern Italy, it would follow *a fortiori* that it did not do so in Spain or Africa. And this is exactly what we find. The independence of the Churches of Spain and Africa is shown simultaneously by the case of the two Spanish bishops Basilides and Martialis. Both had compromised with idolatry in the Decian persecution. Basilides resigned and his resignation was accepted by the bishops of the province, while Martialis was deposed by the same authority; both obtained recognition from the Pope, and returned to Spain; in the state of confusion which followed the Churches in Spain wrote to Cyprian at Carthage. Cyprian ruled that the sentence of the synod of the province was final, that the see left vacant had been canonically filled up, and that the Pope's decision in regard to a matter outside his jurisdiction had no force. In Africa we meet with the same independence shown by Cyprian and the councils over which he presided in the baptismal controversy, and by Aurelius and Augustine in the case of Apiarius in the early years of the fifth century.

And the reason why Western Europe and Africa failed to recognize the authority of the Church of Rome is that they had no historical connexion with it. Though civil officials were perpetually travelling from Rome to all parts of the empire, there is no good evidence that Rome ever sent out a single missionary until centuries later. The story given by Gregory of Tours that seven bishops were sent from Rome to Gaul in 250 has no historical foundation;[2] both the date of St Patrick and his connexion with Rome are doubtful; so is the connexion with Rome

1 *Christian Worship*, p. 39.   2 See below, p. 176, 177.

of Germanus of Auxerre, who could not be called a missionary
in any case. And the first authentic missionary from Rome is,
in consequence, Augustine of Canterbury at the close of the
sixth century. One cause, at any rate, of this want of enterprise
abroad was weakness at home. At the time of the Council of
Nicaea Harnack reckons that except in the remote country
districts half the population of Asia Minor was at least nominally
Christian,[1] but Rome remained the stronghold of paganism.

These lines of evidence converge to a single point, namely that
if we should find Creeds of a common pattern in Northern Italy
in the fourth century we could be certain that they were not
brought thither from Rome, but from some Eastern source; and
therefore if the Creed of Rome resembled them this could only
be due to an engrafting of these Creeds, or some of them, on a
native Roman stock.

II. The Creed of Spain

Apart from the journey which St Paul intended to make, and
may have taken, the earliest notices of Christianity in Spain are
in Irenaeus (*adv. Haer.* I. iii. A.D. 180–185), and Tertullian
(*adv. Jud.* vii. A.D. 197–198); and the latter apparently intends
to indicate a general diffusion of Christianity throughout Spain,
as compared with a more limited expansion in Mauritania, which
he had mentioned just before. Then we have the letter of
Cyprian (*Ep.* lxvii) in which he replied to one received from
Spain. This shows that there were Christian settlements at Leon,
Astorga, Merida and Saragossa, these last possibly forming a
single community; in other words Christianity seems to have
come to Spain from the coast, and travelled up the rivers Douro,
Guadiana, Guadalquivir and Ebro, and the roads beside them.
And it was probably brought from Asia Minor or Syria by
people who spoke Greek, and subsequent generations of Spanish
Christians maintained the connexion with its seat of origin.
Geography, history and liturgiology combine to assure us of this;

1 *Mission and Expansion*, II. p. 184.

and we shall naturally expect to find the same conclusion confirmed by the form of Creed. Of the Creed of the fourth century we have two examples in Priscillian (*c.* 380, L. pp. 10, 11) and Gregory of Elvira (351–392).[1]

Priscillian	Gregory
(Credimus in) unum Deum Patrem omnipotentem;	Credimus in unum Deum Patrem omnipotentem;
Et (in) unum Dominum Jesum Christum	Et in unigenitum Filium Ejus, Jesum Christum,
	Deum et Dominum, salvatorem nostrum,
natum ex Maria virgine ex Spiritu Sancto	natum de Spiritu Sancto ex Maria virgine,
passum sub Pontio Pilato	passum sub Pontio Pilato,
crucifixum...sepultum	crucifixum, et mortuum, et sepultum,
tertia die resurrexisse	secundum scripturas tertia die a mortuis resurrexisse,
ascendisse in caelos,	assumptum in caelos,
sedere ad dexteram Dei Patris omnipotentis,	sedere ad dexteram Patris,
inde venturum et judicaturum de vivis et mortuis,	inde venturum judicare vivos et mortuos;
(Credimus) in Spiritum Sanctum; In sanctam ecclesiam Baptismum salutare;	...Spiritum Sanctum.
(Credimus in) remissionem peccatorum;	Remissionem peccatorum;
(Credimus in) resurrectionem carnis.	Hujus carnis resurrectionem.

The peculiarity of Priscillian's Creed is the order *natum ex Maria virgine ex Spiritu Sancto*, and this has been taken as evidence of his heretical views, but γεννηθέντα ἐξ ἁγίας παρθένου καὶ Ἁγίου Πνεύματος occurs in Cyril of Jerusalem (*Cat.* iv. 9), and *Hic unigenitus Dei de Maria virgine et Spiritu Sancto secundum carnem natus ostenditur* in the *Gelasian Sacramentary* (ed. Wilson, p. 35), and probably the order means that the earlier Spanish Creeds had *natum ex Maria virgine* only, as is found in the Creeds of Antioch and Philadelphia and in all conciliar creeds earlier than the Council of Nike, 359, and that *ex Spiritu Sancto* is a later

1 See Dom Morin's article in the *Revue Bénédictine*, XIX. pp. 229–237.

addition. Both Priscillian's and Gregory's Creeds have the participial form *natum passum*, etc.; this form might be thought to be
due to the treatises from which the Creeds are taken, were it not
that the Mozarabic Missal (Migne, *P.L.* LXXXV. p. 395) has *et in
Jesum Christum...natum de Spiritu Sancto ex utero Mariae virginis*,
and then starts off another sentence: *Passus, ...sepultus, tertia
die resurrexit*, an arrangement which suggests that the original
Spanish Creed was a translation from the Greek—as was probably, in fact, the case—but that as *resurgo* has no past participle
corresponding to ἀναστάντα the translator had to begin a new sentence in order to avoid the harshness which is obvious in the
Creed of Niceta of Remesiana.

Syagrius(?), c. 430

In the Chronicle of Bishop Hydatius under the year 433
occurs this entry: "In the district (or 'assembly', *conventu*) of
Lugo [in north-western Spain] Pastor and Syagrius were ordained
bishops against the will of Agrestius, Bishop of Lugo, and
Gennadius mentions a Bishop Syagrius of whom he says: 'Under
the name of this Syagrius I have found seven books entitled on
the faith and rules of faith'".

Dom Morin[1] thinks that these exist in a MS. of the eleventh
or twelfth century at Reims, of which the first claims to be an
exhortation by Ambrose on the Creed; it runs:

Credimus itaque in Deum Patrem omnipotentem,
saeculorum omnium et creaturarum regem et conditorem.
Et in Jesum Christum, Filium Ejus unicum, Dominum nostrum,
qui natus est de Spiritu Sancto et Maria virgine,
qui sub Pontio Pilato crucifixus et sepultus,
tertia die resurrexit a mortuis,
ascendit in caelos,
sedet ad dexteram Dei Patris,
inde venturus est judicare vivos et mortuos,
Et in Spiritum Sanctum;
Et sanctam ecclesiam catholicam;
Remissionem peccatorum;
Carnis resurrectionem.

1 *Revue Bénédictine*, X. p. 392.

And another piece by the same author (Pseudo-Augustine, Sermon ccxxxvi) containing:

> Credimus in Deum Patrem omnipotentem,
> cunctorum visibilium et invisibilium conditorem.
> Credimus et in Dominum nostrum Jesum Christum,
> per quem creata sunt omnia, verum Deum,
> unigenitum et verum Dei Filium...
> Credimus et in Spiritum Sanctum ex Patre procedentem...
> Ipsum autem Dei Filium...dicimus, hominem
> suscepisse ex Maria semper virgine...
> Passus est...
> Resurrexit tertia die,
> Ascendit in coelum,
> sedet ad dexteram Dei Patris...
> Resurrectionem etiam carnis confitemur...
> Baptisma unum tenemus.

With these we may put extracts from the *Epistola ad Fratrem Graecum Diaconum*, written by Bachiarius, who was most probably a Spaniard, about the middle of the fifth century.

> Pater enim unus ingenitus, Filius unus est genitus, Spiritus Sanctus
>   a Patre procedens, Patri et Filio coaeternus...
> Filium quoque credimus...
> natum esse de virgine et Spiritu Sancto...
> passum et sepultum resurrexisse a mortuis...
> ascendisse in caelum,
> unde venturum expectamus ad judicium vivorum et mortuorum.
> Virginem quoque de qua natum scimus...
> Carnem quoque nostrae resurrectionis fatemur integram.

Further evidence that Christianity reached Spain in Greek would seem to be furnished by the occasional occurrence of "Agyos, Agyos, Agyos, kyrie, o Theos" in the *Sanctus* in the Mozarabic Illation. Though the phrase "Agyos, Agyos, Agyos, Lord God eternal king" in the Diaconal Litany (the old Prayer of the Faithful, an *ectene* reduced to two clauses) would seem to be an imitation of Byzantine custom and not an original part of the Mozarabic rite, this would not appear to be true of the *Illatio* in which the *Sanctus* occurs. Thus we seem to have an original evangelization of Spain coming from the East, not by way of Africa, since the Creed form has none of the peculiarities shown in that of Cyprian, but water-borne by a more direct route, so that if we could recover it we should probably find that the original Creed resembled those of the Marcosians and of the *Epistola Apostolorum*, both in length and structure, and that this was enlarged at some later time by phrases brought by land routes through Northern Italy and Gaul.

III. The Creed of Gaul

"The South of Gaul had been colonized originally from the Eastern shores of the Aegean. Its Christianity came from the same region as its colonization. The Church of Gaul was the spiritual daughter of the Church of proconsular Asia."[1] Lightfoot, from whom these remarks are taken, sees no improbability in Benignus, afterwards the patron saint of Dijon, having been sent to evangelize Gaul, together with his companions Andochius the Presbyter and Thyrsus the Deacon, by Polycarp, Bishop of Smyrna; it is highly probable also that Pothinus, the predecessor of Irenaeus in the episcopate of Lyons, migrated from Asia Minor; Irenaeus himself received his early education in Asia Minor, partly under Polycarp's direct influence. The Epistle of the Churches of Lyons and Vienne,[2] which gives an account of the persecution in the days of Marcus Aurelius (c. 177), is written in Greek "to the brethren in Phrygia and Asia"; and individual martyrs and confessors also addressed letters to the same region; a third of the number of sufferers are Greeks, and at least three of these come from Asia Minor.

Here again Christianity started from the Greek settlements on the coast, such as Massilia, and spread along the sea shore and up the rivers, particularly the Rhône. But though Irenaeus wrote Greek, the civil and ecclesiastical language was Latin.[3]

Duchesne holds that "all the Christians from the Rhine to the Pyrenees formed only a single community, and recognized but one chief, the Bishop of Lyons",[4] but this seems an extreme interpretation of the words of Eusebius, "the parishes (or dioceses, παροικίαι) in Gaul over which Irenaeus presided",[5] and it is more probable that at the time to which Eusebius refers, about

1 *Ap. Fathers*, pt. II, vol. I, p. 446.
2 Eusebius, *H.E.* v. 2, 3 (G. pp. 62–83).
3 Mommsen, *Provinces*, I. pp. 101, 102; and for the end of the first century cp. Juvenal, *Sat.* vii. 147, 148.   4 *Fastes Épiscopaux*, I. p. 40.   5 *H.E.* v. 23.

190, Irenaeus was the leading bishop, the "Primus" who would naturally occupy the chair at episcopal meetings, but not strictly speaking a metropolitan, for the metropolitical system was only being introduced into Gaul in the fourth century. The independence of Lyons towards Rome is shown by the part played by Irenaeus in the Paschal controversy.

No doubt in his time Lyons would possess a rite akin to that of Asia Minor, and of course Christians would make some declaration of their faith before being baptized; but we have no knowledge of its precise form. It could not, however, be much fuller than the contemporary Creeds of Asia Minor, and must be such that subsequent Gallican Creeds could be expanded from it. If we were to take the treatise *Against Heresies*, and extract from it all the possible Creed phrases, we could produce a formula of nearly three hundred words; but this would obviously be a monstrosity, and our best source for obtaining it is his *Epideixis* or *Demonstration of Apostolic Preaching* found in an Armenian translation at Eriwan in 1904. In Chapter III we have "we must needs hold the κανών of the faith without deviation....Faith...bids us bear in mind that we have received baptism for the remission of sins, in the name of God the Father, and in the name of Jesus Christ, the Son of God, who was incarnate, and died and rose again, and in the Holy Spirit of God, and that this Baptism is the seal of eternal life. All things are God's, and therefore God is almighty...", and in Chapter XLI, "which Holy Spirit they [the disciples] had received of the Lord, and they distributed and imparted It to them that believed; and thus they ordered and established the Churches".

From these sentences we might extract a Creed:

> Credo in Deum Patrem omnipotentem;
> Et in Jesum Christum, Filium Ejus,
> natum et mortuum,
> resurrexit;
> Et in Spiritum Sanctum;
> Sanctam ecclesiam;
> Remissionem peccatorum;
> Vitam aeternam.

But though this is near the truth it is probably too long.

It has been sometimes argued that the first clauses of the
Creed of Irenaeus must have run: "I believe in *one* God", because the oneness of God is so often insisted upon in his own
controversial writings, but the arguments do not appear at all
conclusive. In contrast with the polytheism of heathendom and
the dualism of Marcion, Irenaeus must have stressed the fact
that God is one, just as a modern missionary must do, but that
no more proves that "one" stood in his creed in the one case
than in the other. St Paul insists that to the heathen "there are
gods many and lords many, yet to us there is one God, the
Father, . . . and one Lord, Jesus Christ" (1 Cor. viii. 5–6); yet
"one God—one Lord" occurs only once in the large number of
instances of the formula "God, Jesus Christ, Holy Spirit" given
on pp. 17–19, and then in conjunction with "one faith, one
baptism". Moreover Irenaeus insisted almost equally on "one"
as applied to Christ, though it is all but certain that the epithet
did not occur in the second member of his Creed. But of greater
weight is the fact that the word "one" in either connexion does
not occur in any later Gallican baptismal Creed, and these were
all in some degree dependent on the Creed of Irenaeus.

Later Gallican Creeds

Phoebadius, Bishop of Agen, in Aquitaine, before 357, died
after 392.

There are three documents ascribed to him. The first is the
confession of the orthodox bishops at the Council of Ariminum
in 359. This is attributed to him by the Benedictines of St Maur
and by Kattenbusch (*ap. Symb.* 1. p. 172).

Credimus in unum verum Deum, Patrem omnipotentem.
Credimus in unigenitum Dei Filium,
qui ante omnia saecula et ante omne principium
natus est ex Deo, natum autem unigenitum. . . . Deum ex Deo. . . .
Qui de caelo descendit,
conceptus est de Spiritu Sancto, natus ex Maria virgine,
crucifixus a Pontio Pilato,
tertia die resurrexit (a mortuis),
ascendit in caelum,
sedet ad dexteram Dei Patris,
venturus judicare vivos et mortuos.

The second is a document afterwards known as *Fides Romanorum*.
This appears to have been written in 360 or 361, and the greater
part of it is quoted in the apocryphal Acts of Liberius written
in the fifth century. It is attributed to Phoebadius by the
Benedictines, Kattenbusch and Burn, the last of whom gives a
critical text (*Introduction*, pp. 216, 217).

Credimus in unum Deum, Patrem omnipotentem,
et in unum unigenitum Filium Ejus,
Jhesum Christum, Deum et Dominum, Salvatorem nostrum....

*   *   *   *   *

Deus de Deo, lumen de lumine...non creatum sed genitum...
ex Patre, unius substantiae cum Patre...
Spiritum vero Sanctum Deum
non ingenitum neque genitum, non creatum nec factum...vene-
    ramur:

*   *   *   *   *

Credimus Jhesum Christum, Dominum nostrum, Dei Filium,
per quem omnia facta sunt, quae in caelis, quae in terra,
visibilia et invisibilia,
propter nostram salutem descendisse de caelo...
et natum de Spiritu Sancto ex virgine Maria.

*   *   *   *   *

passum sub Pontio Pilato,
crucifixum secundum scripturas,
mortuum et sepultum,
secundum scripturas tertia die a mortuis resurrexisse,
adsumptum in caelum,
sedere ad dexteram Patris,
inde venturum judicare vivos et mortuos.
Expectamus...remissionem peccatorum consecutos,
resuscitandos nos...in eadem carne qua nunc sumus,
sicut et Ipse in eadem carne qua natus passus et mortuus resur-
    rexit...
accepturos ab Eo aut vitam aeternam...
aut sententiam...aeterni supplicii.

And the third is in Chapter 8 of his *de Fide Orthodoxa*.

Quem...passum credimus et sepultum....
Tertia...die resurrexit.
Ascendit in caelos....
Misit nobis Spiritum Sanctum Ipse Dominus Salvator noster,
cujus regnum...non initium habet nec terminum.

Victricius of Rouen (*c.* 390–400), extracted from his *Liber de Laude Sanctorum.*

.   .   .   .   .   .

...de Maria virgine.
passus est, crucifixus, sepultus,
tertia die resurrexit a mortuis,
ascendit in caelum,
sedet ad dexteram Dei Patris,
inde venturus est judicare vivos et mortuos;
Et in Spiritu Sancto....

Leporius of Trèves, a priest of Marseilles, who fell into heresy, and was converted by Augustine at Hippo. On his return (415–420) he presented a confession to the Bishops of Marseilles and Aix, including:

nascitur...de Spiritu Sancto et Maria semper virgine,
Filius Dei
crucifixus est, mortuus,
resurrexit.

Faustus of Riez (450–490), *de Spiritu Sancto* (L. p. 12):

Credo et in Spiritum Sanctum;
Sanctam ecclesiam;
Sanctorum communionem;
Abremissa peccatorum;
Carnis resurrectionem;
Vitam aeternam.

Caesarius of Arles (*c.* 468–542). (Pseudo-Augustine Sermon CCXLIV):[1]

Credite...	in Deum Patrem omnipotentem;
credite	et in Jesum Christum, Filium Ejus unicum, Dominum nostrum.
Credite Eum et	conceptum esse de Spiritu Sancto, natum ex Maria virgine,...
Credite Eum	...passum sub Pontio Pilato,
credite	crucifixum, (credite) mortuum et sepultum,
credite Eum	ad inferna descendisse,...
Credite Eum	tertia die a mortuis resurrexisse,...
Credite Eum	in caelis...ascendisse:
credite quod	in dextera sedet Patris:
credite quod	venturus sit judicare vivos et mortuos.

1 This sermon is now accepted by Dom G. Morin as the work of Caesarius, *S. Caesarii Opera*, 1. p. 50.

Credite	in Spiritum Sanctum,
credite	sanctam ecclesiam catholicam,
credite	sanctorum communionem,
credite	carnis resurrectionem,
credite	remissionem peccatorum,
credite et	vitam aeternam.

Cyprian of Toulon (*c.* 475–556) in a letter to Maximus, Bishop of Geneva (*Monumenta Germ. Hist.* Ep. 3): (L. p. 12).

Credo in Deum Patrem omnipotentem;
Credo et in Jesum Christum, Filium Ejus unigenitum,
Dominum nostrum...
qui conceptus de Spiritu Sancto, natus ex Maria virgine,...
passus sub Pontio Pilato, crucifixus et sepultus,...
tertia die resurrexit a mortuis,
ascendit in caelos,
sedet ad dexteram Patris,
inde venturus judicaturus vivos ac mortuos....

Gregory of Tours (*Historica ecclesiastica Francorum*, *Prologus*), born in Auvergne 540, bishop 573–594.

Credo in Deum Patrem omnipotentem.
Credo in Jesum Christum, Filium Ejus unicum, Dominum Deum nostrum, natum a Patre non factum...
cujus passione mundus redemptus est....
Credo Eum die tertia resurrexisse,...
ascendisse in caelos,
sedere ad dexteram Patris,
venturum ac judicaturum vivos et mortuos.
Credo Sanctum Spiritum a Patre et Filio processisse....
Credo beatam Mariam ut virginem ante partum ita virginem et post partum.

These forms are none of them earlier than the extreme end of the fourth century and show certain amplifications, *conceptus*, ad dexteram *Dei* Patris, *sanctorum communionem*, *vitam aeternam*, and all these phrases travelled to Gaul from regions to the East of it; but the Creed form is structurally, and in phrase, the same as that found in the fourth century in Spain on the one side and Northern Italy on the other. And the liturgical influence of Rome did not reach Gaul before the sixth century, and in the sixth century Gallican bishops all wore the pallium, and all priests wore armlets (*manicae*, ἐπιμανίκια), which suggests Byzantine influence.[1]

The third canon of the Second Council of Vaison in 529, which was a Provincial Council of the Metropolis of Arles, orders the use of the *Kyrie eleison* at lauds, mass, and vespers. It begins: "Et quia tam in sede apostolica, quam etiam per totas orientales atque Italiae provincias...". The fifth canon orders that in the *Gloria Patri* the clause *sicut erat in principio* should be inserted with the object of refuting heresy. It begins: "Et quia non solum in sede apostolica, sed etiam per totum Orientem, et totam Africam vel Italiam...". This was certainly an exaggeration in the second case as regards the Eastern Churches, and probably in the first also as regards Africa, since in the African Church there is no trace whatever of the *Kyrie eleison* in the Mass previous to the Vandal invasion; but it marks the beginning of deference in Gaul towards Roman liturgical authority. Probably to much the same time and movement in Gaul or Burgundy belongs the *de Sacramentis*, a treatise obviously based on Ambrose's *de Mysteriis*, and including, besides many Gallican usages, a Canon which appears to be an adaptation of the Roman.[2]

Later in date are the Creeds of Venantius Fortunatus, who was ordained priest and consecrated bishop at Poitiers between 560 and 600, and Eligius of Noyon, 588–659.

Venantius Fortunatus, *Carminum* XI 1:

> Credo in Deum Patrem omnipotentem;
> Et in Jesum Christum, unicum Filium,
> qui natus est de Spiritu Sancto ex Maria virgine,
> crucifixus sub Pontio Pilato,
> descendit ad infernum,
> tertia die resurrexit,
> ascendit in caelum,
> . . . . .
> judicaturus vivos et mortuos;

---

[1] See St German of Paris, *Epp.* i and ii (Migne, *P.L.* LXXII. 97); *Conc. Matiscon.* I. can. 6 (where *episcopus* is the right reading). "It would seem that in the East, and also in countries following the Gallican use, the *pallium* was worn indiscriminately by all bishops" (Duchesne, *Christian Worship*, p. 389).

[2] See C. Atchley, *J.T.S.* xxx. pp. 281–286.

Credo in Sanctum Spiritum;
Sanctam ecclesiam;
Remissionem peccatorum;
Resurrectionem carnis.

This Creed appears to be quoted with some omissions, but the only additional clause is *descendit ad infernum* which was undoubtedly derived from Aquileia, since Venantius Fortunatus was born at Ceneta (Ceneda) near Trevisium (Treviso) in North Italy.

Eligius of Noyon, *de Rectitudine Catholicae Conversationis Tractatus*:

Promisistis... credere vos
in Deum Patrem omnipotentem;
et in Jesum Christum, Filium Ejus unicum,
Dominum nostrum,
natum ex Maria virgine,
passum sub Pontio Pilato,
tertia die resurrexisse a mortuis,
ascendisse ad caelos.
Promisistis deinde credere vos
et in Spiritum Sanctum;
Sanctam ecclesiam catholicam;
Sanctorum communionem;
Remissionem peccatorum;
Carnis resurrectionem;
Et vitam aeternam.

This form also is plainly shortened, since it is impossible that in a sermon on the Last Judgement the preacher should not have confessed Christ as Judge in his Creed.

IV. CREEDS OF NORTHERN ITALY

The only bishoprics in Northern Italy which have any serious claim to date earlier than the fourth century are those of Ravenna (Classis), Milan, Aquileia, Brescia, and Verona. Ravenna and Milan appear to have been evangelized about the beginning of the third century, or perhaps a little earlier, and Aquileia rather later. At the Council of Arles in 314 the Bishop of Aquileia was Theodore, and his deacon Agatho, both evidently Greeks. The first well authenticated Bishop of Milan is Merocles (304–315), probably a Greek also. He is said to have been succeeded by Eustorgius in 315, and he by Protasius, who

was present at the Council of Serdica in 343. Protasius was succeeded by Dionysius who was banished by Constantius in 355
when Auxentius the Cappadocian became bishop. Thus all the
known Bishops of Milan before Auxentius bear Greek names.
Both Milan and Aquileia probably became metropolitical sees
between 358 and 361. Harnack would therefore appear to be
abundantly justified in saying that "ecclesiastically, it was a
longer road from Rome to Ravenna and Aquileia than from
Sirmium, Sardica, and Thessalonica. And this state of matters
did not originate in the fourth century; on the contrary, it was
not till then that, owing to the new political conditions of the age,
the Roman Church exercised any perceptible influence over
these towns and districts."[1] The map suggests that the plains of
Lombardy drew their Christianity from the East by way of the
Po in much the same way as the valley of the Rhône was
colonized by Greek settlers from the South and the valley of the
Nile from Alexandria in the North, while the provinces of Venetia
were Christianized by immigrants coming up the Adriatic.

Ravenna, c. 450	Turin, c. 450
Peter Chrysologus, sermons 57–62 (L. pp. 9, 10)	Maximus, *Hom. de Expositione Symboli* 83 (L. p. 10)
Credo in Deum Patrem omnipotentem;	Credo in Deum Patrem omnipotentem;
Et in Christum Jesum.	Et in Jesum Christum.
Filium Ejus unicum, Dominum nostrum,	Filium Ejus unicum, Dominum nostrum,
qui natus est de Spiritu Sancto	qui natus est de Spiritu Sancto
ex Maria virgine,	ex Maria virgine,
qui sub Pontio Pilato crucifixus est et sepultus,	qui sub Pontio Pilato crucifixus est, et sepultus,
tertia die resurrexit (a mortuis),	tertia die resurrexit a mortuis,
ascendit in caelos,	ascendit in caelum;
sedet ad dexteram Patris,	sedet ad dexteram Patris,
inde venturus est judicare	inde venturus judicare
vivos et mortuos;	vivos et mortuos;
Credo in Spiritum Sanctum;	Et in Spiritum Sanctum;
Sanctam ecclesiam;	Sanctam ecclesiam;
Remissionem peccatorum;	Remissionem peccatorum;
Carnis resurrectionem;	Carnis resurrectionem.
Vitam aeternam.	

1 *Mission and Expansion* (2nd ed. 1908), II. p. 258.

The importance of these two Creeds is that in spite of the fact that they belong to the middle of the fifth century, neither of them shows any growth beyond the fourth-century form except the addition of *vitam aeternam* in the Creed of Ravenna.

Aquileia between 399 and 410 Rufinus *in Symb. Ap.* (L. p. 9; H. pp. 37, 38)	Aquileia or Forum Julii (? Udine) 5th or 6th cent. (Hahn[3], pp. 43, 44)
Credo in Deo Patre omnipotente	Credo in Deum Patrem omni- potentem
invisibili et impassibili; et in Christo Jesu,	Et in Jesum Christum
unico Filio Ejus, Domino nostro,	Filium Ejus unicum, Dominum nostrum,
qui natus est de Spiritu Sancto ex Maria virgine, crucifixus sub Pontio Pilato, et sepultus, descendit ad inferna, tertia die resurrexit a mortuis, ascendit in caelos, sedet ad dexteram Patris, inde venturus est judicare vivos et mortuos; Et in Spiritu Sancto; Sanctam ecclesiam; Remissionem peccatorum; Hujus carnis resurrectionem.	qui natus est de Spiritu Sancto ex Maria virgine, sub Pontio Pilato crucifixus est, et sepultus, tertia die resurrexit a mortuis, ascendit in caelum, sedet ad dexteram Patris, inde venturus est judicare vivos et mortuos; Credo in Spiritum Sanctum; Sanctam ecclesiam catholicam; Remissionem peccatorum; Carnis resurrectionem; Et vitam aeternam.

There is no doubt that the weight of MS. authority is in favour of *in Deo Patre, in Jesu Christo, in Spiritu Sancto*, in the Creed of Rufinus, which means that there is strong reason to think that the writer or writers of the MS. or MSS. wrote *in* with the ablative. But *in* with the ablative in these clauses when it occurs elsewhere in Creeds is due to what may be called "the carelessness of scribes", and the form is so strange in Rufinus's Creed that it is incredible that it was in the Creed of Aquileia, that is, that Rufinus actually wrote it, and in Chapter VI he writes *unicum hunc esse Filium Dei, Dominum nostrum*. The ablatives used to be supported by quoting Venantius Fortunatus, but the latest editor of a critical text, F. Leo (*Monumenta Germ. Hist.* 1881), gives the accusative throughout. The real peculiarity is that the

scribe is perfectly consistent in his use of the ablative, instead of
mixing the two cases as we get elsewhere. But there are people
who habitually say "between you and I",[1] and the less educated
Berliner regularly says "mich" when he should say "mir".

Invisibili et impassibili. Rufinus writes: "Before I begin to dis-
cuss the meaning of the words, I think it well to mention that in
different churches some additions are found in this article. This
is not the case, however, in the Church of the city of Rome. The
reason being, as I suppose, that on the one hand no heresy has
had its origin there, and, on the other, that the ancient custom is
maintained that those who are going to be baptized should re-
hearse the Creed publicly, that is in the hearing of the people, the
consequence of which is that the ears of those who are already
believers will not admit the addition of a single word. But in
other places, as I understand, additions appear to have been
made on account of certain heretics, by means of which novelty
in doctrine, it was believed, might be excluded. We, however,
follow that order which we received when we were baptized in
the Church of Aquileia." And: "I should mention that these
two words [*invisibilis* and *impassibilis*] are not in the Creed of
the Roman Church. They were added in our Church as is well
known on account of the Sabellian heresy, called by us 'the
Patripassian', that which says that the Father Himself was
born of the Virgin and became visible, and affirms that He
suffered in the flesh. To exclude such impiety, therefore, concerning the Father, our forefathers seem to have added the
words." Rufinus went to Rome in 397 or 398 and came back to
Aquileia in 399, but the public recitation of the Creed at Rome,
though no doubt customary, would not appear to have been of
universal obligation, for Augustine says of a time some forty
years earlier, that the presbyters would have given Victorinus
leave to make his profession in private.[2]

Rufinus's statement that he intends to give the Creed in the
form delivered to him at the time of his baptism, carries back to
about 370.

1 Cp. Shakespeare, *Merchant of Venice*, III. ii (end–Antonio's letter).
2 *Conf.* VIII. 5.

Ut ergo excluderetur talis impietas de Patre [the Sabellian heresy] *videntur haec addidisse majores.* Sabellianism was taught in Rome towards the end of the second century, but this would appear to be before Aquileia was evangelized. Towards the middle of the fourth century something like it was taught by the followers of Marcellus of Ancyra; but this is clearly too late, and the only epoch in which it flourished which will suit the language in which Rufinus refers to it is about the year 250, when it was maintained in Libya, where it gained such a hold that even certain bishops were infected by it.[1] Aquileia was on a navigable river, the Natiso, and probably there was considerable commercial intercourse between it and the great towns of northern Libya such as Ptolemais, to which Dionysius of Alexandria refers as a stronghold of Sabellianism. The phrase added to the Creed of Aquileia has an Eastern sound, and resembles the language used in the Epistle of Ignatius to Polycarp, c. 3, "Await Him... the eternal, the invisible...the impassible"; Melito, *Frag.* 13, "Invisibilis videtur; neque erubuit; incomprehensibilis prehenditur, neque indignatur; incommensurabilis mensuratur, neque repugnat, impassibilis patitur, neque ulciscitur"; and in a letter thought by Routh[2] to have been written before the condemnation of Paul of Samosata in 269, "God is ingenerate, one, without beginning, invisible, immutable"; cp. also the Creed of Auxentius of Cappadocia, *invisibilem, impassibilem, immortalem.*

The order *Christus Jesus, unicus Filius Ejus.* The more usual order is *Jesus Christus, Filius Ejus unicus. Christus Jesus* occurs in the Creed of Peter Chrysologus at Ravenna; but in no other Creed of Northern Italy. On the other hand it is in the Creed of Marcellus of Ancyra and in three Creed-like passages of Irenaeus (I. 2, L. p. 3; III. iv. 2; and IV. xxvii. 2), and this order may very possibly be an Eastern symptom; and Ravenna and Aquileia were from their position peculiarly exposed to Eastern influences. This is almost certainly true of the second half of the phrase. Τὸν μονογενῆ Αὐτοῦ Υἱόν occurs in the Fourth formula of Antioch in 341; in the formula of the Third Council of Antioch in 345; in the Creeds of the First and Third Councils of Sirmium in 307

---

1 Eusebius, *H.E.* VII. xxvi. 1.   2 *Rel. Sacr.* III. p. 290.

and 357, and in that of the *Apostolic Constitutions*; and the Council of Philippopolis in 343 has *unigenitum Ejus Filium*. The full phrase *de Spiritu Sancto ex Maria virgine* would seem to have come to Aquileia from the Balkans; compare the Creeds of Jerome and Niceta.

Descendit ad inferna probably travelled by a similar route. "Before Rufinus wrote (*c.* 400 A.D.) a similar clause ($\epsilon i s$ $\tau \grave{a}$ $\kappa a \tau a \chi \theta \acute{o} \nu \iota a$ $\kappa a \tau \epsilon \lambda \theta \acute{o} \nu \tau a$ [$\kappa a \tau \epsilon \lambda \eta \lambda \upsilon \theta \acute{o} \tau a$]) had already made its appearance in the three allied *formulae* of Sirmium (359), Nike in Thrace (359), and Constantinople (360)....The Sirmian formula was composed by Mark of Arethusa in Syria."[1] Next we find it in Jerome's Creed from Pannonia. Rufinus says: "'He descended into hell' is not added in the Creed of the Roman Church, neither is it in that of the oriental churches. It seems to be implied, however, when it is said that 'He was buried'" (c. 18).

Inde. Eastern Creeds have "coming" or "about to come" either alone or with "and" or "again", but in a recapitulation under the article dealing with the Holy Spirit in the Creed of the Council of Nike in 359 we find: $\tau \grave{o}$ $\Pi \nu \epsilon \hat{\upsilon} \mu a$ $\tau \hat{\eta} s$ $\grave{a} \lambda \eta \theta \epsilon \acute{\iota} a s \cdot$ $\ddot{o} \pi \epsilon \rho$ $\kappa a \grave{\iota}$ $A \grave{\upsilon} \tau \grave{o} s$ $\grave{a} \pi \acute{\epsilon} \sigma \tau \epsilon \iota \lambda \epsilon \nu$ $\grave{a} \nu \epsilon \lambda \theta \grave{\omega} \nu$ $\epsilon i s$ $\tau o \grave{\upsilon} s$ $o \grave{\upsilon} \rho a \nu o \acute{\upsilon} s$, $\kappa a \grave{\iota}$ $\kappa a \theta \acute{\iota} \sigma a s$ $\grave{\epsilon} \nu$ $\delta \epsilon \xi \iota \hat{q}$ $\tau o \hat{\upsilon}$ $\Pi a \tau \rho \acute{o} s$, $\grave{\epsilon} \kappa \epsilon \hat{\iota} \theta \epsilon \nu$ $\grave{\epsilon} \rho \chi \acute{o} \mu \epsilon \nu o s$ $\kappa . \tau . \lambda .$, though the main body of the Creed has $\grave{\epsilon} \rho \chi \acute{o} \mu \epsilon \nu o s$ simply. Then we find *inde* in Niceta, Mai's Arian Fragments, and Jerome.

Hujus. Rufinus says: "This last article, which affirms the resurrection of the flesh, concludes the sum of all perfection with succinct brevity....And accordingly our Church, in teaching the faith, instead of 'the resurrection of the flesh', as the Creed is delivered in other churches, guardedly adds the pronoun *this* in 'the resurrection of *this* flesh'. 'Of this', that is, of course, of the person who rehearses the Creed, making the sign of the Cross upon his forehead while he says the word, that each believer may know that his flesh, if he have kept it clean from sin, will be a vessel of honour useful to the Lord, prepared for every good work, but that if defiled by sins it will be a vessel of wrath destined to destruction." The word *hujus* is almost cer-

1 Sanday, *J.T.S.* III. p. 17.

tainly connected with the Origenistic controversy, as is indicated in his comment by Rufinus. Jerome's translation of the letter of Epiphanius to John of Jerusalem (Venice, 1766, 1. p. 248 B): *Quis autem patienter ferat Origenem lubricis argumentationibus resurrectionem carnis hujus negantem?* all but asserts what Rufinus implies.

This one word seems peculiar to the Creed of Aquileia, as Rufinus says, for in the sermon of Niceta it is probably part of the comment and not of the text of his Creed; but with this exception not only is the Creed of Rufinus of the same family as the Creed of Niceta, of Marcellus, and of the *Psalter of Aethelstan*, but every peculiarity of it can be shown to have Eastern affinities. Quite obviously, therefore, it is not the Creed of Rome, nor does Rufinus claim that it is, but the fact that he compares the two shows that they must have some common resemblance, only we have no means so far of saying how close was their likeness

NOTE

The *Disciplina Arcani* and the Creed

Rufinus gives two synonyms for *symbolum* as applied to the Creed. *Symbol*, in Greek, he says, answers to both *Indicium* and *Collatio* in Latin. *Collatio* means a joint contribution, and this the Apostles made, each contributing his several sentence. This story is, of course, a myth.[1]

As regards the second meaning, *Indicium*, or *Signum*, Rufinus says that many of the vagabond Jews went about naming the name of Christ but not delivering their message on the exact traditional lines: "The Apostles therefore prescribed this formulary as a sign or token by which he who preached Christ truly might be recognized." And he draws a parallel between the Creed and the use of a watchword in war, "so that if one is met with of whom it is doubtful to which side he belongs, being asked the symbol, he discloses whether he is friend or foe. And for this reason, the tradition continues, the Creed is not written on paper or parchment, but retained in the hearts of the faithful, that it may be certain that no one has learnt it by reading, as is sometimes the case with unbelievers, but by tradition from the Apostles" (c. 2; H. pp. 122, 123). This is part of the so-called *Disciplina Arcani*. When we have got rid of Rufinus's embroidery we get down to what we may take to be substantial facts. In times of persecution some sign would be needed from a stranger by which it would be known whether

1 See Chapter XI.

he was a Christian, otherwise a spy or informer might easily enter the
Christian assembly and subsequently denounce its members. This
evidence might, of course, be furnished by letters from the bishop of
the diocese from which he came, but such a method might be sometimes impossible and at others dangerous. The Creed would obviously
supply a ready test if, as we know to have been the later practice, it was
only taught to candidates at the end of their catechetical course, when
their sincerity and faithfulness had been under scrutiny, and if it was
kept as a secret not to be revealed. This, then, would appear to have
been what the *Disciplina Arcani* stood for in early times. Then, secondly,
if heretics framed a Creed for themselves, as did the Marcosians, the
"Symbol" would furnish a test of orthodoxy. It is this traditional
usage which explains the conduct of Augustine; he is afraid that others
besides Christians might get to know the Creed, and so might be able
to misuse the Christian watchword. Finally, it is this practice, which
survived as a religious custom after its original value had passed, that
explains the use of the Creed as a part of their defence by persons
accused of heresy. Eusebius might plead with some show of justice that
the orthodoxy of his Creed proved him not to be an Arian, but over and
over again the Creed quoted had no bearing on the particular point at
issue. Thus Marcellus, who was present at the Council of Nicaea and
heard Eusebius give his Creed, and knew of his subsequent acquittal,
quotes a Creed as part of his defence in his letter to Pope Julius. Thus
Auxentius quotes his Creed to the Emperors Valentinian and Valens,
and Charisius quotes his Creed at the Council of Ephesus. So, too,
Caelestius and Pelagius quoted their Creed in their letter to Pope
Zosimus. This custom of quoting a Creed in spite of the fact that it was
irrelevant to the subject under discussion, needs an explanation. The
explanation is found in the fact that it was the survival of a much older
usage when the power of quoting the Creed was a real *Indicium* or
Signum that the producer was an orthodox Christian.

THE CREED OF MILAN

The Creed of Milan is known to us from phrases contained
in a treatise called *Explanatio Symboli ad Initiandos*, almost certainly based on a Lecture or Sermon delivered by Ambrose, and
from three treatises, *de Fide et Symbolo*, *de Genesi ad Literam*,
and *Enchiridion*, and five sermons, *in Traditione Symboli*, Nos.
212, 213, 214, 215, and *ad Catechumenos* of Augustine. Of the
sermons, 212 and 215 give the Creed of Milan after it had been
amalgamated with the Creed of Africa, but the peculiarly African
matter is easily detachable. These documents not only show
minor diversities, but the MSS. of a single sermon or treatise

differ slightly among themselves, and in a sermon on the Creed preached before a council of bishops at Hippo in 393 while he was still a presbyter Augustine says: "The dissertation is of such a kind that the combination of words which is given to cate- chumens to commit to memory does not occur."[1]

I give the resulting form with this caution, and put beside it the phrases from the *Explanatio*.

Augustine	*Explanatio*
Credo in Deum Patrem omni- potentem;	Credo in...Patrem omnipoten- tem;
et in Jesum Christum,	et in Jesum Christum,
Filium Ejus unicum, Dominum nostrum,	Filium Ejus unicum, Dominum nostrum,
qui natus est de Spiritu Sancto	qui natus est...Spiritu Sancto
ex (*or* et) Maria virgine,	ex Maria virgine,
passus sub Pontio Pilato,	sub Pontio Pilato passus,
crucifixus, et sepultus,	...et sepultus,
tertia die resurrexit a mortuis,	tertia die resurrexit a mortuis,
ascendit ad (*or* in) caelos (*or* -um)	ascendit...
sedet ad dexteram Patris,	sedet ad dexteram Patris,
inde venturus est judicare	. . . . . .
vivos et mortuos;	...et mortuos;
Et in Spiritum Sanctum;	Et in Spiritum Sanctum;
Sanctam ecclesiam;	In ecclesiam sanctam;
Remissionem peccatorum;	In remissionem peccatorum;
Carnis resurrectionem.	In...resurrectionem.

The *Explanatio ad Initiandos* was published by Cardinal Mai in 1833 from a MS. Cod. Vat. 5760 saec. ix, x, which came from Bobbio. Two other MSS. are known, Cod. Lamb. saec. xiii from Lambach, and Cod. S. Gall. 188 saec. vii, viii from St Gallen, and all these have been edited by Caspari.[2] The two last probably go back to a common original, and give a more polished recension of the text, filling up the blanks in the concluding portion by phrases of a later date. They attribute the treatises the one to Maximus of Turin, and the other to Augustine, but by a com- parison with their authentic works this attribution is seen to be wrong. The Bobbio MS. has *Beati Ambrosii, Episcopi Medio- lanensis Explanatio*, and the treatise is now generally accepted as being his. It bears witness to conflict with Arianism, and be-

1 *Retractations*, i. 17.   2 *Quellen*, ii. p. 48; iii. p. 196.

longs to some diocese in North Italy. As it consists of a series of lecture notes certain allowances have to be made.

It has several interesting features. (1) It says that the Apostles met together and composed the Creed, and assigns the twelve clauses of the Creed to the Twelve Apostles, and asserts that it was brought to Rome by St Peter. (2) In contrast with the use of Aquileia it orders the sign of the cross to be made at the very beginning of the recitation. (3) It objects strongly to any additions being made to the text, as at Aquileia (*catholici in hac parte*), and says such additions had been misused by the Arians. (4) It asserts that the form given is that in use at Rome (*Hoc autem est symbolum quod Romana ecclesia tenet*, cp. the letter of Ambrose to Pope Siricius in 389, *Ep.* liii. 5: *Credatur symbolo apostolorum quod ecclesia Romana intemeratum semper custodit*, the earliest mention of the Apostles' Creed). (5) But for a single word this claim is no doubt justified; the last three clauses begin with the word *In* and the text calls attention to this: *Quae ratio est? Quia qui credit in auctorem, credit et in opus auctoris.*

Rufinus strongly objected to this phrasing: "It is not said '*In* the holy Church', nor '*In* the forgiveness of sins', nor '*In* the resurrection of the flesh'. For if the preposition 'in' had been added, it would have had the same force as in the preceding articles. But now in those clauses in which the faith concerning the Godhead is declared, we say '*In* God the Father', '*In* Jesus Christ His Son', and '*In* the Holy Ghost', but in the rest where we speak not of the Godhead but of creatures and mysteries, the preposition 'in' is not added....By this monosyllabic preposition, therefore, the Creator is distinguished from the creature, and things divine separated from things human."

And Rufinus was followed by Venantius Fortunatus, who says: "Ergo una divinitas in trinitate, quia dixit symbolum: *Credo in Deum Patrem et in Jesum Christum et in Spiritum Sanctum*. Ergo *in* ubi praepositio ponitur, ibi divinitas adprobatur ut est: *credo in Patrem, in Filium, in Spiritum Sanctum*. Nam non dicitur *in sanctam ecclesiam*, nec dicitur *in remissionem peccatorum*, sed *Remissionem peccatorum*."[1]

1 *Carminum* XI. 1.

Bishop Pearson says: "To *believe* with an addition of the pre-position *in*, is a phrase or expression ordinarily conceived fit to be given to none but God Himself, as always implying, besides a bare act of faith, an addition of hope, love, and affiance. An observation, as I conceive, prevailing especially in the Latin Church, grounded principally upon the authority of St Augustine. Whereas among the Greeks, in whose language the New Testament was penned, I perceive no such constant distinction in the deliveries of the Creed"; and he supports his view by numerous examples. Until recently no sermon of Augustine was known in which he quoted the word *in* in these last clauses, but in 1930 there was published a volume entitled *Sancti Augustini sermones post Maurinos reperti*, including a *Tractatus de Symbolo*, and in it we find "*In sanctam ecclesiam*", "*In remissionem peccatorum*". "*Post haec, Carnis resurrectionem*" (pp. 447, 448, 449). When we remember that Cyril of Jerusalem delivered his Catechetical Lectures while still a presbyter, and that Augustine delivered in a Council of bishops while still a presbyter the sermon which was afterwards put into the form *de Fide et Symbolo Liber* and gives the Milanese Creed without the African additions, we shall have little hesitation in assigning this *Tractatus* to the time shortly after his ordination by Valerius in 391, before he had decided that *in* ought to be omitted from the African Creed combined with the Creed of Milan. When also we recollect that all the bishops of Milan down to and including Auxentius were apparently Greeks, and that numerous Greek Creeds either have *in* with these clauses or carry on the construction from the previous clause, *In the Holy Spirit*, we shall recognize this feature as evidence that Christianity had reached Milan from Greek-speaking countries.

The Creed of Auxentius is, as we have seen, the Creed of Cappadocia, with his personal additions, some of them designed to cloak his unorthodoxy; but there is no reason to think that Arian bishops substituted another Creed for that traditional in the diocese to which they were appointed. We may take it, therefore, that the Creed of Milan as quoted by Ambrose, or rather by one of his auditors, and by Augustine, went back before the date of the documents in which it appears.

The Text of the *Explanatio* abbreviated

Symbolum graece dicitur, latine autem collatio....Sancti ergo Apostoli in unum convenientes, breviarium fidei fecerunt....Sed... quod et quae primo tradita sunt a majoribus nostris, dum quasi fraude alii, alii diligentia, fraude haeretici, diligentia catholici; dum ergo illi fraudulenter conantur inrepere, addiderunt quod non opus est.

Ergo Apostoli sancti convenientes fecerunt symbolum breviter. Signate vos....Frequenter admonui quod *Dominus noster, Jesus Christus, Filius Dei* solus istam carnem suscepit...non enim ex virili *natus* est semine sed generatus *Spiritu,* inquit, *Sancto ex Maria virgine....*

Sed dicis mihi, postea emerserunt haereses. Quid ergo? Vide simplicitatem, vide puritatem, Patripassiani cum emersissent, putaverunt etiam *catholici in hac parte* addendum *invisibilem et impassibilem,* quia Filius Dei visibilis et passibilis fuerit....Ex illo remedio Arriani invenerunt sibi genus calumniae, et quoniam *symbolum Romanae ecclesiae nos tenemus,* ideo visibilem et passibilem *Patrem omnipotentem* illi aestimarent et dicerent; vides quia symbolum sic habent, ut visibilem Filium et passibilem designarent....Hinc symbolum: *Credo unicum Dominum nostrum.* Sic dicite: *Filium Ejus unicum.* Non unicus Dominus? Unus Deus est, unus et Dominus; sed ne calumnientur et dicant, quia una persona, dicamus *Filium* etiam *unicum, Dominum nostrum.* Quia de divinitate Patris et Filii venitur ad incarnationem Ipsius, *qui natus et sepultus,* habes et passionem Ipsius et sepulturam. *Tertio die a mortuis*; habes et *resurrectionem* Ejus. *Ascendit, et sedet ad dexteram Patris....*Duo habes; surrexit a morte, *sedet ad dexteram Patris.*

Sane accipe rationem quemadmodum credimus in auctorem; en forte dicas, sed habet *in ecclesiam,* sed habet et *in remissionem peccatorum,* sed habet *in resurrectionem.* Quid ergo? Par causa est. Sic credimus *in Christum,* sic credimus *in Patrem,* quemadmodum credimus et *in ecclesiam,* et *in remissionem peccatorum,* et *in carnis resurrectionem.* Quae ratio est? Quia qui credit in auctorem, credit et in opus auctoris....

In ecclesiam sanctam, et in remissionem peccatorum. Credo ergo ex fide, quia omnia tibi peccata remittuntur. Ergo dixi apostolos symbolum composuisse. Si ergo mercum istarum negociatores et collatores pecuniae hanc habent legem, ut siqui symbolum suum violaverit, improbus et intestabilis habeatur, multo majus cavendum est nobis, ne de majorum symbolo aliquid detrahatur; cum habeas in libro Apocalypsis Johannis..."siqui", inquit, "addiderit aut detraxerit judicium sibi sumit et poenam". Sic unius Apostoli scripturis nihil est detrahendum nihil addendum, quemadmodum nos *symbolo quod accepimus ab Apostolis traditum atque compositum,* nihil debemus detrahere, nihil adjungere. *Hoc autem est symbolum quod Romana*

ecclesia tenet, ubi primus apostolorum Petrus sedit, et communem sen-
tentiam eo detulit.

Ergo quemadmodum duodecim Apostoli, et duodecim sententiae
Signate vos. Quo facto: *Credo   virgine*; habes incarnationem Filii,
quemadmodum dixi. *Sub Pontio Pilato passus   et sepultus*; habes
passionem et sepulturam. Ecce quattuor sententiae.... *Tertia die et
mortuos.* Ecce aliae quattuor sententiae. *Et in Spiritum Sanctum resur-*
rectionem. Ecce secundum duodecim apostolos, et duodecim sententiae
comprehensae sunt.

Summary

So far we have said nothing of the Creed of Rome, because at
least up till the middle of the fourth century Rome had a distinct
rite of its own. But certain facts have been brought prominently
before our notice. Liturgical authorities seem agreed that outside Rome and its immediate neighbourhood all the Christian
churches to the West of the Adriatic used the same Liturgy with
local variations, and the forms of Creed, which are the portions
of the liturgy best known to us at this time, enforce the same
lesson. But if we seek this Creed in its least developed fourth-
century form, we find it in the interior of Asia Minor, in that of
Marcellus, the *Psalter of Aethelstan*, and its translation into
Latin in the *Codex Laudianus*. In the Creeds of Remesiana and
Aquileia it has adopted some additional matter, and these are in
fact slightly more developed than the Creed of Milan; but the
mind of the West moved more slowly than that of the East, and
the fifth-century Creeds of Gaul are less exuberant than those
of Antioch and Philadelphia of approximately the same date.
But all these Creed forms show a fundamental unity of pattern
and suggest that in the fourth century the "European" or
"Western" rite was in large measure identical with the rite of
Asia Minor and Syria, though in later times it naturally expanded in different ways until in the West it was brought into
some measure of uniformity by the spread of Roman usage.

We have given many examples showing a transference of
liturgical language from its home among the "Oriental" Churches
by the land route to Spain. Are we not obliged to take the further
step and, as the most fitting name for a Creed so wide-spread is
"The Old Catholic Baptismal Creed", to recognize that though

rites developed into the Mozarabic, the Gallican, the Ambrosian, the Danubian or Moesian, the Byzantine, the Syrian, yet in the fourth century, or at least in its early years, the only classification which would not misrepresent the fact is the Roman, the Egyptian, the Palestinian—not yet sufficiently overborne to be ranked as Syrian—and the Old Catholic Rite or Liturgy?

This conclusion, based on liturgical evidence, is supported by two considerations of a more general kind, the first that of the spread of the Syrian race, and the second that of the position of Antioch as the home of Syrian Christianity, whence it spread to the further East. Cumont writes: "The ever increasing traffic with the Levant induced merchants to establish themselves in Italy, in Gaul, in the Danubian countries, in Africa and in Spain....The Syrian emigrants were especially numerous... Italy...ordered slaves from Phrygia, Cappadocia, Syria and Alexandria...."

"The Syrians' love of lucre was proverbial....They succeeded in establishing themselves on all coasts of the Mediterranean, even in Spain. At Malaga an inscription mentions a corporation formed by them. The Italian ports where business was especially active, Pozzuoli, Ostia, later Naples, attracted them in large numbers. But they did not confine themselves to the seashore; they penetrated far into the interior of the countries, wherever they hoped to find profitable trade. They followed the commercial highways and travelled up the big rivers. By way of the Danube they went as far as Pannonia, by way of the Rhone they reached Lyons. In Gaul they were especially numerous.... Thus the Syrians spread over the entire province as far as Treves, where they had a strong colony."[1]

And Harnack draws the moral: "When one recollects that Antioch was the mother-church of Gentile Christianity, the spread of Christianity can be illustrated even from the standpoint of Syrian trade activity."[2]

1 *Oriental Religions in Roman Paganism*, pp. 23, 24, 107, 108.
2 *Mission and Expansion*, II. p. 140.

The Creed of Rome

We have no direct quotation of the Roman baptismal Creed which can be dated with certainty earlier than the Tome of Leo in 448. The particular phrases which he gives are:

> Credo in Deum Patrem omnipotentem;
> Et in Jesum Christum, Filium Ejus unicum Dominum nostrum,
> qui natus est de Spiritu Sancto et Maria virgine,

and

> crucifixus *mortuus* et sepultus.

References in Leo's sermons (1) make it somewhat doubtful if the Creed had "*et Maria*" or "*ex Maria*", and (2) suggest that some of the remaining clauses should be filled up:

> tertia die ascendit in (*or* ad) caelos,
> sedet ad dexteram Patris,
> venturus judicare vivos et mortuos.

We can check and enlarge this incomplete form from three other sources. First we have the Creed of Milan, and the author of the *Explanatio ad Initiandos* asserts that this was identical with the Creed of Rome in his day; but we note that no other Latin Creeds had *in* with the clauses following *in Spiritum Sanctum*, a construction which seems to have jarred upon the Latin mind.

Secondly, though Rufinus cannot be relied upon as an authority when standing alone, because while he tells us that the Roman Creed has not the Aquileian additions *invisibilis et impassibilis*, *descendit ad inferna*, *hujus* (carnis) he does not tell us in what other respects it may have differed; yet he implies a general likeness, and Rufinus when checked by Leo, Ambrose, and Augustine is on quite another footing.

Thirdly, we have the later *Textus Receptus*, which is that now in use, and this is the fourth-century Creed of Rome in an expanded form.

Putting these various sources together we need have little hesitation in writing it down as follows:

> Credo in Deum Patrem omnipotentem;
> Et in Jesum Christum, Filium Ejus unicum, Dominum nostrum,
> qui natus est de Spiritu Sancto ex (*or* et) Maria virgine,

passus sub Pontio Pilato,
crucifixus et sepultus,
tertia die resurrexit a mortuis,
ascendit ad (*or* in) caelos,
sedet ad dexteram Patris,
inde venturus est judicare vivos et mortuos;
Et in Spiritum Sanctum;
Sanctam ecclesiam;
Remissionem peccatorum;
Carnis resurrectionem.

We can feel confident that this was the form of Creed in use at Rome when Ambrose became Bishop of Milan in 374; but it is impossible to say how much earlier. Ambrose was chosen as bishop while still a catechumen, and the Creed was not taught to catechumens until just before their baptism. He would seem to imply in his letter to Pope Siricius in 389 that it had been in use for a considerable time, but since he imagines that it had been brought to Rome by St Peter, we cannot place much reliance on his historical statement.

NOTE

Extracts from Leo's Sermons

xxv. 2. Consummato passionis et resurrectionis triumpho...renovat tamen nobis hodierna festivitas *nati Jesu ex Maria virgine* sacra primordia...sicut cum *Christo* in *passione crucifixi*, in *resurrectione* resuscitati, in *ascensione ad dexteram Patris* collocati....

xxvii. 6. Idem erat...per humanam infirmitatem *crucifixus, mortuus, et sepultus,* per divinam virtutem *die tertia* resuscitatus, *ascendit ad caelos, sedet ad dexteram Dei Patris.*

xxix. 5. Idem est a paterno non divisus throno, et ab impiis *crucifixus* in ligno. Idem est super caelorum altitudines victor mortis *ascendens.* ...Idem postremo est qui in eadem qua *ascendit* carne *venturus* sicut judicium sustinuit impiorum, ita *judicaturus* est de omnium actione mortalium.

xxxiii. 4. Negent Eum pro mundi salute *crucifixum,*...negent Eum *sepultum* ac *die tertia* suscitatum, negent Eum *in dextera Patris* super omnes caelorum altitudines elevatum et ut tota *Apostolici* veritate *Symboli* sublata...negent a Christo *vivos et mortuos judicandos.*

xlv. 3. Hoc fixum habete in animo, quod dicitis in *symbolo.* Credite consempiternum *Patri Filium Dei*...hunc corporaliter *crucifixum, mortuum,* suscitatum, et super altitudines caelestium dominationum elevatum, *in Patris dextera* constitutum ad *judicandum vivos et mortuos* in eadem carne quo *ascendit, venturum.*

lx. 2. Hac fidei regula, dilectissimi, quam in ipso exordio *Symboli* per auctoritatem *Apostolicae institutionis* accepimus, *Dominum nostrum Jesum Christum*, quem *Filium Dei omnipotentis unicum* dicimus, eundem quoque de *Spiritu Sancto natum ex* (al. *et*) *Maria virgine* confitemur.... *Ipsum crucifixum et mortuum et die tertia* credimus suscitatum.

lxv. 5. Secundum propositum voluntatis suae *Jesus Christus crucifixus* et *mortuus et sepultus est.*

lxviii. 4. Quis vere *Christum passum, mortuum* et resuscitatum colit, nisi cum Ipso *patitur et moritur et resurgit?*...*Natis de Spiritu Sancto* quantumque superest mundani temporis, non sine *crucis* susceptione ducendum est.

Qui ascendit in caelos, non deserit adoptatos; qui *sedet ad dexteram Patris,* Ipse totius habitator est corporis.

lxxi. 4. Per omne ergo hoc tempus, dilectissimi, quod inter *resurrectionem Domini* et *ascensionem* Ejus exactum est, hoc providentia Dei curavit...ut *Dominus Jesus* vere agnosceretur resuscitatus qui vere erat *natus et passus et mortuus.*

lxxii. 2. *Dominus noster Jesus Christus*, quadragesimo post *resurrectionem* die...elevatus *in caelum*...mansurus *in Patris dextera*... *ad judicandos vivos et mortuos* in eadem carne, in qua *ascendit*, adveniat.

lxxii. 3. Hanc fidem *ascensione Domini* auctam. Unde et ipsi beati Apostoli...atrocitate tamen Dominicae *passionis* expaverant, et veritatem *resurrectionis* Ejus non sine haesitatione susceperant....Totam enim contemplationem animi in divinitatem *ad Patris dexteram consedentis erexerant.*

lxxii. 4. Cum autem *ascendentem ad caelos Dominum* sequaces discipulorum oculi...suspicerent.

Sicut enim concipiendum Christum *de Spiritu Sancto* beatae virgini angelus nuntiavit, sic et editum *de virgine* vox caelestium pastoribus cecinit, sicut *resurrexisse a mortuis* supernorum nuntiorum prima testimonia docuerunt, sic *ad judicandum* mundum in ipsa carne *venturum* angelorum officia praedicarunt.

CHAPTER VII

HOW CREEDS GROW

I. The Interrogatory Creed of Rome. II. The Roman Declaratory Creed of the Fourth Century (R), and the *Textus Receptus* (T). III. The Creed of Antioch and the Nestorian Creed. IV. The Creed of Nicaea (N) and the Creeds of Jerome, Epiphanius and Constantinople (C).

IT is not often that we can catch a Creed at different stages of its growth. We have, however, two examples connected with Rome, the Interrogatory Creed at three different epochs, and the Declaratory Creed of the fourth and of the eighth centuries. In both cases the Creed grew merely by means of additions without corresponding omissions, and with no alterations in the order of words except when necessitated, e.g. "natus est de Spiritu Sancto ex Maria virgine" to "conceptus est de Spiritu Sancto natus ex Maria virgine".

I. THE INTERROGATORY CREED OF ROME

Gelasian Sacramentary[1]	*Gregorian Sacramentary*[2]	*Modern Form*
Credis in Deum Patrem omnipotentem?	Credis in Deum Patrem omnipotentem, *Creatorem caeli et terrae?*	Credis in Deum Patrem omnipotentem, Creatorem caeli et terrae?
Credis et in Jesum Christum,	Et in Jesum Christum,	Credis et in Jesum Christum,
Filium Ejus unicum, Dominum nostrum,	Filium Ejus unicum, Dominum nostrum,	Filium Ejus unicum, Dominum nostrum,
natum,	natum,	natum,
et passum?	et passum?	et passum?
Credis in Spiritum Sanctum;	Credis in Spiritum Sanctum;	Credis in Spiritum Sanctum;

1 Probably written in Central Italy between 475 and 525, incorporating the Roman Canon and Ordinary of the Mass and other *ordines*, e.g. Baptism, Penance, and Ordination. Added to in France in the sixth century, so forming our *Gelasianum*, which dates from the end of the seventh or early in the eighth century. Sinclair, *Theology*, XXXII. pp. 142–155.

2 A revised edition of the Roman Mass Book made by Pope Gregory I (590–604) (Bishop, *Liturgica Historica*, p. 81). Subsequently revised by Gregory II (715–731) and sent by Hadrian (772–795) to Charlemagne after 783. Sinclair, *loc. cit.*

Gelasian Sacramentary	Gregorian Sacramentary	Modern Form
Sanctam ecclesiam;	Sanctam ecclesiam catholicam;	Sanctam ecclesiam catholicam;
		Sanctorum communionem;
Remissionem peccatorum;	Remissionem peccatorum;	Remissionem peccatorum;
Carnis resurrectionem?	Carnis resurrectionem?	Carnis resurrectionem; Et vitam aeternam?

II. ROMAN DECLARATORY CREED

R. c. 400	Textus Receptus (T.), c. 740
Credo in Deum Patrem omnipotentem;	Credo in Deum Patrem omnipotentem,
	Creatorem caeli et terrae;
Et in Jesum Christum,	Et in Jesum Christum,
Filium Ejus unicum, Dominum nostrum,	Filium Ejus unicum, Dominum nostrum,
qui natus est de Spiritu Sancto,	qui conceptus est de Spiritu Sancto,
ex (or et) Maria virgine,	natus ex Maria virgine,
passus sub Pontio Pilato,	passus sub Pontio Pilato,
crucifixus, et sepultus,	crucifixus, mortuus, et sepultus, descendit ad inferos,
tertia die resurrexit a mortuis,	tertia die resurrexit a mortuis,
ascendit ad (or in) caelos,	ascendit ad caelos,
sedet ad dexteram Patris,	sedet ad dexteram Dei Patris omnipotentis,
inde venturus est judicare vivos et mortuos;	inde venturus est judicare vivos et mortuos;
Et in Spiritum Sanctum;	Credo in Spiritum Sanctum;
Sanctam ecclesiam;	Sanctam ecclesiam catholicam;
	Sanctorum communionem;
Remissionem peccatorum;	Remissionem peccatorum;
Carnis resurrectionem.	Carnis resurrectionem;
	Vitam aeternam.

III. THE CREED OF ANTIOCH AND THE NESTORIAN CREED (L. pp. 18–20)

In the East it is certain that the Creed of the so-called Nestorians of Mesopotamia was derived from that of Antioch. 'Solum verum" is omitted; "Dominum nostrum" changed to "one Lord", and "ex Eo" to "from His Father", the Syriac representing, no doubt, the Greek ἐκ τοῦ Πατρός. The whole of the rest, where we have the text of the Creed of Antioch, consists of additions.

Antioch	Nestorian
et solum verum	*omitted*
nostrum	one
ex Eo	from His Father
add	men and for our salvation
,,	from heaven
,,	and was incarnate by the Holy Ghost
,,	and became man, and was conceived,
,,	and He suffered,
,,	and He sat at the right hand of God the Father.

After this point the Antiochene Creed is defective.

IV. THE CREED OF THE COUNCIL OF NICAEA, N, AND THE CREEDS OF JEROME, EPIPHANIUS, AND CONSTANTINOPLE, C.

Similarly the Creed of Jerome consists of an amalgamation of the Creed of the Council of Nicaea, the local baptismal Creed of Stridon, and certain phrases added by Jerome himself. Jerome has the triple *Credo*, once with each Person of the Trinity, instead of the single "We believe"; he substitutes "God" for "the Father" in the second clause; he omits "only begotten", the explanatory clause "that is of the essence of the Father", and "of one substance with the Father", "for us men", and "was incarnate". All the rest consists of additions, and there is no interference with the original order of words.

The Longer Creed of Epiphanius reproduces the Nicene Creed verbally down to the article dealing with the Incarnation, with the two exceptions that Epiphanius reads "invisible and visible" in the first clause and adds "visible and invisible" after "the things in heaven and the things in (*or* on) earth". He adds two clauses shown to be explanatory by the introductory "that is", the latter of considerable length. There are also two other explanatory clauses not so designated, "the same in flesh", and "in the body itself", and probably none of them was intended for recitation by the catechumen in his delivery of the Creed,

The Creed of Nicaea and its Derivatives

Alterations only are given and referred to the Nicene Creed as the standard

N. (L. p. 20; H. p. 3)	Jerome	Ep. (L. pp. 17, 18; H. pp. 16-18)	C. (L. pp. 31, 32; H. pp. 20-22)
Πιστεύομεν	Credo		
πάντων	om.		ποιητὴν οὐρανοῦ καὶ γῆς,
ὁρατῶν τε καὶ ἀοράτων ποιητὴν		ἀοράτων τε καὶ ὁρατῶν	ὁρατῶν τε πάντων κ. ἀοράτων
Καὶ	Credo		
γεννηθέντα ἐκ τοῦ Πατρὸς	natum de Deo		τὸν μονογενῆ τ. ἐκ τ. Π. γ.
μονογενῆ	om.		πρὸ πάντων τῶν αἰώνων.
τουτέστιν ἐκ τῆς οὐσίας τοῦ Π.	om.		om.
Θεὸν ἐκ Θεοῦ			om.
	(omnipotentem de omnipotente)		
	ante saecula		
ὁμοούσιον τῷ Πατρί	om.		om.
τά τε ἐν τ. οὐρανῷ κ. τ. ἐν τ. γῆ	om.	ὁρατά τε καὶ ἀόρατα	om.
τὸν δὲ ἡμᾶς τοὺς ἀνθρώπους	om.		
	de caelo		ἐκ τῶν οὐρανῶν
καὶ σαρκωθέντα	conceptus est de Spiritu Sancto	[τουτέστι γεννηθέντα τελείως	ἐκ Πνεύματος Ἁγίου
καὶ ἐνανθρωπήσαντα	natus de Maria virgine	ἐκ τ. ἀ. Μ. τ. ἀειπαρθένου διὰ Π. ʿΑ.]	καὶ Μαρίας τῆς παρθένου
παθόντα	om.	[τουτέστι...βασιλεύς]	
	(passione) sub Pontio Pilato	[δὲ τὸν αὐτὸν ἐν σώματι]	σταυρωθέντα τε ὑπὲρ ἡμῶν
	(sub Herode rege)		ἐπὶ Π. Π. κ. παθ. κ. ταφέντα
	crucifixus, sepultus		
	descendit ad inferna		
	(calcavit aculeum mortis)		
τῇ τρίτῃ ἡμέρᾳ	(apparuit apostolis)		κατὰ τὰς γραφάς
	(post haec)	om.	
	sedet ad dexteram Patris	[ἐν αὐτῷ τῷ σώματι]	κ. καθεζόμενον ἐκ δεξιῶν τ. Π.
	inde	ἐνδόξως καθίσαντα ἐν δεξιᾷ τ. Π.	καὶ πάλιν...μετὰ δόξης
		[ἐν αὐτῷ τῷ σώματι ἐν δόξῃ]	οὗ τ. βασιλείας οὐκ ἔσται τέλος
		οὗ τῆς βασιλείας οὐκ ἔσται τέλος	Καὶ εἰς τὸ Π. τὸ ʿΑ. κ.τ.λ.
Καὶ εἰς τὸ Ἅγιον Πνεῦμα	Credo in Spiritum Sanctum, etc.		
See pp. 181, 182.	See pp. 75, 76.	See pp. 209, 210.	See pp. 220, 221.

but they are rather hints to the catechist. He omits "the third day", and then comes an addition, probably from the local baptismal Creed of Cyprus: "He sat gloriously at the right hand of the Father", where "gloriously" is probably no more intended to be recited than the next clause, "in the body itself in glory". And finally, in all probability from the Cypriote Creed, he adds "of whose kingdom there shall be no end". Then he begins the third article with "And in the Holy Spirit", which is as far as the Nicene Creed takes us.

A comparison with these two examples will make it clear that the Constantinopolitan Creed is also based on the Nicene. Here indeed we do encounter some other alteration in the order of the words, but each alteration is *necessitated by the additions made* and all these additions have Antiochene affinities but for the single clause "who with the Father and the Son together is worshipped and glorified" which appears to be a new coinage, and is obviously directed against Macedonianism, a heresy to which the Church of Constantinople was peculiarly exposed.

In short, what we learn from the comparison is that while words are occasionally omitted, some for fairly obvious reasons, and others for no reason that we can see, and while additions are made—particularly the clauses "of the Holy Ghost and Mary the virgin", "crucified under Pontius Pilate", "sitteth at the right hand of the Father", and in some cases "of whose kingdom there shall be no end"—yet, unless by the necessity of taking in additional matter, *words are never altered in order*.

This is sufficient to condemn any such thing as the genealogical tree noticed in Chapter I for the Roman Declaratory Creed.

CHAPTER VIII

THE EARLY BAPTISMAL CREED OF ROME

I. Elimination and the Maximum Limit. II. Synthesis: (*a*) The Earliest Apostolic Preaching. (*b*) The Threefold Formula. The Order "Jesus Christ". (*c*) The Enlargement of this Formula. The First Two and the Last Three Clauses. The Third and Fourth Clauses. (*d*) The Sevenfold Formula of the Gelasian Sacramentary. This Formula not an Abbreviation.

THERE is no writer who quotes the Roman Creed earlier than the author of the *Explanatio Symboli ad Initiandos*. Accordingly if we desire to get back to the form current, let us say, 150 years earlier, there are two methods we can employ: we can take the fourth-century Creed, and subtract from it, and here we shall be helped by the discovery of "How Creeds Grow", that is we are assured that simple subtraction, either of whole phrases or of parts of phrases that would seem to be of late date, will restore to us something like the earlier form; or we can build up from the earliest elements, checking our reconstruction as far as we are able by references or semi-quotations in Roman writers, whether given under some such heading as *Regula Fidei* or not. If we find a particular collocation of words often recurring in an author who belonged to the Church of Rome, then, though he may not be quoting from the Creed, or have it consciously in his mind, he is nevertheless probably giving a Roman turn of speech, and the Creed would take shape under the same influences, and so he may be cited as an indirect witness to it.

I. ELIMINATION AND THE MAXIMUM LIMIT

Pursuing our first method, and being conservative in our rejections, we should arrive at something like the following:

> I believe in God the Father almighty;
> And in Jesus Christ, His only Son, our Lord,
> who was born,
> suffered, *or* was crucified, [*probably not both*]

rose again (the third day?),
ascended,
sitteth on the right hand of the Father,
is to come to judge the quick and the dead;
And in the Holy Ghost;
Holy Church;
Forgiveness of sins;
Resurrection of the flesh.

This form is probably too full for the date at which we are aiming; but it is difficult to know what more to omit. At any rate this form may be regarded as giving us our maximum limit.

II. SYNTHESIS

(a) *The Earliest Apostolic Preaching*

Now let us try the other method.

The earliest Apostolic preaching of which we have record had as its nucleus the Messiahship and Lordship of Jesus, one or both. Thus St Peter's speech at Pentecost as given by St Luke leads up to a climax in "Let all the house of Israel know assuredly, that God hath made Him both Lord and Christ, this Jesus whom ye crucified" (Acts ii. 36). So in his second speech "that He may send the Christ (*or* Messiah) who hath been appointed for you, Jesus" (Acts iii. 20). So: "Every day, in the temple and at home, they ceased not to teach and to preach Jesus as the Christ" (Acts v. 42); "straightway in the synagogues he proclaimed Jesus, that He is the Son of God", "proving that this is the Christ" (Acts ix. 20, 22); "Jesus Christ, He is Lord of all" (Acts x. 36).

Correspondingly, the earliest confession of faith demanded was faith in the Messiahship or Lordship of Jesus, and this would run, "I believe that Jesus is the Christ, or (the) Lord", "I believe in Jesus as the Christ, or (the) Lord", or "I believe in Jesus Christ the Lord". When we find "Lord Jesus", as in St Stephen's speech, or "Christ Jesus", the words "Lord" and "Christ" in the mind of the speaker have ceased to be predicative, and by familiarity become titles. This form agrees with the texts quoted in Chapter II.

(b) The Triple Formula

But we are not now trying for a Creed built on a simple formula of one clause, but on a triple formula, which, as we saw, would appear to have run originally "God, Jesus Christ, Holy Spirit".

The order "Jesus Christ"

Nevertheless it has been supposed that in the Roman Creed the original order was not "Jesus Christ", but "Christ Jesus". Fortunately in Clement we have a writer who was a "Roman of Rome". He invariably writes "Jesus Christ", except in two passages both reminiscent of St Paul: "and we therefore being called through His will in Christ Jesus" (c. 32). And "so therefore let our whole body be saved in Christ Jesus" (c. 38). There is one other passage in which Lightfoot reads "Christ Jesus": "the sceptre of the majesty of God our Lord Christ Jesus" (c. 16), but here he does so on the sole authority of the Alexandrine MS. against the Constantinopolitan and Syriac Versions, a quotation in Jerome, and the more recently discovered Latin Version, a combination which is decisive. The most important of the other twenty quotations are as follows:

Grace to you and peace from almighty God by Jesus Christ be multiplied (Preface).
As God lives and the Lord Jesus Christ and the Holy Spirit (c. 58).
The grace of our Lord Jesus Christ be with us and with all those everywhere who are called by God through Him (c. 65).

Next we come to the letter of Dionysius, Bishop of Rome, to his namesake of Alexandria. Dionysius was probably not of Roman stock; his letter is too short—some seventy lines in all—to determine his regular usage; the words occur only once: "It is needful to have believed in God the Father Almighty, and in Christ Jesus His Son and in the Holy Spirit" (sub fin.); and he has the non-Roman order "Holy Spirit" instead of the regular Roman order "Spiritus Sanctus". It is obvious that his authority cannot be set against that of Clement.

Finally Novatian. Novatian in the de Trinitate has "Christ Jesus" five times and "Jesus Christ" eight times. Of these three would seem to be connected with the Creed.

"Eadem regula veritatis docet nos credere post Patrem etiam in Filium Dei Christum Jesum" (L. p. 6). But this is almost immediately resumed in: "Hunc enim Jesum Christum iterum dicam hujus Dei Filium" (c. 9); "Est ergo credendum secundum praescriptam regulam in Dominum unicum verum Deum, et in Eum quem misit Jesum Christum" (c. 16); "Hoc ergo credamus siquidem fidelissimum, Dei Filium Jesum Christum, Dominum et Deum nostrum" (c. 30). So far the proportion in favour of "Jesus Christus" is about two to one. But the nearest actual quotation from the Creed is at the end of *de Cibis Judaicis* (c. 7): "Regulam veritatis per omnia custodientes, Deo gratias agere debemus per Jesum Christum, Filium Ejus, Dominum nostrum."

Thus the undoubted use of the fourth century is confirmed by a twofold probability, the one drawn from the New Testament and the other from the general practice of Roman authors including, in Novatian, what looks like an actual adaptation from the Creed of his day. And supposing "Christ" to have retained the suggestion of the "Messiah", or "the Anointed", then it would naturally have followed the subject of which it was predicated in accordance with the general Latin usage, as we see, for instance, in "Maria virgo", which, when it was introduced into the Creed, was no mere title (still less the name of an order of "virgins" to whom Mary belonged), but expressed definite belief that Mary conceived "non ex virili semine", as the author of the *Explanatio* puts it.

And lastly the word ΙΧΘΥΣ, meaning Ἰησοῦς Χριστός, Θεοῦ Υἱός, Σωτήρ, is of such frequent occurrence in the catacombs, and had such an intimate connexion with baptism (cf. Tertull. *de Bapt.* c. 1), that we must allow it some weight in discussing a baptismal formula.

Accordingly there is good reason to think that the baptismal questions ran:

> Dost thou believe in God?
> Dost thou believe in Jesus Christ?
> Dost thou believe in the Holy Spirit?

Supposing this to be so, when and why would this short formula be enlarged?

(c) The Enlargement of the Threefold Formula. The First Two and the Last Three Clauses

The most probable answer to this question would be "as a safeguard against heresy". If we then ask from what heresies the early Church of Rome suffered, the names that suggest themselves are Marcion and his disciple Apelles, Praxeas and Noetus, and Sabellius. All these heresies were of a gnostic character, and there were three points on which they differed from the Church of Rome, which in common with the Church of Africa "knew one God, the Creator of the universe; and Christ Jesus from the Virgin Mary, the Son of God the Creator; and the resurrection of the flesh" (Tertull. *de Praescr.* 36; L. p. 5). Their special views are described by Tertullian in the neighbouring chapters: "Marcion introduced, in addition to the Creator, another God of goodness only; Apelles made the Creator some glorious angel or other.... Valentinus traced the sin of one Aeon to God the Creator". That is, all these heresies denied, in one form or another, the contact of God with matter, in creation, in the incarnation and the reality of our Lord's human body, and in the resurrection of the flesh.

To assert the Creatorship of God one of the words added in the first clause may have been "Father", but this may have been added to the baptismal formula much earlier. It might have come in specifically from the Lord's Prayer; it might have come in from ordinary Christian usage imitating our Lord's regular method of address: "Ye received the spirit of adoption, whereby we cry, Abba, Father" (Rom. viii. 15); "If ye call on Him as Father" (1 Pet. i. 17); or it might have come in from the blending of the Matthaean formula with that already in use.

But in early Christian writings it was also employed metaphorically of God as the source from whom all things proceeded. Thus Clement: "Father and Creator of the whole world" (c. 19): "Maker and Father of the ages" (c. 35). We have already seen parallels in Justin Martyr (cp. L. p. 3); and so in Novatian *de Trinitate* "(Ipse) qui virtutum omnium et Deus et Parens est" (c. 2); cp. Irenaeus "Pater universorum", *adv.*

Haer. IV. xxxiv. And if "Father" was already present in the formula or was thought by itself insufficient, then "almighty" could be added to it.

In the next clause, the addition against Marcion, if it were not already present, would be "His Son", asserting that the historic Jesus Christ is the Son of God the Father, the Creator. So Tertullian: "It has been already ruled with sufficient clearness that Christ must be understood as belonging to [i.e. 'Son of' or 'sent by'] no other God than the Creator...whilst proving Christ to be the Creator's, we are effectually shutting out the God of Marcion" (*adv. Marc.* III. 1).

The last clause will obviously be "the resurrection of the flesh". Marcion and the Gnostics held that the redemption of matter was impossible so the fleshly character of the resurrection would be emphasized. "Marcion denies the resurrection of the flesh (carnis resurrectionem)" (Tertull. *adv. Marc.* V. 19).

Probably also in controversy with heresy there would be introduced a clause about the Church. Hippolytus says of Carpocrates and his followers: "Carpocrates affirms that the world and the things in it were made by angels far inferior to the unbegotten Father, and that Jesus was generated of Joseph...[these heretics] have themselves been sent forth by Satan for the purpose of slandering before the Gentiles...the divine name of the Church" (*c. Haer.* VII. 20). Carpocratian doctrines were brought to Rome by Marcion in the episcopate of Anicetus (155–167), but considering how constantly "the Church" is opposed to heretical societies, such a clause need not be specially anti-Carpocratian. If, as is probable, some epithet were attached to "the Church", that would almost certainly be "holy", and perhaps "the divine name of the Church" implies this.

At some time or other, and probably quite early, the epithet "only" or "only-begotten" was added to the second clause— its presence in nearly all forms of Creed suggests this—but the motive of its addition is not so clear. "Monogenes" is a common Greek word to express a natural relationship, and is so used in the Gospel of St Luke, and in the Epistle to the Hebrews; the use of it to express the relation of our Lord to God the Father is purely Johannine. In John i. 18 it is doubtful whether the substantive is "God" or "Son", but St John regularly uses "the Son of God" not of the eternal relation of God the Son to the Father within the Blessed Trinity, for which his title is "Logos", but of the incarnate or historic Christ, and whatever be the date when the word was first added, there is no doubt that this is its meaning in the Creed. It is probable that it was from the Johannine school that the word "Monogenes" was taken over by the Gnostics as the name of one of their Aeons, and in several passages Irenaeus vindicates for the Church a pre-emptive right to the word (i. i. 19, 20; i. iv); so it may have been adopted either to oppose the teaching of Gnosticism, or else to emphasize the uniqueness of Christ's human sonship towards the Father as compared with that of Christians.

Similar language might be used of the other addition, "our Lord". The meaning of the phrase was not "the Lord over us", but "whom we recognize as Lord", as opposed to all forms of Gnosticism, and on the lines of Eph. i. 20, 21: "And made him to sit at his right hand in the heavenly places, far above all rule and authority and power and lordship, and every name that is named, not only in this world, but also in that which is to come; and he put all things in subjection under his feet"; Rom. xiv. 9, "Lord of both the dead and the living"; and Phil. ii. 9–11, "Wherefore God highly exalted him and gave unto him the name which is above every name; that at the name of Jesus every knee should bow...and that every tongue should confess that Jesus Christ is Lord, to the glory of God the Father".

But "our Lord" may well have been in the baptismal Creed of Rome before the coming of Gnosticism, since the confession in baptism of the Lordship of Christ seems to have been very early, and "Lord" is almost a standing epithet in Clement.

So far the Creed would run:

Dost thou believe in God the Father almighty?
Dost thou believe in Jesus Christ, His only Son, our Lord?
Dost thou believe in the Holy Ghost;
Holy Church;
The resurrection of the flesh?

The Third and Fourth Clauses

But we have not yet dealt with the question in what terms the reality of our Lord's human body was to be asserted, in contrast to the spiritual nature of the Godhead. Let us first put the question from the other side and ask what were the epithets used of deity which were inapplicable to manhood and contrasted with it? We know, for instance, that the Creed of Auxentius contained "Invisible, impassible, immortal", and that the two former were added to the Creed of Aquileia against Sabellianism; but language of this kind was far earlier than Sabellius.

Thus Ignatius writes: "There is one physician, fleshly and spiritual, generate and ingenerate, in man God, in death true life, both from Mary and from God, first passible and then impassible, Jesus Christ our Lord" (*Eph.* 7); and, "Await Him who is above every season, the timeless, the invisible, the visible for our sakes, the untouchable, the impassible, the passible for our sakes" (*Ep. to Polyc.* 3). So Tertullian: "Thus the condition (census) of the two substances displayed Him as man and God, in regard to the one born, in regard to the other not born; in the one fleshly, in the other spiritual; in the one weak, in the other exceedingly strong; in the one living, in the other dying" (*de Carne Christi,* 5).

So Irenaeus: "Summing up man in Himself, the invisible became visible, and the incomprehensible became comprehensible, and the impassible passible, and the Word man" (*adv. Haer.* III. xvii. 6).

Now let us glance at the teaching of the early heretics.

The Gnostics in general: "They will have it that the Word and Christ never came into the world; that the Saviour also did not become incarnate nor suffer...while others say that Jesus was born from Joseph and Mary, and that the Christ from above descended upon Him, being without flesh and impassible" (Iren. *adv. Haer.* III. xi. 8).

The Valentinians: "They maintain that in the invisible and ineffable heights above there exists a certain perfect, pre-existent Aeon, whom they...describe as being invisible and incomprehensible. Eternal and unbegotten, he remained throughout innumerable cycles of ages in profound serenity and quiescence" (Iren. *adv. Haer.* I. i. 1).

That against such teaching the Church fought by maintaining the opposite truth is shown over and over again; that antitheses are not foreign to the mind of Rome can be seen from Leo's Tome (H. pp. 208, 209); and that heresy was a real motive for making additions to Creeds is manifest not only from the Creed of Nicaea, but from many others. Hence it is not unlikely that against docetic heresies the Creed of Rome should have been enlarged; but we may be sure that if this was the case, the terms used would not be descriptive of status, but historical. Such words as *passibilis, visibilis, mortalis* would be felt to be foreign intrusions in a Roman Creed, and would be represented by *passus, visus, mortuus.* If then we select from the large number of possible words which are as a matter of fact found in Creeds, we shall find ourselves confronted with a list such as this:

Dost thou believe in Jesus Christ, etc.

Who was incarnate,
    and was made man,
    and was born,
    and suffered,
    and was crucified,
    and died,
    and was buried?

Clearly this list is far too long, but any of these expressions is possible; how then are we to make a selection?

Fortunately history seems to have made the selection for us. Tertullian asserts that Praxeas taught at Rome (towards the end of the second century), and that what he taught was this: "Pater natus et Pater passus, ipse Deus Dominus omnipotens, Jesus Christus" (*adv. Prax.* 2).

The words look as though Praxeas had taken over an already well-established formula and twisted it round for his own purposes. Now we know how that formula ran, "Deus Pater omnipotens, et Jesus Christus Dominus"; at least that was part of it; let us then subtract and see if we can obtain the remainder.

The result is "natus" and "passus". Both these words occur
on our list, and it would seem that history was really working
for us; but it may nevertheless be a mere piece of verbal
jugglery.

At the beginning of the next century Hippolytus accused
Callistus of having held the opinions of Noetus, and the opinions
of the Noetians are as follows:

For they say thus—that one and the same God is the Creator and
Father of all things; and that when it pleased Him He appeared to just
men of old, though invisible, but that when He is not seen, He was
invisible (but when He is seen He is visible), and incomprehensible
when He does not wish to be comprehended, but comprehensible when
He is comprehended. So, according to the same account, He is un-
conquerable and conquerable, ingenerate (and generate), immortal and
mortal.... For in this manner he thinks to establish the unity [of God],
alleging that one and the same being subsists under the name of Father
and Son.... That this person suffered by being nailed to the tree, and
that He commended His spirit unto Himself, and died and did not die,
and raised Himself the third day, and was buried in the tomb, and
pierced by the spear, and nailed down with nails.... Callistus attempted
to confirm this heresy.... He put forward Zephyrinus..., and induced
him publicly to assert (Ἐγὼ οἶδα ἕνα Θεόν, Χριστὸν Ἰησοῦν, καὶ πλὴν
Αὐτοῦ ἕτερον οὐδένα γεννητὸν καὶ παθητόν) "I know one God, Christ
Jesus, and beside Him no other generate and passible" (Hipp. c. Haer.
IX. 10, 11).

Here we have another list of antithetical epithets:

| invisible | incomprehensible | unconquerable | ingenerate | immortal |
| visible | comprehensible | conquerable | generate | mortal; |

or, translating them into the only terms possible in the Roman
Creed:

| seen | comprehended | conquered | born | died |

and in the latter half of the paragraph, "suffered, dead, risen,
buried, pierced, nailed".

We might have even more difficulty in selecting from this list,
but again history seems to come to the rescue and selects just
two terms "generate" and "passible", or in the language of the
Roman Creed "natus" and "passus".

Once more, in the fourth century Pope Damasus put up over

the tomb of Felix and Philippus, the sons of Felicitas, an inscription containing the following lines:

> Qui natum passumque Deum repetisse paternas
> Sedes, atque iterum venturum in aethere, credit,
> Judicet ut vivos rediens pariterque sepultos.

It is really impossible to believe that the identical phrase "natus et passus" should appear in successive centuries in Rome, each time in reference to belief, by mere accident, or unless it was embodied in a well-established formula, and, it will be observed, a formula which is exactly such as the prevalence of heresies known to have existed in Rome in the second century would be likely to cause to be framed, and which exactly agrees with the Roman baptismal Creed of the later date.

But besides these external quarrels there was an internal dispute which began as early as the time of Hermas and reached its culmination in the days of Callistus:

"In some quarters, for a while, it was held that for certain grave sins the Church ought not to give absolution. The history of the question is obscure; but it was already being discussed in the middle of the 2nd century, when the *Shepherd* of Hermas was a manifesto in favour of 'one repentance' for all sins....And when the Roman bishop Callistus (218–223)...notified that it was his practice to absolve sins of the flesh after penance, he was doubly attacked. Tertullian, who, fifteen years before, as a Catholic, in the *de paenitentia* had treated all sins as remissible after penance, now, as a Montanist, assailed Callistus with characteristic bitterness....Later Hippolytus, now an anti-pope and the bishop of a schism, assailed the memory of Callistus on this among other grounds, holding with Tertullian that Idolatry, Homicide, and Unchastity are irremissible. But whereas Tertullian had represented that Callistus refused to absolve Idolatry and Homicide, and therefore charged him with inconsistency in absolving Unchastity, the complaint of Hippolytus is that Callistus was 'the first to devise a concession to men's passions by declaring that he absolved all sins'."[1]

Harnack's theory is that the primitive Church was conceived of as "a communion of saints", and that down to the end of the second century final exclusion from the Church was the penalty of lapse into sin. This primitive conception was replaced during the third century by the idea that the Church is a *corpus per-*

1 Brightman in Swete's *Essays*, pp. 374, 375.

mixtum, a training school for salvation. According to this view the relaxation granted by Callistus represents an innovation, and marks the first stage in the transformation of the conception of the Church. Less familiar is the contention of Funk that the ministry of reconciliation, though inherent in the Church and recognized by it, came into activity at a comparatively late period. From this point of view the action of Callistus was a piece of "ecclesiastical opportunism" due to the situation of the Church at the time.

But however this may be, the relaxation marks a critical turning point, and it would be at least a plausible conjecture that the phrase "Forgiveness of sins" was incorporated into the Creed of Rome in the time of Callistus, or at any rate earlier than the time of Novatian, for "by the middle of the 3rd century the rigourist attitude towards the remission of sins had disappeared in Africa and Italy—even Novatian did not adopt it".[1] And if *sancta* was not already an epithet of the Church, it might be highly expedient to add that though it reconciled sinners to its communion, the Church never lost its sanctity. It is perhaps some confirmation of this view that the phrase "Forgiveness of sins" is absent from the *Apostolic Tradition* of Hippolytus.

(d) The Sevenfold Formula

Accordingly before the middle of the third century we have good reason to think that the baptismal interrogations would run:

> Credis in Deum Patrem omnipotentem?
> Credis in Jesum Christum, Filium Ejus unicum,
>   Dominum nostrum,
> natum et passum?
> Credis in Spiritum Sanctum;
> Sanctam ecclesiam;
> Remissionem peccatorum;
> Carnis resurrectionem?

This is, I think, a fair conclusion from the evidence. The form is exactly such a Creed as might well have been developed from the threefold formula under the pressure of circumstances which we know to have been those of the Church of Rome in the second

---

1 Brightman, *op. cit.* p. 375.

and third centuries; it is such as to give a basis from which the fourth-century Creed might be developed in accordance with "the law of growth"; and it is a genuine Roman form, for it is that of the Gelasian Sacramentary.[1]

It is probable that when Creeds were quite short the interrogatory and declaratory forms were—but for the triple "Credis" and the single "Credo"—identical. There is little direct evidence except that they began in the same way in the fourth century in the Balkans, as is shown by Mai's Arian Fragments, and were probably alike throughout in Egypt, as is shown by the different versions of the shorter form of the Egyptian Church Order. When the western declaratory Creed grew to the length it acquired in the fourth century, all the evidence there is goes to show that the interrogatory form was the shorter of the two.

This Formula not an Abbreviation

But it has been argued that the Gelasian form, instead of being early, is an abbreviation from the declaratory Creed made at a later date. Such a view appears to be absolutely untenable on two independent grounds. The local Creed, as distinct from conciliar Creeds, which might be called into requisition whenever need arose, was employed solely in connexion with baptism, and the great season for adult baptism in Rome was immediately before Easter.

At this time the declaratory Creed, from which the Gelasian is supposed to be an abbreviation, contained "*tertia die resurrexit a mortuis*". Is it conceivable that anyone should, in making an abbreviation, omit *this* article, when the whole baptismal ceremonial spoke of death and resurrection, and when the time of Easter was selected as specially suitable for baptism, just because it emphasized this special doctrine?

The second reason seems equally conclusive. It is this. The declaratory Creed ran "*Qui natus est—passus*", etc. Would not this form be retained in any abbreviated form to be made by

1 Cp. Turner, *History and Use of Creeds*, p. 11: "These questions and answers may be regarded, then, as the first stage of the process by which the Creed was developed out of the baptismal formula."

merely omitting certain articles? But we may go further. If it is evidence that the Creed of Niceta came to Remesiana from the East, because Western Creeds had uniformly *qui* with the indicative, and Niceta's Creed has past participles, is it not equally clear that the Gelasian Creed arose at a time when the Roman Church was speaking Greek, and that *natum et passum* represent a Greek original γεννηθέντα καὶ παθόντα?

But if we may go thus far, it would seem to follow that the *qui* with the indicative of the later declaratory form was adopted at Rome under some form of collaboration or pressure from the provincial churches where it was already established.

There is, of course, no difficulty about the survival of an early form through many centuries; the Creed of the Dair Balaizah Papyrus is found in a rite at least three centuries later; the Creed of Constantinople is used in the East unchanged to-day; our own baptismal Creed is found in full in the seventh century; and, more significant still, though the Roman declaratory Creed has had *qui* with the indicative from the fourth century at the latest, yet the baptismal interrogations of to-day still retain the participles "natum" and "passum", a proof, if any were needed, of the traditional sanctity of the formula, and the innate conservatism of the Roman Church.

CHAPTER IX

THE ENLARGEMENT OF THE ROMAN CREED

I. The Creeds of Spain, Gaul, and Northern Italy; their resemblance to (a) each other, (b) Eastern Creeds, (c) the Creed of Rome. II. The Conservatism of Rome. III. A Probable Motive and Date for the Enlargement.

I. The Creeds of Spain, Gaul, and Northern Italy. Their Resemblance to (a) each other, (b) Eastern Creeds, (c) the Creed of Rome

THE problem for solution is this: supposing the set of baptismal questions put to the candidate in Rome *c.* 220, which taken together may be called the Interrogatory Creed, was identical with that preserved in the Gelasian Sacramentary, how did the corresponding Declaratory Creed, or positive affirmation of his faith by the candidate, come to have the form it possessed in the last quarter of the fourth century as testified by the sermons of Augustine, the *Explanatio Symboli ad Initiandos*, and the phrases derived from Leo's Tome and Sermons of *c.* 450?

At first sight there seem to be no available data; but this problem is closely connected with a second, namely, How is it that in the fourth century the Creeds of Spain, Gaul and Northern Italy so closely resembled (a) each other, (b) Eastern baptismal Creeds of a somewhat earlier date, and (c) this later form of the Creed of Rome?

This second problem is not so difficult of solution, and though the answer to it may not be demonstrably certain, it is at any rate so highly probable as to be almost indisputable.

Within this period, the third and fourth centuries, it is generally acknowledged (a) that "provincial rites", that is the rites current in Spain, Gaul, and Northern Italy—we might add Africa—differed in structure and in detail from the contemporary Roman rite; (b) that in spite of minor variations these provincial rites so closely resembled each other that they can be classed together as a single rite; and (c) that they contained many oriental features and might justly be regarded as a scion of the Eastern family transplanted to a Western soil.

This, then, is the situation with which we are faced. We find running throughout the Western provinces a single type of Creed from *c.* 380 onwards. It contains, in some examples, certain phrases which existed earlier in the East, and we can trace the road by which they travelled. The effect of omitting them, where they occur, is only to enhance the similarity of the remainder. It is not due to prescription by the authority of Rome, for Rome exercised no jurisdiction in this region such as would enable it to impose its Creed; nor can we date the desire of ritual uniformity in the mind of the Roman bishop before the pontificate of Damasus, even if so early.

This developed form cannot be much earlier in the West than the Council of Nicaea, as it contains the phrases "of the Holy Ghost and Mary the virgin", and "under Pontius Pilate", and to judge by analogy we should say it could not have come into being before the middle of the fourth century. But in the early portion of the third century the Roman Creed had the participles "*natum, passum*", whereas in Gaul and Northern Italy we find *qui* with the indicative. The participial form at Remesiana and in Spain we judged to be due to independent translations from the Greek. Are we not forced to conclude that the provincial creeds have not been assimilated to the Roman form, but *vice versa*, that the Creed of Rome has been enlarged, and has changed the participial construction to *qui* with the indicative, owing to some kind of contact with the provincial Creeds, and with the Creeds of Gaul and Italy rather than with those of Spain? And in consequence is not the question before us really found to be, "When and in what circumstances did such contact occur, and what motive could have urged the Church of Rome towards such a change?"

II. THE CONSERVATISM OF ROME

If we read the history of the Eastern Church between the middle of the second and the end of the fourth century, we are struck with its amazing fertility and development. There are notable schools of theology at Alexandria and Antioch, besides others of less repute scattered over Asia Minor; there is a marked growth of organization, and councils and synods are held at frequent intervals and in many localities; there are Christian writers of all sorts, doctrinal, expository, apologetic, devotional, and historical. Everywhere we seem to be breathing the air of adventure and exploration; we are conscious of the rapid and widespread growth of new ideas and new expressions in matters of faith and experience. The same phenomenon is exhibited in pictorial form in the map. By the time of the Council of Nicaea Christianity has permeated heathen society throughout Asia Minor. It has thrust itself on the north-west nearly to the borders of Italy, and farther south has established itself in strength on the Illyrian coast. It has crossed the Adriatic, and taken firm root along the east coast of Italy and round the Gulf of Tarentum.

Much the same state of things, though less developed, shows itself in the Western provinces. On the secular side there is the spread of Roman civilization and the Latin language. There is a vast educational movement, and this tends to sharpen the intellect and accustom the mind to new ideas. A further stimulus is supplied by the increase of trade, which was for the most part in other than Italian hands. By the time of the Council of Nicaea non-Roman Christianity has taken possession of the northern fringe of the Mediterranean, and pushing inland has penetrated to Britain. Southern Gaul is largely, though not predominantly, Christian, and the new religion has been established in Southern Spain, and is preached and practised over the greater part of the Iberian peninsula. In Northern Italy we find a wedge of Eastern Christianity on a Western soil.

And now turn to Rome. Even if we grant to Roman missionary zeal all Italy except the extreme East and South, and add to it Sicily, and a small portion of Sardinia, how meagre is the total as compared with either the East, or the Western provinces over which Rome had the start of 100 years! And if we look to other fields, we find similar results. Teachers of all kinds, orthodox and heretical, flock to Rome, but there is no native school of theology. From the days of Clement to those of Paulinus of Nola there is no great theological writer who is not either of foreign parentage or born or nurtured on foreign soil. Examine any Christian Latin author within this period, and you will find that he has drunk from Eastern sources; nowhere south and west of the Apennines do you meet with anything more than the codification and arrangements of other men's thoughts. From the Eastern point of view the West, where the East has not fertilized it, appears unoriginative and sterile.

Nevertheless Rome was all the while performing a useful function. Heresies beat upon it, but for the most part they failed to move it. Seeds were carried thither from exotic climes, but they took but shallow root, and soon the plants withered away.

The position of theological correctness, which the Roman Church managed to hold, must be accounted for. It was the result of various causes. One was the essential conservatism of the Roman Church. The conservatism of the West...was a wise conservatism which recognized the strength of the Church's tradition, and the weight of the teaching of the past....A second cause was her want of originality. The Church of Rome produced no heretic and no theologian. Destitute of imagination, destitute of creative power, she was never carried away by doctrinal innovations. She received slowly, weighed carefully, and judged solemnly.[1]

Another characteristic of Rome was its attachment to forms. The cataclysmic upheavals of its youth were all but forgotten; the greatest of political revolutions, the change from republican, or at least aristocratic, government to empire was accomplished under a combination of constitutional precedents.

Perhaps the most striking example of the perpetuation of ancient customs is given by the christianizing by Pope Nicholas in the ninth century of the ancient Roman marriage rite of the "confarreatio".[2] Nicholas was not a pedantic antiquarian; he did not deliberately search among old manuscripts for traces of an obsolete pagan ceremony; even if it had fallen into complete practical desuetude it still survived, handed down by a living tradition.

1 *Church Quarterly Review*, XXVI (July 1888), p. 464; cp. G. F. Browne, *Theodore and Wilfrith*, p. 83.

2 See Duchesne, *Christian Worship*, pp. 433, 434.

And this conservation of formulas showed itself especially in the realm of law. The Law of the Twelve Tables was constantly re-embodied in later codes. The Praetorian Edict tended to become "perpetual" until it was made obligatory. The mis-wording of a contractual stipulation might render it legally invalid. And in religious rites formulas would be handed down and repeated, even if they had become all but unintelligible. That Rome was still the stronghold of paganism is shown by the possibility of revival under Julian, but the official heathen religion was now almost entirely a matter of forms and ceremonies which had once been significant and alive. So court ceremonial was stiffened and rigidified under Diocletian, and after Diocletian's persecution the Bishop of Rome became a great social personage, while imperial officers were chosen, as we saw in the case of Ambrose, from those learned in the law.

From every side, therefore, we seem assured that a religious formula once adopted by the Roman Church would tend to remain unaltered, a tendency strikingly exemplified by the maintenance of the Interrogatory Creed till we find it in the Gelasian Sacramentary. The Declaratory Creed would naturally not be surrounded by the same halo of sanctity as invested the formula used in the act of ministration of baptism, but nevertheless there would be a strong feeling against any alteration, and it would need a powerful motive and a peculiar combination of circumstances to effect the change. It was a formula which was wrought out phrase by phrase in conflict with heresies, and as such entitled to honour, and about it we may well believe there was the same feeling which moved Athanasius to insist on the danger of touching the formula of Nicaea. Nevertheless the Nicene Creed had to be enlarged at Constantinople to safeguard the faith against novel teachings.

III. A PROBABLE MOTIVE AND DATE FOR THE ENLARGEMENT

Supposing, then, we think that there is any force in this analogy, we shall ask, what were the later heresies with which Rome found itself in conflict? Arianism, but for the lapse of

Liberius owing to political pressure, found no resting place in Rome. Though Marcellus came to Rome, he came as a suppliant, and even if he were more heretical than he has been represented, yet he could not have preached his heresy there, or he would not have been acquitted. Macedonianism must have been recognized as a danger, or Damasus would not have added to the Nicene Creed *neque facturam, neque creaturam, sed de substantia Deitatis*; but Macedonianism, like Arianism of which it was an offshoot, seems not to have domiciled itself in Rome, and clearly it has not affected the Roman Declaratory Creed, nor did the additions to the Nicene made by Damasus prove permanent. But with Apollinarianism it is otherwise. Its danger was certainly recognized by Rome, since in the same Council (probably 380) in which Damasus enlarged the Nicene text, he condemned Apollinarianism by anathemas, clearly based on those passed in the Alexandrian Council of 362 under Athanasius. Moreover, the particular phrase "of the Holy Ghost and the virgin Mary" was added to the Nicene Creed at the Council of Constantinople in 381 (see below, p. 198) against this heresy. Nor would the Creed of Rome probably have been revised until the fear of persecution was allayed by the Edict of Toleration in 313.

Nor again would the need for a fuller Creed be felt until the advent of a pope with a widely extended view, to whom the short Creed of the early third century had come to look antiquated by contrast with other baptismal Creeds, such as that of Marcellus, to which circumstances had directed his attention. The sense of the isolation of Rome in the matter of religious usages was slow to make itself felt. The first definite evidence we have is in the decretal of Siricius in 385, "Catholicorum episcoporum unam confessionem esse debere apostolica disciplina composuit. Si ergo una fides est, manere debet et una traditio, si una traditio est una debet disciplina per omnes ecclesias custodiri". The decretal is addressed to Himerius, Bishop of Tarragona in Spain, and it is in the course of this same instrument that we find a strong assertion of the Petrine claims, a circumstance which shows that by the "apostolica disciplina" is meant that of the Church of Rome.

But perhaps better known is the letter of Innocent I to Decentius, Bishop of Gubbio, in 416:

"If the bishops of God wish to possess the ecclesiastical traditions as they have been handed down from the blessed Apostles, let there be no diversity or variation in ordinations and consecrations. But as long as everyone thinks he must maintain not what has been handed down, but what seems good to himself, different uses are sure to be kept and employed in different places or churches, and there is made a scandal. . . . For who is there who does not know or perceive that all ought to observe what has been handed down to the Roman Church by Peter the Prince of the Apostles, and kept up to this day, and nothing which has not authority or which seems to take a model elsewhere ought to be added or introduced? Especially as it is evident that in all Italy, Gaul, Spain, Africa, Sicily, and the adjacent islands no one has founded churches except those whom the venerable Apostle Peter or his successors have constituted bishops."

On this letter several remarks may be made. What the Pope is tilting at is clearly the non-Roman elements in the usage of Eugubium, not more than one hundred miles distant, and within his own metropolitan jurisdiction. Beyond that he looks to the *fons et origo mali*, the Western provincial rite. His "history" is no more to be trusted in the case of Africa than in that of Gaul or Spain, and he shows clearly that the Roman rite, and in consequence the Roman Creed, had not been introduced by papal authority in the countries he mentions. This desire for uniformity might perhaps be dated back to the pontificate of Damasus, but certainly not earlier. There would seem, then, good reason for thinking that the enlargement of the Roman Declaratory Creed took place about the latter half of the fourth century, and probably during the pontificate of Damasus.

And Damasus seems particularly appropriate; the alteration would be likely to meet with some opposition, but Damasus had the "temerity", as Athanasius would have called it, to add to the Nicene Creed. But if we accept provisionally the pontificate of Damasus as giving the most likely period for revision, we must clearly put it in the earlier portion of his reign. And here we are met with what may be more than a coincidence.

In December 371 Damasus held a council by command of the Emperor Valentinian, and its decrees were signed by Damasus

himself and by ninety bishops of Italy and Gaul. With Damasus
was associated Valerian, Metropolitan of Aquileia. The letter is
addressed to the bishops of Illyria, and states that a report had
been received from the brethren in Gaul and Venetia (certain
MSS. read "the Bessi", but this reading seems improbable).
It deals with Arianism and Macedonianism, condemns Auxentius
of Milan, who nevertheless continued to retain his see; and it
repudiates the Council of Ariminum. This Council was also attended by Dorotheus, a deacon of Antioch, whom Basil had sent
with a letter to Rome by way of Alexandria, whence he brought
also a letter from Athanasius. Liberius had been out of communion with Athanasius in 362, and though the latter had doubtless sent him a copy of the decrees of the Alexandrian Synod
when communion had been restored, yet no action against the
Apollinarians seems to have been taken at Rome before 380. It
is possible, therefore, that Dorotheus called the attention of
Damasus to the decree sent to his predecessor. It would seem
likely that this gathering of Italian and Gallic bishops may have
suggested to Damasus the expediency of revising his Creed; at
any rate we seem to have here both the earliest and the most
favourable opportunity for such action.

CHAPTER X

THE *TEXTUS RECEPTUS*, T[1]

Not known in Rome in the time of Gregory the Great: his profession of faith. Alternative theories of composition: (*a*) Rome; (*b*) Southern France, first half of the sixth century; (*c*) Northern France, Switzerland or North Italy, seventh century. Appendix: The Longer Creed of the *Egyptian Church Order*.

THE *Textus Receptus*, T, is formed from the baptismal Creed which in the fourth and fifth centuries ran, as we have seen, with slight modifications, from the East, through Asia Minor, the region of the Danube, Northern Italy, Gaul, and Spain, and, after the return of Augustine from Milan, in Africa also, and was grafted on to the old stock of the Creed of Rome. In Syria and Asia Minor it received additions which partially disguised its original outline, but in the West this is easily visible.

To this Creed were added from time to time one or more of the phrases *Creatorem caeli et terrae, conceptus, mortuus, descendit ad inferna*, or *ad inferos, Dei...omnipotentis, Inde, Credo, sanctorum communionem* and *vitam aeternam*.

The result of the addition of all of them is the *Textus Receptus*, but this also varied slightly in different localities until the spread of the influence of the see of Rome blotted out these local peculiarities, and standardized the form employed there. Nevertheless there is an earlier form which survives in English and in other tongues translated from it, and for dioceses in communion with the see of Canterbury possesses a higher authority than that taken from the Roman Book of Hours which has been incorporated into Morning and Evening Prayer, since it is used in the English Book of Common Prayer in baptism, and in the Office for the Visitation of the Sick.

In the second member it has "only-begotten Son" instead of "only Son", representing a Latin *unigenitus* instead of *unicus*; it omits "from the dead", inserts "at the end of the world" after "shall come again", and ends "everlasting life after death".

1 For the text see p. 118; H. p. 42.

The Apostles' Creed was not said in the Roman Hours Office before the ninth century,[1] so that while it is theoretically possible that monks, for the most part Irish, should have brought to England the form which afterwards came to be adopted in Rome, yet it is far more probable that they would bring one of the many variants from it, as apparently they actually did.

The earliest known of these Irish importations is that contained in the Antiphonary of Bangor (L. pp. 13, 14), near Belfast, where a monastery was founded by Comgall in 558. The MS. is dated between 680 and 691, and contains a collection of hymns, collects and canticles, including the *Te Deum*, for use in the Hours Office on Saturdays, Sundays and feasts of martyrs. The Creed has some remarkable variants from the Roman form of the *Textus Receptus*; it introduces *Credo* before and *Deum omnipotentem* after the mention of each of the three Persons of the Blessed Trinity, besides adding two more *Credo*'s at the end, *Credo vitam post mortem et vitam aeternam in gloria Christi*, and it closes: *Haec omnia credo in Deum*. In the first clause it reads *omnium creaturarum visibilium et invisibilium Conditorem*, instead of *Creatorem caeli et terrae*, a form somewhat similar to that in the Creed of Jerome, *omnium visibilium et invisibilium Factorem*; it omits the word *mortuus*, and it has *ad inferos* instead of the more usual *ad inferna*, a reading which is found also in the *Quicumque Vult*. In other respects the Creed follows the lines of T, and this suggests that T was composed not later than 650 or 660.

Of the ninth century there is also an Anglo-Saxon MS. at the Lambeth Library (No. 427) containing the Psalter, hymns and canticles including the *Te Deum* and *Quicumque Vult*, with interlined Latin translation underneath. This contains the Creed in the T form. The Scottish *Book of Deer* (L. p. 14) has the Creed in the T form except for *ad inferna* in place of *ad inferos*.

The Durham Rituale quotes in the Office of Prime only the first and last lines of the Creed, the Anglo-Saxon being translated from the Latin and written above it. It ends: *Carnis resurrectionem in vitam aeternam.*

1 Bishop, *Liturgica Historica*, p. 144 n.

Our problem is, then, not altogether a simple one; T is R+ several words and phrases found, but for the single word *Dei*, in the Creeds of Jerome, Niceta, and Mai's Arian Fragments. These phrases came to Rome already incorporated into some existing Creed. It is fairly certain that Rome had not adopted them as early as the time of Gregory the Great (590–604), since his confession of faith (Migne, *P.L.* LXXVII. p. 1327) would seem to be founded solely on the Constantinopolitan Creed and R with Gregory's own additions.

> Credo in unum Deum omnipotentem Patrem
> et Filium et Spiritum Sanctum,
> tres Personas, unam substantiam;...
> Confiteor unigenitum Filium
> consubstantialem et sine tempore natum de Patre,
> omnium visibilium et invisibilium Conditorem,
> lumen ex lumine, Deum verum de Deo vero...
>
> Conceptus et　　　　　　　　　　　　　　　(from C)
> natus ex Spiritu Sancto et Maria virgine...
> qui...sub Pontio Pilato crucifixus est et sepultus
> tertia die resurrexit a mortuis...
> ascendit in caelum,
> sedet ad dexteram Patris,
> unde venturus est judicare vivos et mortuos...
> Confiteor...unum baptisma,
> unam apostolicam et universalem ecclesiam
> in qua sola possint laxari peccata.　　　　　(from R)

Here *Conceptus* is very possibly Gregory's own addition. If so he has omitted the characteristic T phrases *descendit ad inferna* or *inferos*, *Dei...omnipotentis*, *sanctorum communionem*, and *vitam aeternam*, and would seem to have paraphrased *Creatorem caeli et terrae* into *omnium visibilium et invisibilium Conditorem*, and *sanctam ecclesiam catholicam* into *unam apostolicam et universalem ecclesiam*. Moreover, if Gregory had had the full form, T, we might have expected that by the time of Adrian it would have spread as far as Naples and have been brought to England in 668 instead of the shorter form which we find in the *Psalter of Aethelstan* and *Titus*. Again, if we compare the Interrogatory Creed in the Gregorian Sacramentary with the modern form, we notice that the former contains *Creatorem caeli et terrae* and *catholicam,* and that the latter has in addition *sanctorum com-munionem* and *vitam aeternam*; so that while the middle section remains unaltered, the first and third sections, but for the single word *Credis* instead of *Credo,* are precisely the same as in T. This suggests that the enlarged Creed reached Rome in two recensions, a shorter, slightly before or in the time of Gregory, and the fuller form at a later date, since it is probable that additions would be made to the declaratory more readily than to the interrogatory Creed, and the earlier phrases may have been incorporated by Gregory himself.

As apparently making against the view is the fact that there is in the library of Corpus Christi College, Cambridge, a manu-script No. 468, probably written in England, entitled *Psalterium Latinum et Graecum Papae Gregorii,* containing, besides the psalter, the Lord's Prayer, the usual hymns, and the Creed in parallel columns, in Latin and in a Greek translation in Roman characters. This gives T with the sole omissions of *est* after *venturus* and of *et* before *vitam aeternam.* The Greek version has *pantocratora* in the first clause but *pantodinamu* in the sixth. The two things that appear certain about this MS. are that the scribe imagined that the original emanated from Gregory the Great, and that this attribution is wrong.

Caspari[1] who is followed by Burn[2] attributes it to Gregory III (731–741), but there is no foundation for this view except the title.

The Greek version, save for some differences in spelling, is identical with that of *Codex Sangallensis* 338 of the tenth century. Caspari thinks that this also was written in Rome, carried thence to England, and brought back by Irish monks to St Gallen; but Hahn[3] holds it more probable that it was written in St Gallen not much earlier than the date of the MS.

The old form, R, maintained itself in some parts of Italy even after T had been adopted as the baptismal Creed in Rome; the MS. *Canonici Liturg.* 343 in the Bodleian shows that it was used in Tuscany even towards the end of the twelfth century.

---

1 *Quellen,* III. pp. 11, 215.   2 *Introduction,* p. 233.
3 *Symbole,* p. 102.

We can, I think, assert quite definitely that T was not *composed* in Rome, and, considering how much Roman liturgical usages owed to Charlemagne, it is no unlikely presumption that it was adopted there under his influence.[1]

Ruling out Rome as the place where T was composed, a second competitor is Southern Gaul in the time of Caesarius of Arles (Bp. 502–542). An extract from his sermon has already been given.[2]

There is no difficulty in supposing that Creed phrases from the region of the Danube might have been transported to Southern Gaul in his time. Not all the Goths were Arians; there would appear to have been some Catholics among them, and in any event both parties would seem to have used the same baptismal Creed. Alaric invaded Italy at the very beginning of the fifth century, and some ten years later Ataulf led his hosts into Gaul and actually went to Arles before passing on into Spain. Nor again is it necessary that a preacher should quote every word of the Creed on which he is commenting; so it might well be thought that Caesarius had the full text behind him; but he has omitted *Creatorem caeli et terrae, Dei...* *omnipotentis*, and *Credo* before *in Spiritum Sanctum*. Dr Burn[3] has pointed out that the first phrase is not to be found in any purely Gallican Creed before 700, and it would seem improbable that if Caesarius was commenting on the full *Textus Receptus* he would have omitted all of them; while if it had been brought to Gaul at so early a date we should have expected that *Creatorem caeli et terrae, mortuus, Dei...omnipotentis*, would have been found in the Creeds of Phoebadius of Agen, Cyprian of Toulon, Gregory of Tours, Venantius Fortunatus and Eligius of Noyon. On the whole, therefore, the weight of probability would seem to be against this location.

There remains what I may call the Northern theory, that T was composed in the seventh century, and probably towards the

1 Cp. Edmund Bishop, *Liturgica Historica*, p. 16: "Rome itself seems to have taken the least possible interest in all that was going on; and ended in accepting from the hands of a stranger, in place of the old *Gregorianum*, the mass book thus compiled in France."

2 See pp. 97, 98. 3 *J.T.S.* III. p. 497.

beginning of it, in Northern Gaul or Switzerland and from thence taken to Northern Italy, or, alternatively, in Northern Italy and thence taken by way of Switzerland to Northern Gaul.

The arguments in favour of this view do not compel assent, but are much more weighty than for any other. From the neighbourhood of the Danube to the Lake of Constance and beyond there were two main routes. The great imperial road which started from Constantinople, after leaving Remesiana, stretched up the valley of the Drave by way of Sirmium to Poetovio. Here it forked, the northern branch following the course of the Drave through Noricum and the Dolomite country over the Pass of the Brenner into Rhaetia and the Bavarian highlands to Bregenz at the eastern end of the Lake; while the southern branch went to Aquileia and thence into the plains of Lombardy. On this route the road to the north from Chiavenna, near Lake Como, as far as Curia (Coire or Chur), had been made as early as the time of Augustus and at Curia there were Christians at latest from the beginning of the fifth century; thence it followed the valley of the Rhine and so reached Lake Constance rather further to the West. This was naturally the more travelled highway of the two and was taken by Venantius Fortunatus in 565 on his way to Austrasia. Twenty years later the Irish monk Columban, who had been trained at Bangor under Comgall, crossed over into Gaul, and in 590 or 591 founded the monastery at Luxeuil (near Vésoul in Burgundy), whence he was carried prisoner to Besançon, and in 610 was shipped from Nantes to return to Ireland. Being blown back by contrary winds he made his way to Metz to the court of Theodoric, King of Austrasia, where he was visited by monks from his old monastery. Thence he went to the Lake of Zürich, but had to flee to Lake Constance where he was hospitably entertained by the Christian priest Willimar at Arbon. Then he went to Bregenz, and after preaching in that neighbourhood for three years, left behind his disciple Gall—afterwards the founder of the monastery of St Gallen—and crossed the Alps by the same road as Venantius Fortunatus, though in a reverse direction, into

Lombardy, the king of which, Agilulf, assigned to him in 613 a tract of land between Milan and Genoa where he founded the monastery of Bobbio.

"In the fifth and sixth centuries what remained of the Upper Danubian provinces was divided between the two Italian metropolitan sees of Milan and Aquileia. Rhaetia Prima (Coire) was under the jurisdiction of Milan";[1] and this arrangement persisted until the erection of Mainz into an archbishopric by Karloman in 743, before which time there was no metropolitan see to the north of Milan. Thus, if during these centuries a Christian travelled by either route into Switzerland, he would almost certainly come across a Creed of the Milanese type, for Willimar was by no means the only Christian near Lake Constance.

The *Textus Receptus*, or something like it, is found in four sermons falsely ascribed to St Augustine, Nos. 240–243, the Gallican Missal, a sermon called from its initial words *Simbolum graeca lingua est*, to which I shall refer by the abbreviated title *Sim.*, the Missal of Bobbio, and later on in the treatise of Priminius.

The so-called Gallican Missal was written in France *c.* 700, but it is not a missal, but a combination of portions of two sacramentaries, the first of the Bobbio type partly Romanized, and the second purely Gallican and probably connected with Auxerre. The baptismal office is in the first portion, but both contain Creeds resembling T followed by expositions, though owing to defects in the MS. the exposition in the second portion is a mere fragment. The first sermon is obviously taken from some monastic collection, since after the exposition of the clause *conceptus de Spiritu Sancto*, it continues: "Jam jam, si jubetis, haec quae dicta sunt, caecitati vestrae sufficiant, et die crastina, secundum sanctam consuetudinem vestram, per ministerium fratrum nostrorum ea quae restant maturius audietis." Though the Creed is complete, the sermon omits *Creatorem caeli et terrae, descendit ad inferna, a mortuis* and *remissionem peccatorum*. It has some connexion with Pseudo-Augustine *S.* 243.

1 Duchesne, *Christian Worship*, p. 31.

The Creed in the second sacramentary omits *descendit ad inferna*, and reads *ascendit victor ad caelos* and *abremissione peccatorum*. The exposition draws, among other sources, on Pseudo-Augustine *S.* 242, which also seems to have been utilized in the first sermon in the Missal of Bobbio.

The sermon *Sim.* has points of peculiar interest. It is found in three MSS.; the first, *Codex Sessorianus* 52, now in the Victor Emmanuel Library at Rome, was written in the eleventh or twelfth century, but the collection of documents of which it forms part came from the Abbey of Nonantola, a town in North Italy nine miles north-east of Modena, and was apparently made in the ninth century, so the original of which the *Codex Sessorianus* is a copy cannot have been later than this. The collection contains also the seventh *Ordo Romanus* in which at the baptism of an infant T is employed, but there is a reference to the custom of reciting the Constantinopolitan Creed over the catechumen on the Thursday in Holy Week at the *redditio symboli*.

The two other MSS. are the one at Vésoul in Burgundy (No. 73) of the eleventh century, and the other at St Gallen (*Codex Sangallensis* 782) of the ninth century. This last is the shortest and gives the most primitive text of the three, in spite of the fact that both it and the Vésoul MS. have *victor* before *ad caelos*, like the Auxerre Sacramentary, a word which is absent from the *Codex Sessorianus*.

On the clause on the Forgiveness of Sins the sermon enumerates seven ways in which remission may be obtained. Any enumeration of this kind is rare, the number seven in this connexion exceedingly so. The seven methods are by (1) baptism; (2) penance; (3) martyrdom; (4) forgiveness of enemies; (5) true contrition, that is, as the sermon explains, by works of mercy; (6) almsgiving; (7) suffering (*doloribus multis*), but for the last item the Vésoul MS. substitutes *per praedicationem*, that is by converting a sinner.

There is no reasonable doubt that this list is based on Rufinus's translation of Origen, *Hom. in Levit.* 4, where Origen is finding Christian equivalents to the seven forms of Jewish sacrifices for sin. Origen's list gives (1) baptism; (2) martyrdom; (3) almsgiving; (4) forgiving our brethren their trespasses; (5) converting a sinner; (6) abundance of love; (7) penance. Rufinus's translation was read by Walafrid Strabo of Reichenau (a monastery at the eastern end of the Lake Constance founded by Priminius) and afterwards of Fulda (founded by Boniface), and by Angelomus of Luxeuil (founded by Columban), and MSS. of it are found at Laon and Chartres, as well as at Paris where it was read by Aeneas, as it was at Orléans by Jonas. We may take it therefore that the translation, which was written by Rufinus at Aquileia, travelled into Lombardy and thence north to the Lake of Constance and through the gap of Belfort between the Vosges and the Jura into Northern France.

Next we come to Priminius,[1] a Benedictine monk, not apparently Irish, as has been asserted, but Anglo-Saxon.[2] About the year 724 he was consecrated rural bishop of Meltis,[3] and subsequently went thence to the Lake of Constance where he founded the Abbey of Reichenau, and later on others in Bavaria and Alsace, and finally the Abbey of Hornbach near Zweibrücken in the Rhenish Palatinate. He wrote a treatise entitled *Dicta Abbatis Priminii de singulis libris canonicis scarapsus*[4] (L. p. 133; H. p. 42). In it he quotes T in three different contexts, the first narrating the legend of its apostolic origin and assigning each clause to an Apostle, the list agreeing with that given in the Missal of Bobbio, except that this gives the last clause to Matthias, while Priminius assigns it to Thomas in addition to the sixth, probably by error of the copyist. The second is in an account of the service of Baptism, in which he has much in common with Martin of Braga, but gives T instead of Martin's Creed, quotes the Roman prayer of unction, and speaks of the act of baptism as following immediately the recitation of the Creed, which was a distinctively Roman custom. On the other hand Priminius employs the full form T in the interrogations, whereas Rome was using a shorter form. The third,

1 For the right spelling of his name see Morin, *Revue Charlemagne*, I. pp. 87–89.

2 See Hauck, *Kirchengeschichte Deutschlands*, 3rd ed. I. p. 347.

3 "Meltis castellum" is probably Meltburch in Brabant, Morin, *Rev. Bénéd.* XXIX. 262–273.   4 *Scarapsus* probably = *excerpsus*, excerpt.

an incomplete quotation, is in a summary of teaching on Faith and Morals. The first two quotations read *ad inferna* instead of *ad inferos* (this clause is not quoted in the summary); the summary gives *surrexit* instead of *resurrexit*; the first quotation reads *sedit*, the second *sedet*, and both omit *est* after *venturus*.

And now we come to the Bobbio Missal (*Cod. Paris. Lat.* 13,246, L. pp. 12, 13). Edmund Bishop says of it: "When we find in the seventh century at Bobbio, a monastery founded by the Irish, a 'Missa Romensis' which is identical with a mass found in Ireland containing a *commemoratio defunctorum* (or diptychs) specially designed for Ireland and dating from 630–640, the conclusion seems inevitable that the two mass texts [meaning this and the Stowe Missal] derive from a common progenitor either in Ireland or among the Irish in quite the early years of the seventh century."[1]

"None of the Masses go beyond the *Sanctus*, which implies that they all terminated in the same way as the *missa Romensis cottidiana* at the beginning of the Missal. In the part before the Preface, the prayers are mostly arranged according to the Gallican use, and placed under Gallican rubrics; in nearly one-third of the Masses, however, the prayers are preceded by Roman rubrics, and are arranged according to the Roman method. The compiler, nevertheless, has shown such a want of skill, that in the Masses of Roman type the prayers are mostly Gallican and *vice versa*. He even places purely Gallican invitatories under the rubrics belonging to Roman prayers."

"The name of St Ambrose occurs in the Canon of the Mass, a peculiarity not met with in any other Gallican or Frankish Sacramentary."[2]

"There can be no doubt that the missal is of Irish composition, not improbably at Bobbio itself. Duchesne was not aware of the intimate connexion between it and the original portion of the Stowe Missal"[3]; and Bishop thinks that it is not by accident that one of the MSS. of the *Orationale Hispano-Gothicum* was found in the Verona Library.[4]

1 *Liturgica Historica*, p. 92.   2 Duchesne, *Christian Worship*, pp. 158, 159.
3 Bishop, *op. cit.* p. 58 n.   4 *Op. cit.* p. 179.

With slight variations (neglecting peculiarities of spelling and the mixture of accusatives and ablatives) the Bobbio Missal contains T no less than four times. The first (*H.B.S.* p. 56) is a statement preliminary to an exposition, and reads in the second section *unigenitum sempiternum*, followed by *Conceptus...natum ...passus...sepultum*, and then starts a series of new clauses, *Descendit ad inferna...sedit*, and omits *est* after *venturus*. The second (*H.B.S.* pp. 56, 57) is the exposition, which omits *Creatorem caeli et terrae*, reads *Et in Jesum Christum unicum Dominum nostrum* without *Filium*, but explains the clause by *Credo ergo Filium Dei unigenitum ab ingenito, viventem a vivente, verum de vero*, and continues with *qui* with the indicative and then *passum...sepultum, Descendit ad inferna* (with no connecting *qui*)...*Sedit ad dexteram Patris omnipotentis* omitting *Dei*, which is nevertheless in the previous text, and omitting *est* after *venturus*. The third is in the Baptismal Interrogations (*H.B.S.* pp. 74, 75), giving past participles from *natum* to *sepultum* (omitting *mortuum*), and then continuing abruptly, without *qui*, *Descendit ad inferna...sedit...inde venturus* without *est*, and ending *vitam habere post mortem in gloria Christi*. The renunciation is *Abrenuncias satanae pompis ejus luxuriis suis saeculo huic*, which is not the Roman form, but the act of baptism follows immediately after the recitation of the Creed, which was a distinctively Roman custom. The interrogative Creed used is not that of the Roman sacramentary but T. The fourth is in the *Additamenta Varia* at the end (*H.B.S.* p. 181), assigning the several clauses to individual apostles in agreement with Priminius except as to the last item. This also omits *Creatorem caeli et terrae* and has in the second section *Deum et Dominum nostrum, natum de Maria virgine per Spiritum Sanctum*, omits *mortuum* and has *Descendit ad inferna* without *qui*, omits *a mortuis* and *est* after *venturus*, and in the third section omits *sanctorum communionem* and has instead *per baptismum sanctum remissionem peccatorum*. It ends *Carnis resurrectionem in vitam aeternam*.

And now let us turn to some peculiarities of words and phrases. *Creatorem caeli et terrae* ultimately goes back to Ἐν ἀρχῇ ἐποίησεν ὁ Θεὸς τὸν οὐρανὸν καὶ τὴν γῆν (Gen. i. 1). The teaching embodied in the phrase was naturally in the Church from the earliest days (cp. Acts xvii. 24) and is found in the Rule of Faith of Irenaeus, Tertullian, and Origen. In the fourth century something of the kind is a commonplace of Eastern Creeds, and was in the Creed of Africa before the return of Augustine. The actual words are in the Creed of the Council of Antioch in 324–325, in the Creed of Jerusalem in 348, and in that of the Acacian Council of Seleucia in 359, and the fact that they were introduced into the Constantinopolitan Creed in 381, together with the parallel phrase Πίστευε τὸν σύμπαντα κόσμον, ὅσος τε ὁρατός, καὶ ὅσος ἀόρατος, ἐξ οὐκ ὄντων παρὰ Θεοῦ γενόμενον, καὶ προνοίᾳ τοῦ ποιήσαντος διοικούμενον in Gregory Nazianzen (*Orat.* xl, *de Baptismo*), would seem to indicate that they were already in the local baptismal Creed of Constantinople and spread thence to the West, where we find them in the Creed of Remesiana and in Mai's Arian Fragments, and later in the varieties of the *Textus Receptus*.

In the second section *Dominum et Deum* is quoted in Mai's Arian Fragments VII as the conclusion of the Preface in the Canon of the orthodox Danubian rite, and probably comes from John xx. 28, but it appears to have been used by Arians to disguise their heresy: *Filius autem Patri non est Deus sed omnis creaturae Dominus et Deus est Filius* (Frag. IV); *Credentes in Patrem per Filium Dominum et Deum nostrum Jesum Christum* (Frag. XIV). The Creed of Asterius, quoted by Marcellus (*ap.* Euseb. *c. Marcell.* 1. 4), has Πιστεύειν εἰς Πατέρα Θεὸν παντοκράτορα, καὶ εἰς τὸν Υἱὸν Αὐτοῦ τὸν μονογενῆ Θεόν, τὸν Κύριον ἡμῶν Ἰησοῦν Χριστόν: the Arian Council of Constantinople in 360 ὁ Κύριος καὶ Θεὸς ἡμῶν: Ulphilas *in unigenitum Filium Ejus, Dominum et Deum nostrum*: Germinius, Arian Bishop of Cyzicus and afterwards of Sirmium, *Dominum Deum nostrum*: so when we find it in Spanish Creeds (L. p. 11) it is probably a Gothic importation.

Similarly *sempiternus* is explained by the Arians: *Sempiternum autem sic dicimus Filium, quia cum initium habeat Filius, finem tamen (non) habiturum, sed mansurum in sempiternum* (Frag. VI); but when we get both words together in the Bobbio and Gallican

Missals, *Filium Ejus unigenitum sempiternum*, the combination probably ultimately runs back to the *Te Deum, venerandum Tuum verum unigenitum Filium* and *Tu Patris sempiternus es Filius*.

In 614 or 615 John, the disciple of Gall, was consecrated Bishop of Constance on Gall's nomination, and at his consecration Gall preached a sermon containing the Roman form of renunciation and the words *Sempiternus...Deus, cum coeterna Sapientia, hoc est Filio sempiterno, et Charitate, sibi et Filio consempiterna, id est Spiritu Sancto; de virginis utero Dominum... et Deum...devicto mortis imperio resurrexit*, language which strongly resembles the *Te Deum*.[1]

Conceptus. The only Eastern Creed which has συλληφθείς is that of the Nestorians. *Conceptus* is in the Creed of Jerome and in those of Phoebadius of Agen, Caesarius of Arles, Cyprian of Toulon, and Eligius of Noyon. In the Creed of Gregory the Great it is most probably his own addition; it occurs regularly in T.

Mortuus is in the Creed of the Council of Philippopolis in 343, the Macrostich in 345, and in the Creeds of the Council of Sirmium in 351 and 359, of Nike in 359 and of Constantinople in 360; then we find it in the Creeds of Niceta of Remesiana, Leporius of Trèves, Caesarius of Arles and in all the various versions of T.

Descendit ad inferna. For the earlier history of this phrase see p. 105. Besides Rufinus we find *ad inferos* in the *Quicumque Vult* and the Bangor Antiphonary; *ad infernum* in Venantius Fortunatus; *ad inferna* in the Gallican and Bobbio Missals and Priminius and most provincial forms of T. *Ad inferos* was most probably preferred at Rome because of the occurrence of *Unde et memores sumus...Christi Filii Tui Domini Dei nostri...ab inferis resurrectionis* in the canon of the Gregorian Sacramentary.

The three phrases *descendit ad inferna, resurrexit vivus* and *ascendit victor* would seem to be closely connected. The doctrine of the Descent into Hades is associated by Cyril of Alexandria with the delivery thence of the patriarchs, and this was often understood to be involved in the meaning of the phrase in later

---

1 Canisius, *Lectiones Antiquae*, i. pp. 785, 788, 790.

times. Thus in *Sim.* we find: *Sicut Ipse tertia die resurrexit [a mortuis facta praeda in inferno et vivus exit de sepulchro.*

In the Creed of Niceta *vivus* is probably drawn from 1 Pet. iii. 18, *vivificatus autem in spiritu. Vivus a mortuis* occurs also in a Creed of Aquileia (or Udine ?), in the Spanish Creeds, Ildefonsus of Toledo (*c.* 660), Etherius and Beatus (785) and in the Mozarabic Liturgy.

Catholic is a common epithet of the Church in Eastern Creeds, and occurs as early as the Creed of the *Dair Balaizah* papyrus. In the province of Antioch we find it in the *Apostolic Constitutions*, and Charisius of Philadelphia, then in Niceta and Jerome, then in Faustus of Riez, and Caesarius of Arles.

Sanctorum communionem. With the early history of this phrase we shall deal in the final chapter. It is in the Creeds of Niceta and Jerome, and then in those of Faustus of Riez and Caesarius of Arles.

Vitam aeternam. This or its equivalent is common in Eastern Creeds, going back as early as Cyprian, and it was probably in the Creed of Irenaeus. We find it in the Creed of Marcellus of Ancyra, and further West in those of Niceta and Jerome.

There can, I think, be little doubt that our baptismal Creed with its "only begotten Son" (*unigenitum*) and "everlasting life after death" (*vitam aeternam post mortem*) goes back to Irish versions of T, and was imported into England before the Roman form of the Hour Offices became current. It is difficult to trace the immediate ancestry of "shall come again at the end of the world", but the phrase ἐπὶ συντελείᾳ τοῦ αἰῶνος (cp. Mt. xiii. 39, 40, 49; Heb. ix. 26) occurs in the Creed of the *Apostolic Constitutions* and in the Fourth Formula of the Council of Antioch in 341.

It is impossible to decide where the whole of the Danubian phrases first came to be attached to the already existing baptismal Creed, but we can, I think, say that the amalgamation took place at some point or points on the road from Bobbio to Northern France, and in the quite early years of the seventh century; and if a nearer definition is required, then probabilities would seem to point to the neighbourhood of the Lake of Constance.

APPENDIX

THE LONGER CREED OF THE *EGYPTIAN CHURCH ORDER*

The *Egyptian Church Order* is known to us through various documents, the general relation of which as given by Dom Connolly[1] is as follows:

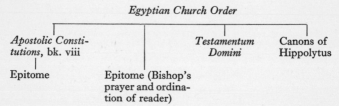

Egyptian Church Order

| *Apostolic Constitutions*, bk. viii | | *Testamentum Domini* | Canons of Hippolytus |

Epitome — Epitome (Bishop's prayer and ordination of reader)

Thus these secondary documents are supplementary authorities for the text in various portions.

The original of the *Egyptian Church Order* is most probably the *Apostolic Tradition* of Hippolytus, written in Greek, but this is no longer extant; it exists, however, in various translations, of which the closest and most accurate is the Latin of the Verona Fragments published by Hauler in 1900. Unfortunately these are only fragments, and we must resort to other documents to fill in the hiatus. There is also a translation (1) in Ethiopic, which may be only an Ethiopic translation of an Arabic translation of a Coptic translation of the original Greek; and (2) in Coptic and (3) in Arabic. The Ethiopic rests upon a Greek text other than that of the Coptic and Arabic, and there are indications that it represents an earlier and better Greek textual tradition than do our present Coptic and Arabic versions, better even in some respects than does the Latin,[2] that is, it lies nearer to the form which must have been the common source of the Ethiopic, Coptic, and Latin versions, and also of *A.C.* viii, and of the *Testamentum Domini*. The three oriental versions have been published by Horner as *The Statutes of the Apostles*; the Canons of Hippolytus are to be found in Turner's *History and Use of Creeds and Anathemas*, p. 92, and all six versions in *J.T.S.* xxv. pp. 134, 135. Our present concern is with the Longer Creed as presented in the four versions of the *Egyptian Church Order*, the *Testamentum*, and the Canons of Hippolytus, with occasional reference to the *Apostolic Constitutions* as a supplementary support.

---

1 *Texts and Studies*, vol. VIII, no. 4, p. 133.
2 Connolly, *op. cit.* p. 5.

The text of the Creed is as follows:

Ethiopic	Arabic and Coptic
Dost thou believe	Dost thou believe (Copt. Thou believest)
in the name of our Lord Jesus Christ,	in Jesus Christ our Lord (Copt. our Lord Jesus Christ),
the only Son of God the Father,	the only Son of God the Father,
that He became man in an incomprehensible miracle	that He became man by an incomprehensible miracle (Copt. by a miracle for our sake in an incomprehensible unity)
by the Holy Spirit	from the (Copt. in His) Holy Spirit
and by Mary the virgin	and (Copt. om.) from Mary the (Copt. holy) virgin
without seed of man,	without seed of man,
and He was crucified in the time of Pontius Pilate,	and was crucified (Copt. for us) in the time of Pontius Pilate,
and He died by His own will for our salvation,	and (Copt. om.) died by His own will to save us withal,
and rose from the dead on the third day,	and rose from the dead on the third day (Copt. om. "from the dead")
and released the captives,	and (Copt. om.) released the captives,
and ascended into the heavens,	and (Copt. om.) ascended into the heavens,
and sat down at the right hand of the Father,	and (Copt. om.) sat at the right hand of the (Copt. His good) Father (Copt. in the height),
and He shall come to judge the living and the dead	and He shall come (Copt. comes again) to judge the living and the dead
at His appearing and His kingdom?	at (Copt. according to) His appearing and His kingdom?
And dost thou believe in the Holy Spirit, the good and the sanctifier,	Dost thou believe (Copt. And thou believest) in the Spirit the holy, the good, the sanctifier (Copt. in the holy good and life-giving Spirit, purifying the universe);
and in the holy Church?	in the holy Church? (Copt. ends)
And dost thou believe the resurrection of the body which shall happen to all men;	And dost thou believe in the resurrection of the body which shall happen to everyone;
and the kingdom of the heavens;	and the kingdom of the heavens;
and eternal judgment?	and eternal judgment?

Latin version (Hauler, p. 110)	Testamentum Domini, ii. 8	Canons of Hippolytus, can. xix
(Credis in Deum Patrem omnipotentem?)	Dost thou believe in God the Father almighty?	Dost thou believe in God the Father almighty?
Credis in Christum Jesum, Filium Dei,	Dost thou believe also in Christ Jesus, the Son of God, who came from the Father, who is of old with the Father,	Dost thou believe in Jesus Christ, the Son of God,

Latin version (Hauler, p. 110)	*Testamentum Domini,* II. 8	Canons of Hippolytus, can. xix
qui natus est de Spiritu Sancto	who was born of Mary the virgin	whom Mary the virgin bore
ex Maria virgine,	through the Holy Spirit,	of the Holy Spirit, who came to save the human race,
et crucifixus sub Pontio Pilato,	who was crucified in the days of Pontius Pilate,	who for us was crucified in the time of Pontius Pilate,
et mortuus est, et sepultus,	and died,	who died,
et resurrexit die tertia vivus a mortuis,	and rose the third day alive from the dead,	and on the third day rose from the dead,
et ascendit in caelis,	and ascended to heaven,	ascended to heaven,
et sedit ad dexteram Patris,	and sat at the right hand of the Father,	sat at the right hand of the Father,
venturus judicare vivos et mortuos?	and cometh to judge the living and the dead?	and will come again to judge the living and the dead?
Credis in Spiritu Sancto;	Dost thou believe also in the Holy Spirit	Dost thou believe in the Holy Spirit, the Paraclete, who emanates from the Father and the Son?
Et sanctam ecclesiam; Et carnis resurrectionem?	in the holy Church?	

The existence of this Creed might be fatal to the theory stated above, but only on one condition, namely, that it could be shown that this Creed was the official interrogatory Creed of the Church of Rome in the time of Hippolytus. But this must be held to be at least doubtful. It is by no means demonstrable even in regard to the whole rite of which it forms part. Of this Fr. Trenholme writes: "The Liturgy in his book is his own, rather than that of the Roman Church of the time, so far as to its detailed language. But its general order and chief formulae are those of the universal Church in the first ages; the skeleton whereon all the historic Liturgies seem to have been subsequently built up."[1]

So E. C. R(atcliff) writing in the *Guardian*, No. 4810, p. 86, says: "All the connexions of the *Apostolic Tradition* are with the East...and the earliest of them with Syria. Though the treatise was composed with reference to the circumstances of the Roman Christian Community early in the third century, one is led to wonder whether Hippolytus belonged to, and drew his adherents from, some group of Christians which, although Roman in domicile, was oriental in origin, connexions, and traditions. That oriental groups existed, and that Christians in Rome still fell into groups according to their *lieu d'origine* at the end of the second century, is not a novel idea to readers of La Piana" (*Harvard Theological Review*, XVIII. pp. 201–277).

[1] *Church Quarterly Review*, XCIII, Oct. 1921, p. 74.

Dom Gregory Dix, the latest editor, writes: "The actual phrasing of the prayers, though not their purport and outline, is manifestly his own composition....But...there remains a much larger part of the contents...which represents the mind and practice not of St Hippolytus only but of the whole Catholic Church of the second century." "The Latin version made about or after A.D. 400 is evidence of a circulation in the West, but there are very strong grounds for attributing a *Syrian* origin to the codex from which it was made, if not to the translator himself" (*Apostolic Tradition*, pp. xliv, xlv; cp. p. liv). And he thinks that the *Epiclesis* is an interpolation in the Latin and Ethiopic versions (p. 79).

Dom Capelle (*Recherches de Théologie*, Ap. 1933, pp. 146 ff.) has shown that each of the extant authorities makes independently a considerable addition in the baptismal rite in order to bring it into line with fourth-century practice.

Of Hippolytus himself but little is known. He would appear to have been of Eastern origin, and by modern writers has been reckoned: (1) Bishop of Portus, (2) Bishop of the Greek-speaking congregation at Rome alongside of the bishop of the Latin-speaking congregation, (3) an anti-pope. In any event he may have had a Creed of a longer and more Eastern type than the official Roman Creed. In later times he was so completely ignored by the Roman Church that Pope Damasus had no authentic information about him. And if the Creed was simply the Creed of his followers, and if the Church of Rome let him drop out of its historical recollection, it may equally well have ignored his Creed. But this possibility being once granted, the Creed of the Egyptian Church Order ceases *ipso facto* to be an obstacle to the view that the official interrogatory Creed of the Roman Church was that of the Gelasian Sacramentary.

And the Creed, even in the comparatively simple form given in the Hauler fragments, seems far more akin to Eastern baptismal Creeds than to those of the West.

Thus *Filium Dei*, which is certified by its appearance in the *Testamentum Domini* and the Canons of Hippolytus, instead of *Filium Ejus* which is the Roman form, occurs in the Creed of Jerusalem, the Nicene Creed, the First Formula of Antioch, and the Creeds of Sirmium, Nike, and Constantinople. The order *Christus Jesus* can hardly be accidental, though even in the Hauler fragments the order varies: "Pater Domini nostri Jesu Christi" (pp. 103, 108, 110); "per puerum tuum Christum Jesum" (pp. 105, 107, 109, 115); "in nomine J.C." (p. 111); "in Christo Jesu" (pp. 111, 112); "in Domino J.C." (p. 113). It looks as though Hippolytus had no feeling on the matter either way, but *Christus Jesus* is in no Western Creed up to and including the time of Leo except that of Aquileia, a city specially exposed to Eastern influences.

The phrases *de Spiritu Sancto et Maria virgine*, and *sub Pontio Pilato* we have already discussed; it is sufficient here to say that they first come to light in the Creed of Auxentius of Cappadocia, and seem to be imported into the West from the East. *Mortuus*, again, is in the Eastern Creeds of the *Apostolic Constitutions*; Macarius of Egypt, Sirmium, Nike, and Constantinople, Jerome, and Niceta; but not in any Western Creed before the time of Leo. *Vivus*, which is certified by the *Testamentum Domini*, appears first in Niceta of Remesiana, then in Martin of Bracara, a native of Pannonia, in the Mozarabic Liturgy, in several Spanish Creeds, Ildefonsus, Etherius, Beatus, and in the Creed of Theodulf of Orleans, who was of Spanish extraction. It adds no new fact to the resurrection, but may very possibly be connected with the "Harrowing of Hell" (cp. 1 Pet. iii. 19; Jn. v. 21; 1 Cor. xv. 45). Its place in the Creed of Jerome is taken by "trod down the sting of death", and in the oriental versions of the *Egyptian Church Order* by "released the captives". *In caelis* instead of *caelos* may be a mere copyist's error; if not, it is paralleled in the Creed of Auxentius of Cappadocia, and in the Creed of Sirmium as given by Hilary of Poitiers, while *in caelo* occurs in the Creed of Philippopolis in 343. For *sedit*, however, this plea will not avail. All the versions have "sat"; but the Western provincial Creeds, and the later Roman Creed, have *sedet* consistently; καθίσας, however, occurs in the Creed of Cyril of Jerusalem, the Fourth Creed of Antioch, the Creed of Nike in 359, and the Confession of Theodore of Mopsuestia; καθεσθείς in the *Apostolic Constitutions*, the Second Creed of Antioch (Athanasius also gives it in the Fourth instead of καθίσας), and in the Creed of Sirmium in 351.

We may discount these facts as we please, but we cannot resist the impression either that the Creed is Eastern, or at least that in its present form it has been worked over in the East.

And the non-Roman character of the Creed is no less apparent if we compare it with Western interrogatory Creeds.

The Creeds of the martyrologies are probably none of them authentic, but taken together they afford an indication of the general length to which Creeds of the reputed dates might be expected to run. The second member is as follows:

Palmatius, *c.* 220	Stephanus, 259	Venustianus, 303
Et in Jesum Christum, Filium Ejus? Qui natus est de Spiritu Sancto ex Maria virgine?	Et in Jesum Christum Dominum nostrum?	Et in Jesu Christo, Filio Ejus? Et in Eum qui passus est et resurrexit? Et in Eum qui ascendit in caelos, et iterum venturus est judicare vivos et mortuos et saeculum per ignem? Et in adventu Ipsius et regnum Ejus?
An unknown author Hahn³, p. 36 in Dominum Christum, Filium Ejus unicum, Dominum, natum ex Maria virgine, passum, **et sepultum?**		

Even that of Venustianus, in spite of its curious addition of *et saeculum per ignem* and *et in adventu Ipsius et regnum Ejus*, is simpler in structure than the Creed of Hippolytus, and the others are very much more brief.

And with these compare:

de Sacramentis	Maximus of Turin	Gelasian Sacramentary
In Dominum nostrum	In Jesum Christum,	Et in Jesum Christum,
Jesum Christum,	Filium Ejus,	Filium Ejus unicum,
et in crucem Ejus?	qui natus est	Dominum nostrum,
	de Spiritu Sancto et	natum,
	Maria virgine?	et passum?
	(*al.* conceptus est...et	
	natus est ex)	

If any of these, or any combination of them, represents the Roman tradition, then the "Creed of Hippolytus" may conceivably be his, but can hardly be regarded as the official interrogatory Creed of the Roman Church.

Finally there is a third test, though a somewhat unfair one, namely to compare the Creed of Hippolytus with the *Declaratory* Creed of Rome in the fourth century. Even by this test its claim must be disallowed. It is of approximately the same length, but

	H.	R.
(1)	Christum Jesum *has been altered to*	Jesum Christum
(2)	Dei *has been altered to*	Ejus
(3)		Passus *has been added*
(4)		Mortuus *has been omitted*
(5)	Resurrexit die tertia	
	has been altered to	tertia die resurrexit
(6)	Vivus *has been added*	
(7)	(in caelis *has been altered to*	in *or* ad caelos)
(8)	Sedit *has been altered to*	Sedet
(9)		Inde *has been added*
(10)	In Spiritu Sancto (cp. Rufinus)	
	has been altered to	In Spiritum Sanctum
(11)		Remissionem peccatorum *has been added*

Additions, of course, may be normal, but if we omit nos. (3) and (10) and grant that (7) is a mere scribal error in Hippolytus, we still have seven variations, all small and all pointless, and it is precisely such variations for no assignable reason that do not seem to occur.

To sum up. It is quite conceivable that Hippolytus may have adopted a Creed suitable to his own temperament and to that of the mixed congregation over whom he seems to have held sway. The omission of *remissionem peccatorum* may be an authentic touch. Even so, the Creed looks too long for his time. It may have been worked over and elaborated, but to allow this is to give away any case that may be rested on it. As it stands, it abounds in Easternisms; it is out of relation to any Western interrogatory Creed of which we have knowledge; and it would need much adaptation before we could regard it as the parent of the Roman Declaratory Creed of a later time. On the other hand, if we suppose that the Gelasian Creed, with the mere alteration of *Credis* to *Credo*, served a second purpose, then it, and the Creed of Ambrose, and that of the Textus Receptus, are seen to stand in a regular order of succession, the shorter and earlier form being in each case verbally embodied in the later and longer.

[One other point may perhaps be mentioned concerning the whole *Ordo*. After Dom Connolly's exposition it would seem impossible to doubt that it is connected with Rome, but it is noticeable that while it mentions bishops, presbyters, deacons, confessors, widows, readers, virgins, subdeacons and exorcists (? "gifts of healing", but cp. *Apostl. Const.* VIII. 26) it omits acolytes. Under Pope Cornelius (251–253) there were forty-two acolytes on the staff of the Roman Church, which suggests that by his time they were an old established institution. The name points to a time when the liturgical language of Rome was still Greek and therefore to a date earlier than Cornelius. Their main function was to carry the *fermentum* from the Pope's Mass to the other congregations in Rome. This practice would seem to be earlier than the time of Irenaeus (Euseb. *H.E.* v. 24), but of course it does not follow that it then fell to the lot of the acolytes. The original institution of acolytes may have gone back to Pope Victor (188–198). In the biography of Victor in the *Liber Pontificalis* we read: "Hic fecit sequentes cleros", not followed by any other indication. Harnack concludes: "So mag auch die Nachricht, dass unter Viktor die Akoluthen zuerst aufgetaucht sind, auf guter Ueberlieferung beruhen" (*Mission*, 4th ed., 1924, p. 863, note). The absence of acolytes from the full list of church officers given by Hippolytus suggests that the organization of the community over which he presided differed from that of the official Church of Rome. Possibly under Hippolytus a similar function was performed by deacons (cp. Just. Mart. *Ap.* 1. 65).]

CHAPTER XI

THE TITLE *SYMBOLUM APOSTOLORUM.*
THE HISTORY OF A LEGEND

THE legend in its latest and fullest form is that the Twelve Apostles met together in Jerusalem before departing on their several missions, and there drew up a Creed of twelve clauses to which each Apostle contributed one, and that this Creed was brought by St Peter to Rome, and thence distributed over Italy, Gaul, Spain, Africa, Sicily, and the adjacent islands by bishops consecrated by him or his successors.

If the title is used in this sense, it is as much a misnomer as that of the so-called "Apostolic" Constitutions.

It has, of course, an element of truth. The name is first found in the fourth century, when the Creed was less full than it is now, but could yet be divided into twelve clauses, and in this form each clause in it could be shown to be apostolic by reference to the New Testament. Moreover, the same form of Creed ran, with slight local variations, over all these countries, and we may add to them Illyria and Asia Minor. Of Macedonia, Greece and Mesopotamia at this time we know too little to pronounce with certainty, while Egypt seems to have had a Creed containing much the same matter, but with a greater variety of form and of independent origin. Nevertheless this baptismal Creed was so widespread that it might almost be called catholic, and it would be a natural inference that it was primitive and apostolic also.

Beyond these two facts the rest is fiction; and the motive for inventing and advocating this fiction, besides the mere pleasure of story-telling, would seem to have been religious rivalry, first between Antioch and Alexandria, and latterly between Rome and Constantinople. And this rivalry manifested itself in much the same form in both places. The Church of Antioch, as we know from the Acts, was originated by refugees who fled from persecution after the death of St Stephen. News of this spreading of

the Gospel came to the ears of the Church at Jerusalem, and
they sent forth Barnabas to take charge of the movement, as they
had sent Peter and John to Samaria; and Barnabas brought Saul
from Tarsus to Antioch. The Church of Antioch could therefore
lay claim to have been founded, or at least organized, by Apostles,
namely by St Barnabas and St Paul, and, as we know from the
Epistle to the Galatians, St Peter had also paid a visit there. On
the other hand the Church of Alexandria had traditionally been
founded by St Mark, who was not himself an Apostle, but the
disciple of St Peter. Antioch could not rival Alexandria in point
of magnificence or of population, nor had it so distinguished a
school of theologians as that successively headed by Athenagoras (?), Pantaenus, Clement, and Origen, but it could lay
claim to a superiority, if it so desired, as being the place where
the Apostles had resided and where two of them had organized
the Church. But this was not enough to satisfy local pride or
vanity. The direct and unquestionable superior of St Mark was
St Peter; and so first the name of St Barnabas, who brought St
Paul to Antioch, is omitted; then St Peter and St Paul are
coupled together; then St Paul's name is omitted; and finally
St Peter, the master of St Mark, is claimed as the sole founder.

By the time of the rise of Constantinople this ecclesiastical
rivalry was of old standing and tended to throw Constantinople
and Antioch together as against Alexandria, which was aiming
at a supremacy over the whole Christian East. Hence we get the
endeavour on the part of Alexandria to thrust Maximus the
Cynic on to the throne of Constantinople, the persecution of
Chrysostom, who came from Antioch, by Theophilus, the
domination of Cyril at the Council of Ephesus in 431, which
condemned Nestorius—also from Antioch—and of Dioscurus at
the later Council of 449 which condemned Flavian of Constantinople.

But the rise of Constantinople had a further effect. Ecclesiastical superiority had naturally tended to fall to the sees of the
greatest civil importance, and it was on the ground of its civil
status that the Councils of 381 and 451 gave to Constantinople
a position second only to the elder Rome. Rome retaliated in

much the same way as Antioch; it dropped out the name of
St Paul as one of its joint founders, and put forward a claim to
submission grounded on the supremacy of St Peter. But the
"blatant worldliness" of the claim of Constantinople at which
Rome raised up its hands in pious horror reverberated beyond
Italy. In the East and in Africa the grouping of dioceses was
already more or less settled; but in Gaul, in opposition to claims
based on the importance of the city, there grew up a custom of
ranking sees according to the antiquity of their foundation.
Something of this kind is indeed to be seen in the East also,
where the autonomy of the Church of Cyprus was secured by
the opportune discovery of the body of St Barnabas; but in
Gaul we get put forward fictitious claims to foundation if not by
Apostles, yet by their direct disciples, and a bid made for the
support of Rome by a pretence of their mission either from
St Peter or from Clement, claims which Rome not unnaturally
tended to regard with a favourable eye; and in the last resort the
great schism between the East and the West was in origin not so
much a question of doctrinal differences as of rival jurisdictions,
and thus ecclesiastical ambition and jealousy has led to the
falsification of history and to a divided Christendom.

All this is illustrated by the story of how the Baptismal Creed
came to be regarded as the composition of the twelve Apostles.

As long as any of these was alive no such jealousy could take
effect, while the early heresies tended to compel the Church to
present a united front; but after their death there was a period
when their personal influence was withdrawn, the canon of
Scripture was as yet only in process of formation, and baptismal
declarations were quite short—of three, or at the most, of six
clauses. Hence, as against heretical innovations, the appeal lay
to the apostolical tradition of which each bishop was in his own
see the official guardian. He was supposed to have received it
from his own predecessor, to maintain it unchanged, and to
transmit it to his successor; and so by regression it was possible
to arrive either at an Apostle or at some one appointed by him.
If, then, amid false teachings of all kinds, anyone wished to learn
the genuine apostolic tradition, he would do best to have recourse

to churches of an apostolic foundation; there the tradition would be least subject to adulteration; those churches were the doctrinal experts, and as such they possessed an *auctoritas* superior to that of others. "Run over the apostolic churches", says Tertullian, "in which the very thrones of the Apostles preside over their own places. Is Achaia near you? you have Corinth; if you are not far from Macedonia, you have Philippi, you have the Thessalonians; if you travel into Asia you have Ephesus; but if you are near to Italy you have Rome and from Rome (*unde*) this *auctoritas* is at hand for us also [in Africa]" (*de Praescr.* c. 36).

It is to be noticed that Tertullian does not mention Antioch, where at least St Peter had resided, but does mention Ephesus, the reputed home of St John, and that all the other churches, except Rome, are wholly Pauline.

But if churches founded by an Apostle possessed a preeminence, Rome had a *potentior principalitas*. It had been founded by the "two most illustrious Apostles Peter and Paul", and in it was to be learnt the consentient tradition of the whole Christian world, because there Christians from all parts were bound to meet (Irenaeus, *adv. Haer.* III. 3). Up to this point we have an appeal to the apostolic faith, but not so far to an apostolic Creed.

Irenaeus takes it for granted that the mention of St Paul as well as St Peter would be gratifying to Rome. So did Ignatius before him. Writing to the Romans (c. 4) he says: "I do not order you as though I were a Peter or a Paul; they were Apostles, I am a convict." Here, similarly, Ignatius regards the two Apostles as shedding on Rome a double glory, but he hints also that there is a common link between himself and his see of Antioch on the one side, and his correspondents on the other, in that both Apostles had taught in each of the two cities. This hint becomes plain if we compare the letter to the Romans written by Dionysius of Corinth (*ap.* Euseb. *H.E.* II. 25): "You have thus by such an admonition bound together the planting of Peter and Paul at Rome and at Corinth. For both of them when they had planted us in our Corinth gave the like teaching." Here also Dionysius takes it for granted that the mention of both the Apostles would be gratifying to the feelings of the Romans, and that the fact that the Churches of both Rome and Corinth had alike been founded and instructed by them created a common tie between them. But in Dionysius we get a stage further, for while St Peter was certainly at Antioch, it is only from the mention of a party of Cephas in St Paul's First Epistle to the Corinthians (i. 12, iii. 22) that it is possible to infer that he was ever at Corinth, and such an inference is most probably false, while it is certain that the foundation of the Church there was solely the work of St Paul (1 Cor. iv. 15).

The earliest mention of any residence of St Peter at Antioch, beyond that made in the Epistle to the Galatians and the hint in Ignatius, is in Origen (*Hom.* v. *in Luc.* ed. Lomm. v. p. 104): "I mean Ignatius the second bishop of Antioch after Peter." Here Origen must not be taken to imply that St Peter was the first local bishop of Antioch, but that he consecrated the first bishop, Euodius, whom Ignatius succeeded, and so was the second.

The *Clementine Homilies* (xx. 23) and *Recognitions* (x. 68 ff.), merely bring St Peter to Antioch and leave him there; but the previous narrative of his journeys is so fantastic that this evidence even for such a visit is entirely worthless. Eusebius in his *History* (III. 36) gives the same account as Origen, that Ignatius was the second bishop in succession from Peter, reckoning Euodius as the first; but in his *Chronicle* (Ann. Abr. 2058 = Claudius 2) he has, "Peter the Apostle when as the first he had founded the Church of Antioch". The idea that St Peter was the founder of the Church at Antioch seems to run clean contrary to the narrative of the Acts, and in any case Eusebius's list of Antiochene bishops is probably as unreliable as his corresponding list for Jerusalem (on which see Turner, *J.T.S.* 1. pp. 529 ff.).

The *Apostolic Constitutions* (vii. 46) says: "Of Antioch Euodius ordained by me, Peter, and Ignatius by Paul"; Pseudo-Ignatius (*ad Magn.* 10): "In Antioch the disciples were called Christians, Paul and Peter founding the Church"; and (*ad Ant.* 7): "Ye have been the disciples of Paul and Peter....Keep in remembrance Euodius your deservedly-blessed pastor, into whose hands the government over you was first entrusted by the Apostles." In both cases St Paul is placed before St Peter, showing some regard for historical truth.

The *Liber Pontificalis* as restored by Duchesne (p. 51) and in the later recension (p. 118) gives to St Peter a seven years episcopate at Antioch, as also does Gregory the Great (*Ep.* vii. 40); the Felician abridgement gives him ten years. Such a tenure is in conflict not merely with the Acts, but also with the Roman tradition of a twenty-five years episcopate there, which is given by the Eusebian *Chronicle* (Ann. Abr. 2058), the "Index" or "Leonine" list, and the "Liberian" list, a dating which would seem to be well established in the third century, since it is found also in the Syriac *Teaching of Addai.*

We note that in the Acts we have St Barnabas and St Paul and a short visit by St Peter; in Ignatius, St Peter and St Paul with a probable reference to their being both together at Antioch; in Pseudo-Ignatius, St Paul and St Peter; in Origen a mention of St Peter alone but not as the first on the list of bishops of Antioch; in Eusebius St Peter as the founder of the Church there; in Gregory and the *Liber Pontificalis* a seven years episcopate of St Peter at Antioch; in the Felician abridgement a ten years episcopate. This growth in definiteness of statement and length of tenure of office as we get further away in time is sufficient to warn us that we are here dealing with a legend; and, with the letter of Dionysius before us, we can say with some confidence that in all probability the sole foundation of the whole story is the mention of St Peter in St Paul's Epistle to the Galatians.

To the Antiochene legend we have a close parallel at Rome. As we have seen, Irenaeus says, "that very great and very ancient and universally known Church which was founded and established at Rome by the most glorious Apostles Peter and Paul" (*adv. Haer.* III. ii. 2), and similarly in the next section, "The blessed Apostles having founded and builded the Church, committed the ministry of the episcopate to Linus...and his successor Anacletus; and after him in the third place from the Apostles, the bishopric is allotted to Clement."

Tertullian (*c.* 200) writes in a similar strain, though he makes Clement and not Linus the first bishop. After describing how the apostolic Churches, when they give an account of their beginnings, are wont to show by the list of their bishops "that their much-venerated first bishop had for his ordainer (*auctor*) and predecessor (*antecessor*) some one of the Apostles or apostolic men", he gives instances: "the Church of Smyrna relates that Polycarp was placed there by John, and the Church of Rome that Clement was in like manner ordained by Peter" (*de Praescr.* c. 32).

Similarly Epiphanius (*Panar. Haer.* xxvii. 6), probably quoting from Hegesippus, says: "At Rome Peter and Paul were the first, being both apostles and bishops; then Linus, then Cletus, then Clement, who was the contemporary of Peter and Paul. He was appointed bishop by St Peter during their lifetime."

Epiphanius tries to reconcile the traditions about Clement by suggesting that Clement was ordained by St Peter, that he at first declined the episcopate, but that he was pressed to take it up after the death of Linus and Cletus. The *Apostolic Constitutions*, as we saw, makes Linus to have been consecrated by St Paul, and Clement after Linus's death by St Peter as second bishop.

Tertullian's account receives a strange though partial confirmation. In the *Datiana Historia Ecclesiae Mediolanensis*, a book compiled by Datius, Bishop of Milan about 536, it is stated that Barnabas, after being appointed with St Paul as Apostle to the Gentiles (Gal. ii. 9), in the fourteenth year after the crucifixion (i.e. according to the chronology of the book A.D. 47) and after working with St Paul for some time, "in the first year of Claudius [i.e. A.D. 42] eight years after Christ's ascension, sailed for Rome, where, as the first Apostle to preach in Rome, he converted Clement". Here it is obvious that the chronology contradicts itself, but A.D. 47 is a very probable date for the departure of Barnabas and Paul from Antioch to Cyprus. If we add eight years to this date instead of to the date of the Ascension, we arrive at A.D. 55, the first year of *Claudius* Nero. The conversion of Clement by St Barnabas appears also in the *Clementine Recognitions* (i. 7), where St Barnabas is brought to Rome apparently solely for this purpose, and as the *Recognitions* is written to magnify the authority and orthodoxy of St Peter, and the introduction of St Barnabas, who is never mentioned again, seems wholly gratuitous, this is probably an authentic touch. Moreover, St Paul (1 Cor. ix. 6) would seem to imply that St Barnabas had been at Corinth, since he speaks of him as well as of himself as labouring with his own hands, as though the Corinthians had witnessed it, and he may have gone to Corinth on his way to Rome; but the tradition that he was sent from Rome by St Peter to be the Apostle of Northern Italy seems devoid of any foundation.

Pseudo-Ignatius (*ad Trall.* vii. 4) says that Linus served St Paul as his minister, Anencletus and Clement served St Peter.

Rufinus, in the Preface to the *Clementine Recognitions*, suggests that Linus and Cletus were St Peter's suffragans during his life-time, and Clement his successor after his death.

So far we seem to have a joint apostolate of St Peter and St Paul at Rome, but of neither, strictly speaking, a localized episcopate; but by the fourth century the tradition of a twenty-five years episcopate of St Peter at Rome is firmly established and St Paul's name is dropped.

Professor Turner (*J.T.S.* XVIII. 115) suggests that the origin of the tradition of St Peter's twenty-five years episcopate at Rome is to be sought in the desire of Christian scholars and antiquaries to effect a complete scheme of succession from the Ascension to their own day; for twelve years our Lord had commanded the Apostles to remain at Jerusalem; for twenty-five years St Peter, transferring himself to "another place" (Acts xii. 17), lived at Rome, and the term of the succeeding bishops was reckoned from the time of his martyrdom; but this supposes the Crucifixion to have taken place in 29 instead of 33 as has recently been decided by the Pope and is all but certain on other grounds; and if this were all, there would seem no good reason for dropping out the name of St Paul from the Roman and the names of St Barnabas and St Paul from the Antiochene list, and some

additional motive must be sought. At Antioch we may say with
some conviction that this motive was the desire for a "*potentior
principalitas*".

It may be a mere coincidence that at the same time that
Antioch seems to have been endeavouring to obtain for itself a
tradition of the highest possible apostolicity, there were being
issued from it, or from its neighbourhood, a series of documents
all claiming to be "apostolic"; the *Didascalia of the Apostles* in
the third century, and the *Apostolic Constitutions* and the
Apostolic Church Order in the fourth. All these assert or imply
a meeting of the Apostles at Jerusalem (other than the Council
of Acts xv), and in the *Didascalia* we find them apparently
drawing up some form of a profession of faith, while the formal
Creed in the *Apostolic Constitutions* is undoubtedly based on the
Creed of Antioch. It is not asserted that the Creed so compiled
was brought to Antioch by St Peter, its bishop, but this is an
obvious inference, and in the fourth century it is definitely stated
that he brought it to Rome.

In the *Didascalia*, cxxiv, we read: "All we the twelve Apostles
came together at Jerusalem, and took thought what should be
done. And it seemed good to us, being all of one mind (cp.
Acts xv. 25), to write this Catholic Didascalia. And we have
established and set down therein that you worship God Almighty
and Jesus Christ and the Holy Spirit; that you use the holy
Scriptures, and believe in the resurrection of the dead; and that
you make use of all His creatures with thanksgiving; and that
men should marry."

A somewhat similar account is to be found in the *Apocalypse
of Peter* (Mingana, *Woodbrooke Studies*, Fasc. 8 *sub fin*.): "All
the Apostles gathered together in the Metropolis where John
preached his Gospel. There each one of the Apostles presented
the book of his profession of faith to Peter, who approved of it
and sanctioned it. Clement sealed the books with the seal of each
Apostle, beginning with the seal of Peter."

And in the *Contendings of the Apostles* (Budge, II. pp. 520,
521): "After all these mysteries had been revealed to me
[Clement] the disciples came together in the great and holy city

of Jerusalem...and there the beloved John preached the preaching of the Gospel. And when my master, Peter, had committed
his faith to his book and had sealed it with his seal, all the
disciples who were in Rome did likewise. Then there arrived
also the books of the disciples who were afar off in which were
written their faiths, and my master Peter read them and found
them to be right and perfect and found that all the disciples were
agreed as to the right faith. Then they set to them as their chief
seal the seal of my master Peter...and at the end of the seals
followed the seal of me, Clement the sinner."

Our next stage is Cassian, who though he wrote in the West,
and at a much later date, c. 429, gives the Antiochene tradition:
"For, as you know, the creed (*symbolus*) gets its name from
being a collection (*collatio*). For what the Greeks call σύμβολος
is in Latin termed 'collatio'. But it is a collection because when
the faith of the whole catholic law was collected together by the
Apostles of the Lord, all those matters which are spread over the
whole body of the sacred writings with immense fulness in detail, were collected together in sum in the matchless brevity of
the Creed." "The Creed, then,...of which we have given the
text above, though it is the creed of all the churches, since the
faith of all is but one, is yet specially that of the Church and city
of Antioch." (*c. Nest.* vi. 3, 6.)

Cassian is undoubtedly right in claiming that our "Apostles'"
Creed belonged peculiarly to the Church of Antioch. It spread
thence by way of the Danube and the imperial road from Constantinople over Moesia and Illyria, and Northern Italy, Gaul
and Spain, being grafted on to the local creed wherever that had
preceded it. We notice also that a second root of the legend is to
be found in the confusion between the Greek σύμβολον, *symbolum*,
a countersign or watchword, and συμβολή, *collatio*, a joint contribution, but even so *collatio* need not imply that each Apostle
contributed one clause; it might equally be used for a com-
pendium of Christian doctrine. And it is in this sense that the
name *symbolum* would seem to be used by Niceta of Remesiana
and Faustus of Riez. Niceta says: "Always keep the agreement
which you made with the Lord, that is this *symbolum*....The

words indeed are few, but it contains all the mysteries. Out of
the whole of Scripture these have been briefly collected"
(*de Symb.* 13).

Faustus of Riez says: "Among the ancients *symbola* were so
called because friends collected together made a combination of
their substance for customary feasts....So the Fathers of the
Churches also, careful for the salvation of the peoples, collected
together from the different books of Scripture testimonies preg-
nant with divine mysteries...and this they named *symbolum*"
(*Hom.* i, ed. Caspari, *Anecdota* I. p. 315).

Our next stopping place is Rufinus of Aquileia, who had been
much in the East. He gives both the meanings of *symbolum*.
"Being therefore on the eve of departing from one another...
being met together...they [the Apostles] compose...this brief
formulary, each contributing his several sentence to one common
summary....To this formulary they gave the name *symbolum*,
for *symbolum* in Greek answers to both *indicium* [a watchword]
and *collatio* in Latin" (*de Symb.* c. 2).

Somewhat earlier in date, though Rufinus is giving a legend
which runs back before *c.* 400, when he wrote, is Ambrose of
Milan, and here for the first time we meet with the title *Symbolum Apostolorum*. Writing to Pope Siricius in 389 he says:
"Let credence be given to the *symbol of the Apostles* which the
Roman Church always keeps and preserves inviolate", where
"inviolate" (*intemeratum*) is a reproach against the Church of
Aquileia for having added to it. And in the *Explanatio Symboli
ad Initiandos*, which in the best MS. is notes of an instruction
almost certainly delivered by him, we are given the precise phrase
in the Creed of Aquileia which moved his wrath, the addition of
"invisible and impassible" after "God the Father almighty".
Here, too, we find the same story as in Rufinus. "The word
symbolum is Greek, in Latin it is *collatio*....So the holy Apostles
coming together made a breviary of the faith...they made the
symbol in short form....So as there were twelve Apostles, there
are also twelve clauses."

But here we come on a further statement: "Now this is the
symbol which the Roman Church holds, where Peter the first of

the Apostles had his see, and brought thither their common sentence" (*sententiam*); and it would seem to be implied that it was brought to Milan by St Barnabas, who, as we have seen, according to the tradition of Milan and Brescia, was sent to Northern Italy by St Peter.

The baselessness of the whole story is manifest, for we have several Creeds of the second century: the *Epistola Apostolorum*, and the Marcosian parody from Asia Minor, the Dair Balaizah papyrus, and the Shorter Creed of the *Egyptian Church Order*, none of which have more than six clauses. But we have not yet finished. If St Peter brought the Creed to Rome and sent it by St Barnabas to Milan, why should he not also send it to Gaul, Spain, Sicily and the Islands and Africa? "Precisely", says Pope Innocent I. "It is evident that in all Italy, Gaul, Spain, Africa and the adjacent islands no one has founded churches except those whom the venerable Apostle Peter or his successors have constituted bishops" (*Letter to Decentius* in 416), and of course they would have carried with them the Roman Creed.

As regards Gaul, Gregory of Tours (*Hist. Franc.* I. 28) says: "At the time seven men consecrated as bishops were sent into Gaul to preach, as we read in the Passion of the holy martyr Saturninus. It is there written: 'In the consulate of Decius and Gratus [A.D. 250], as is faithfully recorded, the city of Toulouse had already its first and greatest bishop in the holy Saturninus. These are the names of those who were sent: to Tours Bishop Catinus [Gatianus]; to Arles Bishop Trophimus; to Narbonne Bishop Paulus; to Toulouse Bishop Saturninus; to Paris Bishop Dionysius; to Clermont Bishop Stremonius; to Limoges Bishop Martialis.'" This story cannot be trusted. Pope Fabian was martyred on January 20th, 250, and was not succeeded by Cornelius until June 251, the see being vacant for a year and a half; consequently 250 would seem an impossible year. But also in 254 Cyprian writes to Pope Stephen (*Ep.* lxviii) about Marcianus, the then Bishop of Arles, who had become a Novatianist, saying that for some years past (*annis istis superioribus*) the faithful had been allowed to die without communion. This letter carries us back to the beginnings of Novatianism in June 251, and Marcianus had for some years occupied the see and was evidently chief bishop of the province; so for once a legend has post-dated an historical event. The *Acta* of Saturninus, from which Gregory quotes, says nothing of the other six bishops, but about Saturninus himself there were three traditions: the one given by Gregory in his *Historia Francorum*; a second that he was sent by Clement of Rome, which Gregory seems to support in his *Gloria Martyrum* (1. 48), "Saturninus, the martyr, as is alleged, was ordained by the *disciples* of the Apostles and sent to the city of Toulouse"; and a third that he was sent by the Apostles themselves. It is clear that we are here in the land of pure fiction.

Similarly Dionysius is said to have been sent to Paris by Clement (Flavius Lucius Dexter, *Chron.*, Migne, *P.L.* xxx. 1, p. 270), and later he was identified with Dionysius the Areopagite (Venantius Fortunatus, if the poem be his, Migne, *P.L.* LXXXVII. 72, 98). And we get a similar story told of Trophimus; and in this case the motive for the invention is plain. In the middle of the fifth century, as I have already said, the position occupied by Constantinople made it convenient in the West to rank metropolitans not by the political importance of each several province, but by the supposed antiquity of its evangelization. It is probable that Christianity in Gaul started from Marseilles (Duchesne, *Fastes Ép.* 1. pp. 76, 103) and spread thence up the Rhône to Lyons and Vienne, and that Arles was a Christian offshoot from Marseilles. At the end of the fourth century all the bishops of Narbonensis Secunda were consecrated by the Bishop of Marseilles; but Marseilles was in the Provincia Viennensis, so the bishops of Narbonensis asked for a metropolitan of their own. The Council of Turin in 401 decided that nothing was to be changed during the life of the venerable Proculus, Bishop of Marseilles, but that after his death their request should be granted. But Patroclus, Bishop of Arles, the favourite of Constantius, obtained the ear of Pope Zosimus, declaring that Trophimus the Ephesian had been sent to Arles by St Peter from Rome. Zosimus himself does not go quite so far as this, but he censures the Council of Turin for exceeding its rights and acting "against the decrees of the Fathers and the

reverence due to St Trophimus, who was sent as first metropolitan of the city of Arles from this see" (*Ep.* v), and says, "to
which [i.e. Arles] Trophimus the Archbishop was first sent from
this see, from whose fountain all the Gauls received the streams of
faith" (*Ep.* i. 3). And a similar statement is made by the bishops
of the province of Arles to Pope Leo in 450: "For it is known to
all the regions of Gaul, nor is it held unknown to the holy Roman
Church, that the city of Arles first among the Gauls merited to
have St Trophimus as its bishop, sent by the most blessed
Apostle St Peter, and thence the gift of faith and religion was
gradually diffused through the other regions of the Gauls."

This legend is not only baseless; it contradicts the story given
by Gregory of Tours, and the legends of the sending of Saturninus and Dionysius by Clement or by the Apostles. The
motive of Zosimus is plain; he wanted to assert jurisdiction in
Gaul where Papal jurisdiction had hitherto been ineffective, and
so lent a ready ear to Patroclus, and as a matter of fact appointed
him his vicar.

The latest stage is the assignment of each clause of the Creed
to a separate Apostle, and here I shall begin with Brit. Mus. MS.
Royal 2 A xx, because, though the assignment is probably not
before the seventh century, the Creed is of the earlier type. This
MS. gives a Latin translation of the same Creed as that found in
Latin in the *Codex Laudianus*, and in Greek transliterated into
Anglo-Saxon characters in the so-called *Psalter of Aethelstan*.
There can be little doubt that the original of the Creed goes back
to Asia Minor in the fourth century (see above, p. 71), but the
marginal notes are in Anglo-Saxon, and found solely in this
Latin version. Unfortunately the list of Apostles is incomplete
and the Anglo-Saxon notes are so scattered that it is impossible
to decide which clauses are to be referred to each Apostle.
Probably the Anglo-Saxon scribe copied from a Creed of the full
form and had difficulties in attaching the names to a form in
which the last clause, *vitam aeternam*, was missing. The list
omits James the son of Zebedee and Andrew, and has Taltheus,
presumably for Thaddaeus, last but one, instead of Judas or
James; otherwise it agrees with Pseudo-Augustine, *S.* 241.

Of the sermons founded on the *Textus Receptus* of the Creed three follow the order given in Acts i. 13, with two slight exceptions, James John for John James, and Matthias to supply the omission of Judas Iscariot. These are Pseudo-Augustine, *S.* 241, the sermon of Priminius, though this by an obvious error repeats Thomas for Matthias, and the third sermon in the Missal of Bobbio.

The first sermon in Codex Sessorianus 52 follows the order of the Roman Canon, the names being added in the margin. The other sermons, Codex Augiensis ccxxix (Karlsruhe) of the year 821, and Ps.-Aug. *S.* 240, omit St Paul's name after St Peter's and add Matthias at the end. The Karlsruhe MS. also omits Simon the Cananaean but a blank space shows that this was an oversight.

None of these assignments can be earlier than the seventh century; and it is obvious that they all are mere guess-work.

PART II

THE NICENE CREED

Chapter XII

ITS ORIGINAL COMPOSITION

The Creed of Eusebius of Caesarea and of the Council of Nicaea. Its Original Composition. Appendix: The Profession of Faith of the Council of Antioch, 324–325.

THE Nicene Creed, N, was made at the Council of Nicaea in 325; the "homoousian clauses", "that is of the substance of the Father" and "consubstantial with the Father", were new matter which had never appeared in any earlier Creed, nor are they to be found in so many words in Scripture. The history and motive of their insertion can be read in any narrative of the history of the Council of Nicaea and need not be retold here.

The remainder of the Creed was old and drawn from already existing confessions of faith and ultimately from Scripture. As regards its composition there are two extreme theories. The first, which has been often repeated, is that it was based exclusively, or almost exclusively, on the Creed put forward at the Council by Eusebius of Caesarea. The second, which is that of Lietzmann, is that it was independent of the Creed of Caesarea, and based on an unknown Creed of some other see.

Our main authority is the letter sent by Eusebius to his diocese to explain his action at the Council (Theodoret, *H.E.* i. 12; G. p. 182):

> When the formulary had been set forth by us, there was no room to gainsay it; but our beloved Emperor himself was the first to testify that it was most orthodox, and that he coincided in opinion with it; and he exhorted the others to sign it, and to receive all the doctrine it contained, with the single addition of the one word "consubstantial". ...But they, under the excuse of adding the word "consubstantial", made the following formula.

Thus against the former theory Eusebius states that the actual Creed differed from that of Caesarea in many other respects besides the addition of the technical term. These differences are, in fact, manifest by a comparison of the two forms: "Word", "Life from Life", "First-born of all creation", "before all ages", "lived among men" have been omitted; "cometh" has been substituted for "about to come", and "Holy Spirit" for "One Spirit Holy"; and if we compare N, the Creed of the Council of Nicaea, with other Eastern Creeds which have been untouched by it, and with the remaining portions of Creeds from which we have taken out obviously Nicene interpolations, we shall find little in N which is exclusively Caesarean. But Eusebius also asserts that the Creed of Caesarea won the approval of the Emperor, and if so, this might be expected to have influenced in some degree the composition of N. Not exclusively, however, for it is probable that the bishops of other great sees, such as Alexandria, Jerusalem and Antioch, would not be content to have the Creeds of their own dioceses entirely passed over,[1] and it would be wise statesmanship to enlist their sympathy for the result by allowing each to contribute to its formation: moreover, if we look at the text of the Creed this is what they would actually seem to have done. The number of phrases dealing with the Incarnation: "came down, and was incarnate, and was made man" and "for us men and for our salvation", of which "for us" occurs by itself in the Creed of Antioch, and "for our salvation" in those of Caesarea, Auxentius of Cappadocia, and the letter of Marcellus to Pope Julius, suggests that we are dealing with a composition rather than with a single original.

The Creed of Eusebius of Caesarea	The Creed of the Council of Nicaea, N.
Πιστεύομεν εἰς ἕνα Θεόν,	Πιστεύομεν εἰς ἕνα Θεόν,
Πατέρα παντοκράτορα,	Πατέρα παντοκράτορα,
τὸν τῶν ἁπάντων	πάντων
ὁρατῶν τε καὶ ἀοράτων ποιητήν·	ὁρατῶν τε καὶ ἀοράτων ποιητήν·
Καὶ εἰς ἕνα Κύριον Ἰησοῦν Χριστόν,	Καὶ εἰς ἕνα Κύριον Ἰησοῦν Χριστόν,
τὸν τοῦ Θεοῦ Λόγον,	τὸν Υἱὸν τοῦ Θεοῦ,
	γεννηθέντα ἐκ τοῦ Πατρὸς μονογενῆ,
	τουτέστιν ἐκ τῆς οὐσίας τοῦ Πατρός,
Θεὸν ἐκ Θεοῦ, φῶς ἐκ φωτός,	Θεὸν ἐκ Θεοῦ, φῶς ἐκ φωτός.
ζωὴν ἐκ ζωῆς,	
Υἱὸν μονογενῆ, πρωτότοκον πάσης κτίσεως,	

1 See Bright, *Age of the Fathers*, I. pp. 87, 94.

The Creed of Eusebius of Caesarea.

The Creed of the Council of Nicaea, N.

πρὸ πάντων τῶν αἰώνων
ἐκ τοῦ Πατρὸς γεγενημένον,

Θεὸν ἀληθινὸν ἐκ Θεοῦ ἀληθινοῦ,
γεννηθέντα οὐ ποιηθέντα,
ὁμοούσιον τῷ Πατρί,

δι᾽ οὗ καὶ ἐγένετο τὰ πάντα

δι᾽ οὗ τὰ πάντα ἐγένετο,
τά τε ἐν τῷ οὐρανῷ καὶ τὰ ἐν τῇ γῇ,
τὸν δι᾽ ἡμᾶς τοὺς ἀνθρώπους

τὸν διὰ τὴν ἡμετέραν σωτηρίαν
σαρκωθέντα,
καὶ ἐν ἀνθρώποις πολιτευσάμενον,
καὶ παθόντα,
καὶ ἀναστάντα τῇ τρίτῃ ἡμέρᾳ,
καὶ ἀνελθόντα πρὸς τὸν Πατέρα,
καὶ ἥξοντα πάλιν ἐν δόξῃ
κρῖναι ζῶντας καὶ νεκρούς·
Πιστεύομεν καὶ εἰς ἐν Πνεῦμα
Ἅγιον.

καὶ διὰ τὴν ἡμετέραν σωτηρίαν
κατελθόντα καὶ σαρκωθέντα,
ἐνανθρωπήσαντα,
παθόντα,
καὶ ἀναστάντα τῇ τρίτῃ ἡμέρᾳ,
ἀνελθόντα εἰς τοὺς οὐρανούς,
καὶ ἐρχόμενον
κρῖναι ζῶντας καὶ νεκρούς·
Καὶ εἰς τὸ Ἅγιον Πνεῦμα.

The Nicene Anathemas

Τοὺς δὲ λέγοντας· ἦν ποτε ὅτε οὐκ ἦν, καὶ πρὶν γεννηθῆναι
οὐκ ἦν, καὶ ὅτι ἐξ οὐκ ὄντων ἐγένετο, ἢ ἐξ ἑτέρας ὑποστάσεως
ἢ οὐσίας φάσκοντας εἶναι, ἢ κτιστὸν ἢ τρεπτὸν ἢ ἀλλοιωτὸν
τὸν Υἱὸν τοῦ Θεοῦ, ἀναθεματίζει ἡ καθολικὴ ἐκκλησία.

In 1905 E. Schwartz published in the *Nachrichten der kgl. Gesellschaft der Wissenschaften zu Göttingen* a Syriac document from a Paris MS. (*Cod. Par. syr.* 62) which purported to be the letter of a Council held at Antioch in 324. If it is genuine it shows that Eusebius of Caesarea was condemned in that Council for Arianism, but in view of the "great and hieratic synod" to be held in the following year at Ancyra—afterwards transferred by the order of Constantine to Nicaea—the sentence upon him was held over. In that case he would have presented his creed as part of the evidence of his orthodoxy. The synodal letter is addressed in the name of fifty-six bishops to Alexander, Bishop of New Rome [Constantinople]. There is little difficulty in accepting the document from the point of view of the historical situation depicted;[1] any objection turns on the form of confession of faith included in it and the technical terms employed.

1 On this see Burn, *Council of Nicaea*, pp. 12–19.

As the Profession of Faith is not easily accessible, I give it in full in an English translation, italicizing the Nicene terms.

"To believe *in one God the Father almighty*, incomprehensible, *unchangeable and unalterable* [ἄτρεπτον καὶ ἀναλλοίωτον, Nicene anathemas], foreknower and Ruler of all, just and good, *Maker* of heaven and earth and of all that is in them, Lord of the law and prophets and of the New Testament. *And in one Lord Jesus Christ, only begotten Son, begotten not from that which is not* [cp. 1 Cor. i. 28 and the Nicene anathemas] but *from the Father, not as made*, but as offspring properly, but begotten inexpressibly and unspeakably, in what way only the Father who generated and the Son who was generated knows; for no one knoweth the Father but the Son, nor the Son—who ever is and is not [one] who was not before—but the Father [Mt. xi. 27]. For we have learnt from the holy Scriptures that He is the only image [Heb. i. 3]; not, assuredly, as though He were ingenerate from the Father, not by adoption—for it would be impious and blasphemous to say this—but the Scriptures call Him begotten Son properly and truly, so that we also believe Him to be *unchangeable and unalterable*, and that He was not generated nor came to be by volition or supposition, so that He should appear to be *from that which is not*, but as it befits Him to be generated, not—a thing which it is not lawful to think—according to resemblance or nature or mixture of any of the things made by Him, but in a way which passes all understanding or conception or reasoning, we confess Him to have been begotten of the unbegotten *Father, God* the Word, true *light*, righteousness, *Jesus Christ, Lord* and Saviour of all; for He is the image not of the volition or anything else, but of the paternal substance itself [Heb. i. 3]. But this Son, God, Word, also having been born of Mary the mother of God and become *incarnate*, having *suffered* and died, *rose* from the dead, and was *taken up into heaven* and sitteth at the right hand of the Majesty on high [Heb. i. 3], *is coming to judge quick and dead*. And further as also the sacred Scriptures teach to believe both our Saviour and one *Spirit*, one catholic Church, the resurrection of the dead, and the judgement of repaying as each has done in the flesh either good or ill, anathematizing those who say or think or preach that the Son of God is a *creature*, or created or made, and that He is not truly offspring or that *there was when He was not* [Nicene anathemas]."

The genuineness of the document is supported by E. Seeberg (*Die Synode von Antiochien im Jahre* 324–325), who points out that phrases in it were used both by Arius and Alexander of Alexandria (see his letter to Alexander of Constantinople, Theodoret, *H.E.* 1. 3) and go back to Lucian. He lays stress on its ante-Nicene character, an impression which it would be difficult for a later forger to produce, and the absence of the Nicene watch-words, while the particular epithet "theotokos", which might at first arouse suspicion, was used by Origen (*in Deut.* xxii. 23, ed. Delarne, 11. p. 391 A), by Hippolytus, according to Georgius Syncellus (*Chronogr.* p. 219), and later by Eusebius himself, e.g. *Vit. Constant.* iii. 43.

There are many inevitable resemblances between this confession of faith and the letter of Alexander of Alexandria to Alexander of Constantinople, but some of them would suggest that the letter was well known to the Council, e.g. the combination ἄτρεπτος καὶ ἀναλλοίωτος; the quotations from Heb. i. 3 "the very image of His substance" and "sat down on the right hand of the Majesty on high", and from Matt. xi. 27; and the mention of scripture in connexion with the Holy Spirit καθὼς ἡμᾶς αἱ θεῖαι γραφαὶ διδάσκουσιν, ἐν Πνεῦμα Ἅγιον ὁμολογοῦμεν. These agreements suggest that Antioch and Alexandria both influenced the phraseology of the Creed of the Council of Nicaea, and that it was not founded in any exclusive sense on that of Eusebius of Caesarea.

APPENDIX

TEXT OF THE PROFESSION OF FAITH OF THE COUNCIL OF ANTIOCH 324–325, AS TRANSLATED INTO GREEK FROM THE SYRIAC BY E. SCHWARTZ

Πιστεύειν εἰς ἕνα Θεὸν Πατέρα παντοκράτορα, ἀκατάληπτον, ἄτρεπτον, καὶ ἀναλλοίωτον, προνοητὴν καὶ ἡγεμόνα τοῦ παντός, δίκαιον, ἀγαθόν, ποιητὴν οὐρανοῦ καὶ γῆς καὶ πάντων τῶν ἐν αὐτοῖς, νόμου καὶ προφητῶν καὶ τῆς καινῆς διαθήκης Κύριον.

Καὶ εἰς ἕνα Κύριον Ἰησοῦν Χριστόν, Υἱὸν μονογενῆ, γεννηθέντα οὐκ ἐκ τοῦ μὴ ὄντος, ἀλλ᾿ ἐκ τοῦ Πατρός, οὐχ ὡς ποιητόν, ἀλλ᾿ ὡς γέννημα κυρίως, γεννηθέντα δὲ ἀρρήτως καὶ ἀλέκτως, διότι μόνος ὁ Πατὴρ ὁ γεννήσας καὶ ὁ Υἱὸς ὁ γεννηθεὶς ἔγνω, οὐδεὶς γὰρ ἐπιγινώσκεται τὸν Πατέρα εἰ μὴ ὁ Υἱός, οὔτε τὸν Υἱὸν εἰ μὴ ὁ Πατήρ, τὸν ἀεὶ ὄντα καὶ οὐ πρότερον οὐκ ὄντα· εἰκόνα γὰρ Αὐτὸν μόνον ἐκ τῶν ἁγίων γραφῶν μεμαθήκαμεν, οὐ, δῆλον ὅτι, ὡς ἂν παρὰ τοῦ Πατρὸς ἀγέννητον ὄντα· οὐ θέσει, ἀσεβὲς γὰρ καὶ βλάσφημον τοῦτο λέγειν, ἀλλὰ κυρίως καὶ ἀληθῶς Υἱὸν λέγουσιν Αὐτὸν αἱ γραφαὶ γεννηθέντα, ὥστε καὶ πιστεύομεν ἄτρεπτον εἶναι καὶ ἀναλλοίωτον Αὐτὸν οὐδὲ θελήσει ἢ θέσει γεννηθῆναι ἢ γενέσθαι ὥστε ἐκ τοῦ μὴ ὄντος Αὐτὸν εἶναι φαίνεσθαι, ἀλλὰ καθὸ γεννηθῆναι Αὐτὸν εἰκός, οὐδ᾿, ὅπερ οὐ θέμις ἐννοεῖν, καθ᾿ ὁμοίωσιν ἢ φύσιν ἢ μῖξιν οὐδενὸς τῶν δι᾿ Αὐτοῦ γενομένων, ἀλλά, διότι ὑπερβαίνει πᾶσαν ἔννοιαν ἢ διάνοιαν ἢ λόγον, ἐκ τοῦ Πατρὸς τοῦ ἀγεννήτου γεννηθῆναι Αὐτὸν ὁμολογοῦμεν Θεόν, Λόγον, φῶς ἀληθινόν, δικαιοσύνην, Ἰησοῦν Χριστόν, πάντων Κύριον καὶ Σωτῆρα, εἰκὼν γάρ ἐστιν οὐ θελήσεως οὐδ᾿ ἄλλου τινός, ἀλλ᾿ αὐτοῦ τοῦ πατρικοῦ προσώπου.

οὗτος δὲ ὁ Υἱὸς Θεὸς Λόγος καὶ ἐν σαρκὶ
ἐκ τῆς θεοτόκου Μαρίας τεχθεὶς καὶ σαρκωθείς,
παθὼν καὶ ἀποθανών,
ἀνέστη ἐκ νεκρῶν,
καὶ ἀνελήφθη εἰς οὐρανόν,
καθῆται δὲ ἐν δεξιᾷ τῆς μεγαλωσύνης τῆς ὑψίστης,
ἐρχόμενος κρῖναι ζῶντας καὶ νεκρούς·
ἔτι δὲ ὡς καὶ τὸν Σωτῆρα ἡμῶν αἱ ἱεραὶ γραφαὶ διδάσκουσιν,
καὶ ἓν Πνεῦμα πιστεῦσαι,
μίαν καθολικὴν ἐκκλησίαν,
τὴν νεκρῶν ἀνάστασιν,
καὶ κρίσιν ἀνταποδόσεως καθὰ ἔπραξέν τις ἐν σαρκὶ εἴτε ἀγαθὰ εἴτε κακά· ἀναθεματίζοντας ἐκείνους οἳ λέγουσιν ἢ νομίζουσιν ἢ κηρύττουσιν τὸν Υἱὸν τοῦ Θεοῦ κτίσμα ἢ γενητὸν ἢ ποιητὸν καὶ οὐκ ἀληθῶς γέννημα εἶναι ἢ ὅτι ἦν ὅτε οὐκ ἦν.

ITS ENLARGEMENT

I. DR HORT'S THEORY

DR HORT suggested in his *Two Dissertations*, published in 1876, that the Constantinopolitan Creed, C, was simply an expansion of the Creed of Jerusalem made by Cyril about the years 362–364. This theory is based on (1) an identity of wording in the first six clauses; (2) a general similarity; (3) the occurrence of C with but few variations in the *Ancoratus* of Epiphanius which was supposed to be completed in 374 or 375; for Epiphanius was residing at Eleutheropolis near Jerusalem until 367, and after leaving kept in touch with it by correspondence. It will perhaps be advisable to take the last point first.

II. THE SHORTER CREED OF EPIPHANIUS

The text of Epiphanius rests on two MSS., both bad and going back to a single lost original; we need therefore have little scruple in admitting the possibility of corruption. The text of C in Epiphanius contains in addition "that is from the substance of the Father", and "the things in heaven and the things in earth", which are in N, but not in the best MSS. of C; and it concludes with the Nicene anathemas, which, as C is a baptismal Creed, are out of place. To put it briefly, the text of C in Epiphanius is a conflate text of C and N, a fact which would be most easily explained by supposing that the *Ancoratus* originally read N, and that some scribe, starting with N, had put either into the text, or in the margin from which they were afterwards

incorporated into the text, the readings of C, with which he would
no doubt be more familiar.

Secondly, the *Ancoratus* gives two Creeds, C, or substantially
C, in chapter 118, and a second Creed, probably the work of
Epiphanius himself, in chapter 119.

If we analyse this second Creed, *The Longer Creed*, we find
that it consists exclusively of (1) N, (2) catechetical explanations,
probably not intended to be recited, and (3) certain additional
clauses which can be paralleled in Creeds of Antiochene affinities, and may be assumed to be derived from the local baptismal
Creed of Salamis in Cyprus, Epiphanius's own diocese.[1] The
conclusion is that neither in this section nor in the *Panarion*,
which is later and contains long discussions against Apollinarianism and Macedonianism, against which in common with
Marcellianism C is specially directed, does Epiphanius show any
knowledge of C. But this Longer Creed in chapter 119, which is
N with additions, is said to be in sequence with (ἀκολούθως)
(L. p. 17 top) that just before given, hence the Creed in chapter
118, where we now read C, should be N.

*The colophon to C in the present text of Epiphanius asserts that
it was made at the Council of Nicaea.*

At the end of the previous chapter, 118, in reference to the
Creed which in our present text immediately precedes it, is this
sentence: "And this creed was handed down from the holy
Apostles and in (the) Church, the holy city, from all the holy
bishops of that time above 310 in number" (L. p. 16). Kattenbusch (I. 257) identified "the holy city" with Jerusalem and
thought the words an interpolation; Lietzmann (see his note)
thinks that Nicaea is intended and suggests an emendation; Holl
(*Griechische Schriftsteller, in loc.*) says no correction is necessary,
"the holy city" is the Church, and refers to *Pan.* H. 75, 77;
H. 86, 11, 6, and the conclusion of the Περὶ Πίστεως I. 6;
II. 5, 9.

In any event "the holy Apostles" is said in reference to the
body of the teaching, and "all the holy bishops above 310 in

---

[1] An analysis of this Creed proving the point will be found at the end of
this chapter.

number" must mean the Council of Nicaea.[1] The occurrence
of the words "the holy city" cannot be twisted to support
Dr Hort's theory; "the holy Apostles, Cyril of Jerusalem, the
Nicene Council", in this order, is an impossible arrangement
both on grounds of relative authority and of historical sequence.
Accordingly Epiphanius here says that the Creed which immediately precedes this sentence, namely C, was handed down
from the Council of Nicaea. Clearer testimony could hardly be
given that N and not C should be read in this chapter.

The Nicene Anathemas inappropriate to C, but appropriate to N

In our present text C is followed by the Nicene anathemas;
but C is a baptismal Creed, and anathemas are inappropriate to
baptismal Creeds, and are never found with them. The one
apparent exception is this Creed of Epiphanius, and there the
reason is obvious. They were not intended to be recited by the
candidate, and Epiphanius deals with them merely because he
found them in the text of N which he had before him.

And C was obviously composed for a Church where Macedonianism was a pressing danger, as is shown by the accumula-
tion of clauses dealing with the Holy Spirit: "The Spirit, the
Holy, the Lord, the Giver of Life, who proceedeth from the
Father, who with the Father and the Son together is worshipped
and glorified, who spake by the prophets". Epiphanius had
himself enlarged the Nicene anathemas against this heresy
(L. p. 18); would he then, in place of his own version, have
affixed to an anti-Macedonian Creed anathemas which had no
reference to Macedonianism?

The Introduction to C advises its recitation by catechumens

Going back to the introduction to C, we find immediately
before the Creed a piece of advice given to those to whom
Epiphanius was writing, that all catechumens are to be taught

---

1 Cf. *Ep. Synod. Dam. ad Illyr.* Theod. II. 17; Soz. VI. 23, "The faith which
was founded at Nicaea according to the authority of the Apostles".

it word for word as the same mother of all, of you and of us,
[teaches]. "The same mother of us all" is the whole catholic
Church.[1] Its Creed is therefore the Creed of Christendom, N,
and not the local Creed of Jerusalem. The *Ancoratus* was written
in answer to a request from an Egyptian Christian named
Hypatius, and a presbyter, Conops, apparently a Pisidian, who,
both in his own name and that of his fellow presbyters, sought
instruction from Epiphanius. On Dr Hort's theory, therefore,
Epiphanius tells them that in Egypt and Pisidia, as well as at
Cyprus, catechumens must be taught the local Creed of Jerusalem in addition to that of their own dioceses, and the Nicene
anathemas which have no connexion with the Creed, and that
this course is to be taken, because this local Creed is the common
Creed of Christendom.

Summarizing these arguments we see that the text of Epiphanius in chapter 118 must originally have read N and not
C, for

(1) The present text of Epiphanius is a conflate text of N
and C.

(2) It ends with anathemas which have no connexion with it,
as C is a baptismal Creed.

(3) C is strongly anti-Macedonian, and if Epiphanius had
written C and had appended anathemas to it, he would
have used his own enlarged anti-Macedonian version (L.
p. 18 top), and not the Nicene anathemas in the original
version.

(4) C is followed in chapter 119 by a longer Creed based on
N which studiously refrains from using any of the
phraseology of C, but nevertheless is said to follow from
that given in the previous chapter.

(5) In the *Panarion*, which is later than the *Ancoratus*, and
deals with Apollinarianism and Macedonianism, Epiphanius shows no knowledge of C.

1 Cp. "this holy faith of the catholic Church"; "all the holy catholic
Church" (L. p. 16 *sub fin.*) and "the catholic and apostolic Church, our
mother and yours" in the anathemas (L. p. 18).

(6) He says that the Creed given in chapter 118 was handed down from the Council of Nicaea;

(7) And that it is the common Creed of Christendom;

(8) And he advises that catechumens should be taught this Creed in addition to their own local Creed.

But if the original text of Epiphanius read N instead of C, Dr Hort's hypothesis is deprived of the only piece of historical evidence that can be quoted in its support, and rests solely on the resemblance of C to J, the earlier Creed of Jerusalem, as enlarged by Nicene additions. We shall revert to this supposed resemblance later.

The Connexion of C with Constantinople

Moreover a necessary part of any theory is that it should account for the attribution of C to the Council of Constantinople from the time of the Council of Chalcedon onwards. Dr Hort suggested that Cyril's orthodoxy was in question in 381, and that he produced his revised Creed in his own defence. Dr Burn rejected this hypothesis as untenable. Cyril had been orthodox for some twenty years, and his orthodoxy could not have been challenged in a Council presided over by Meletius of Antioch. In this claim Dr Burn is undoubtedly right, and Dr Hort's theory is therefore left hanging in the air, since no connexion is made between Cyril's Creed and Constantinople. An alternative is therefore necessary. Following Kunze, Dr Burn suggested that C was used at the baptism of Nectarius. The supposition is not demonstrably true but exceedingly probable.

But would Nectarius, whoever was his instructor, have been baptized with a Creed entirely unconnected with Constantinople, such as, *ex hypothesi*, C was up to this date? Nectarius was to be Bishop of Constantinople, and the Council, which was largely composed of Constantinopolitan bishops, held itself responsible for his orthodoxy; is it likely that they would have approved an alien Creed for the purpose, or that Nectarius, if he had any voice in the matter, would have consented; or that any bishop would have sacrificed the obvious appropriateness of using a Constantinopolitan Creed to his personal prejudice in favour of that of his own diocese? Would it have been courteous to the Council, to the see over which Nectarius was to preside, or to Nectarius himself?

Secondly, would the Council have appointed Cyril or any bishop outside the Constantinopolitan province to instruct Nectarius? Cyril was undoubtedly of eminence and of fame as a catechist, but would local feeling have permitted the appointment of any outsider? Would not such conduct appear to argue the destitution of the province if it could not produce a bishop of sufficient ability from within its own ranks? And, if a man must be named, would not Gregory of Nyssa have done at least as well?

And thirdly, would Nectarius have signalized his appointment by throwing over the official Creed of his diocese for the sake of a personal preference for the Creed in which he had been himself instructed? Nectarius had the mind of a statesman, and was in high favour with the Emperor on that account; could he have made such a *faux pas*?

Yet the whole theory falls to the ground if any of these questions is answered in the negative. Taken together they suggest a strong cumulative probability against the theory of Dr Burn.

III. The Similarity of C to the Creed of Jerusalem

We now come to the supposed resemblance of C to J and N. Here Dr Hort all but supplies his own refutation. He cites as a parallel case the relation of the Creed of the Nestorians (L. pp. 19, 20) to the Creeds of Antioch (L. p. 18) and Nicaea (L. p. 22).

A comparison between the Creed of Antioch and that of the Nestorians has already been made on p. 119. If we take the phrases in the right-hand column, we find that where the Nestorian Creed differs from that of Antioch for the most part

it agrees with N, and that the only differences from both are
the additions:

l. 5. "from heaven",

l. 6. "by the Holy Ghost",

l. 7. "and was conceived" (Lietzmann's ἄνθρωπον γενόμενον
is a Greek translation of a Syriac phrase which represented the
Nicene ἐνανθρωπήσαντα),

l. 9. "and He sat at the right hand of the Father".

After "quick and dead" the Creed of Antioch fails us till we
come to the clause "forgiveness of sins" which also is in the
Creed of the Nestorians. The Creed of Antioch gives "resurrection of the *dead*" and the Creed of the Nestorians "resurrection of *our bodies*", but for this translation of the Syriac
Caspari prefers "of the dead".

In short, except for these three, or possibly four, clauses the
Creed of the Nestorians follows either the Creed of Antioch or
N; this is therefore the sort of result that we should expect
to find if C was based on J and N. But in fact the parallel
breaks down.

The first six clauses correspond verbally with the Creed of
Jerusalem. This is Dr Hort's strong point. Then we continue
with the Nicene insertion, interpolated, as in the Creed of
Antioch under Meletius, to signalize Cyril's transition to the
full Nicene position. And we may go further than that. If Cyril
made his Creed under the influence of Athanasius he may have
inserted "of the Holy Ghost and Mary the virgin" against
what came to be known as Apollinarianism and was condemned
by anathema in the Alexandrian Council of 362. But now we
come to what no doctrinal motive will cover: "from heaven",
"for us under Pontius Pilate", "according to the Scriptures".
It would seem unlikely that Cyril would insert these un-
necessary words into what must have been a hallowed formula.
But in the last part of the Creed his action would seem yet more
strange. Here is no insertion, but a total rewriting. Καθίσαντα
ἐκ δεξιῶν becomes καθεζόμενον ἐν δεξιᾷ, seemingly an arbitrary
change which was sure to be ill-received. Ἐρχόμενον ἐν δόξῃ
becomes πάλιν ἐρχόμενον μετὰ δόξης, καὶ εἰς ἓν Πνεῦμα, τὸν

Παράκλητον becomes εἰς τὸ Πνεῦμα τὸ ἅγιον, τὸ κύριον καὶ τὸ ζωοποιόν, τὸ ἐκ τοῦ Πατρὸς ἐκπορευόμενον, τὸ σὺν Πατρὶ καὶ Υἱῷ συμπροσκυνούμενον καὶ συνδοξαζόμενον.

Obviously the church where such an alteration was made must have been strongly afflicted by Macedonianism. This was undoubtedly true of Constantinople, but was it true of Jerusalem?

Ἐν τοῖς προφήταις becomes διὰ τῶν προφητῶν. The order of the next two clauses is inverted; and καὶ εἰς ἓν βάπτισμα μετανοίας becomes ὁμολογοῦμεν ἓν βάπτισμα and μετανοίας is dropped. Καὶ ἀποστολικήν is added to the clause on the Church. Εἰς σαρκὸς ἀνάστασιν is weakened to προσδοκῶμεν ἀνάστασιν νεκρῶν and εἰς ζωὴν αἰώνιον is changed into the rarer phrase ζωὴν τοῦ μέλλοντος αἰῶνος.[1]

It seems highly unlikely that any bishop would have introduced such arbitrary changes into his diocesan Creed, and especially a bishop of Cyril's eminence and position. These later changes more than balance the probability drawn from the earlier clauses, and Dr Hort's hypothesis is seen not to be broad enough.

IV. THE ALTERNATIVE VIEW

Now let us try once more to fit the facts. Supposing we were dealing with a Church in a situation such as we know to have been the position at Constantinople in 381, afflicted by Arianism, Apollinarianism, Macedonianism, and Marcellianism simultaneously; then all the extra doctrinal matter is accounted for. And suppose it possessed a Creed containing the phrases "Maker of heaven and earth", and "begotten of the Father before all worlds", the first of which was in the Creed of the Council of Antioch in 324 on the one side, and in the Creed of Remesiana and of the Danubian district on the other, and the second in that of Antioch; if we combine these with the early phrases of the Creed of Nicaea, in much the same fashion as was done at Antioch under Meletius, we obtain C exactly down to "came down".

Moreover every single phrase in C additional to N can be traced in Creeds of Antiochene affinities, with the one exception of "who with the Father and the Son together is worshipped and

1 On these changes see Gibson, *Three Creeds*, note C, pp. 169 ff.

glorified". And this appears to be a new anti-Macedonian coinage, unprecedented in any baptismal Creed, but more likely to have been manufactured at Constantinople than anywhere else. And Constantinople probably obtained its Christianity, and therefore its Creed, from Antioch. From a mere analysis of C we should judge that C is far more probably a revised Creed of Constantinople than of Jerusalem.[1] Nectarius was to be baptized in order to become bishop of a church where all the four heresies were present against which C protests. What more likely than that the local baptismal Creed should have been revised in this sense? And if so, the revision must have been made at the time of the Council, and we may say under its authority. Thus we are provided with a much stronger ground for its subsequent attribution to the Council itself.

Beyond the one solid fact of the baptism of Nectarius we have not as yet invoked historical evidence, but this is a fact, whereas that Cyril ever revised his Creed at all is a pure supposition. Now let us turn to history.

(1) TESTIMONIES
(a) Before Nestorius

Before the rise of the Nestorian controversy, that is within forty or fifty years of the Council of Constantinople, it was acknowledged as a fact both by Macedonians and Catholics that additions against novel heresies had been made by that Council to the Creed of Nicaea. This is seen in the following dialogue, falsely ascribed to Athanasius.

Orthodoxus: Why do you condemn the creed put forth by the 318 holy fathers in Nicaea of Bithynia so that you cast about for another?

Macedonius: And why do you condemn the Creed of Lucian?

Orthodoxus: I condemn the addition which you made, and I can prove that the addition is opposed to the original.

Macedonius: Well, did not you add to the Nicene?

Orthodoxus: True, but nothing opposed to it.

Macedonius: Anyhow you added to it.

Orthodoxus: Matters not then in question, which the fathers have now piously expounded.

de Sancta Trinitate, Dial. III. 1 (Migne, P.G. XXVIII. 1204).

1 See the note at the end of this chapter.

The Council of Constantinople, then, added clauses to the Nicene Creed in opposition to the new heresies, namely Apollinarianism, Macedonianism, and Marcellianism.

(b) Nestorius

In 430 in two letters to Pope Celestine Nestorius writes: "Since those holy and inestimable fathers at Nicaea said nothing more about the holy virgin than that our Lord Jesus Christ was incarnate *of the Holy Ghost and Mary the virgin*" (Mansi, IV. 1022), and, "Blind men who did not even remember the expositions of the holy fathers openly calling to them: 'We believe in one Lord Jesus Christ the Son of God incarnate *of the Holy Ghost and Mary the virgin*'" (*ib.* 1024).

So Cyril of Alexandria quotes from Nestorius's sermons: "That your ears may not be shocked by hearing '*was crucified and buried*'.... Then he adds to these: 'We believe in one Lord Jesus Christ the only-begotten Son, who was generated from the Father, the consubstantial with the Father, who came down *from heaven* for us and was incarnate *of the Holy Ghost*'." And "Come now, compare with what he said the rendering of our Creed; let us see if this fellow has made no innovations in it".

Then follows N, and then "Well, now, my fine fellow, tell us where they said about the Son 'incarnate *of the Holy Ghost and Mary the virgin*'" (*Adv. Nest.* I. 6, 8).

In a Syriac fragment (Loofs, *Nestoriana*, p. 378): "I am often compelled to say the same things (for I am afraid of those who change the words), that we believe in one Lord Jesus Christ the Son of God, the only-begotten, begotten of the Father *before all worlds*", and lower down he speaks of certain clergy who said of him, "Before I came we used to make the words of the bishops at Nicaea who say these things of no account".

It is clear (1) that Nestorius is quoting all these phrases from C; and (2) that he calls C the work of the Council of Nicaea; and (3) that Cyril reproaches him for quoting an adulterated instead of the pure text of N. Here then we reach a further point. Judging from this evidence, C was not the Creed of Constantinople enlarged by Nicene phrases, but contrariwise, C was N enlarged by phrases taken from other sources, one of them probably being the local Creed of Constantinople. The only clause in these extracts that has any dogmatic importance is "of the Holy Ghost and Mary the virgin"; this might be intended to be anti-Apollinarian. So far the Nestorian excerpts agree with the Dialogue.

(c) *Flavian of Constantinople*

Flavian writing to Theodosius in 449 says: "Always following the Holy Scriptures and the expositions of the holy fathers gathered together at Nicaea and at Constantinople" (Mansi, VI. 541). Here Flavian attributes expositions to both Councils and appears to place them on much the same level of authority; that is, the Constantinopolitan tradition was that the Council of 381 made an exposition of the Creed. This is reconcilable with the *Dialogue* if we suppose that what they did was to add phrases to N, and among them we should include "of the Holy Ghost and Mary the virgin".

(d) *The Council of Chalcedon*

The First Session. In this session at the reading of the *Acta* of the Council of Ephesus of 449 (the Latrocinium) Eutyches was represented as endeavouring to cover himself for refusing to go beyond the words of N by pleading the resolution of the earlier Council of Ephesus in 431. At this point Eusebius of Dorylaeum and Diogenes of Cyzicus interrupted. The decision of Ephesus, they said, was being strained; the resolution had no such intention; putting forward the Council of Nicaea was a mere pretence; the Creed had received additions from the holy fathers on account of the corruptions of Apollinarius, Valentinus, and Macedonius and others like them, and there had been added to it "Who came down and was incarnate of the Holy Ghost and Mary the virgin", and Eutyches only left them out because he was an Apollinarian. For the holy fathers of a later time (οἱ μετὰ ταῦτα) explained the "was incarnate" of the holy fathers at Nicaea by saying "of the Holy Ghost and Mary the virgin" (Mansi, VI. 632). Their plea, however, was not accepted by the Egyptian party who at once cried out (like Cyril of Alexandria) at any addition to N, adding that Eutyches had quoted correctly. That is, the Council of Constantinople added to the Creed of Nicaea "of the Holy Ghost and Mary the virgin" against the Apollinarians and some other phrase against the Macedonians. This confirms the earlier evidence.

At the close of the same session the imperial commissioners asserted that their master believed in accordance with the expositions of the 318 and of the 150 who succeeded them (οἱ μετὰ ταῦτα); and none of those present appears to have challenged the assertion that both Councils made expositions of the faith. This confirms the words of Flavian.

The Second Session. In this session was read first N (with the addition of πάλιν before ἐρχόμενον), and then C, the Creed of the 150. After hearing the former the bishops exclaimed "This is the faith of the orthodox; in this we all believe; with this we baptize; in this we were baptized. So let there be read what was set forth by the 150 fathers." And after the latter, "This is the faith for all, this is the faith of the orthodox; this we all believe" (Mansi, VI. 956–958).

The Fifth Session. Aetius the archdeacon read the doctrinal formula drawn up by the commission. After the opening statement there followed the recitation first of N[1] and then of C. The formula continues: "The present holy, great, and ecumenical synod decrees that the faith of the 318 fathers shall remain inviolate, and on account of the Pneumatomachi it confirms the doctrine subsequently delivered concerning the substance of the Spirit by the 150 holy fathers who assembled in the imperial city, in order to express by written documents their faith concerning the Holy Ghost" (H. p. 28). Probably to this session also belongs the *Allocutio* addressed to the Emperor Marcian. Here it is stated that the orthodox faith in the Holy Ghost is already expressed (in N), but on account of the Pneumatomachi the fathers (in Constantinople) added "the Holy Ghost is Lord and God, proceeding from the Father" (ἐπειδήπερ ἁπλῆν ἡ πίστις τηνικαῦτα τοῦ Πνεύματος τὴν διδασκαλίαν ἐξέθετο, οὐδενὸς οὔπω

[1] Heurtley, p. 25, here gives a corrupt text with little manuscript support.

περὶ Αὐτοῦ προσερίζοντος (cp. the language of the Pseudo-
Athanasian Dialogue), οἱ μετὰ ταῦτα (an all but technical phrase)
τῆς ἀληθείας ὑπερασπίζοντες...Κύριον Αὐτό, καὶ Θεόν, καὶ ἐκ
τοῦ Πατρὸς ἔχον τὴν ἐκπόρευσιν, κατὰ τὴν τῆς πίστεως διάνοιαν
ἀποφαίνοντες...). The language of the Council of Chalcedon is
not quite exact, but we gather that the Council of Constantinople added to N Κύριον, some word asserting the deity of
the Holy Spirit, and ἐκ τοῦ Πατρὸς ἐκπορευόμενον.

(e) Nicephorus Callistus[1]

Nicephorus Callistus[1] (H.E. XII. 13) states that the Council
added to N an assertion of the equality of honour and identity
of glory of the Holy Spirit with the Father and the Son, and
entrusted the selection of the additional language to Gregory
of Nyssa, καὶ τὴν τοῦ παναγίου Πνεύματος δόξαν, ὡς ἰσότιμον
καὶ ὁμόδοξον τῷ Πατρὶ καὶ τῷ Υἱῷ τῷ συμβόλῳ τῆς ἐν Νικαίᾳ
πίστεως προσετίθεσαν, τοῦ Νύσσης Γρηγορίου τὸ λεῖπον τῷ ἱερῷ
συμβόλῳ ἀναπληρώσαντος, a description which would exactly
suit the clause τὸ σὺν Πατρὶ καὶ Υἱῷ συμπροσκυνούμενον καὶ
συνδοξαζόμενον.[2]

But if the Council added clauses to N against the Apollinarians
and Macedonians, they probably did the same thing against the
Marcellians, and this clause could only be "of whose kingdom
there shall be no end", which is scriptural, and occurs in the
letter of Marcellus to Pope Julius, and in the Creeds of the
Apostolic Constitutions, Armenia, and Epiphanius.

So far, therefore, we have evidence that the Council of Constantinople added to N the dogmatic clauses:

"Of the Holy Ghost and Mary the virgin,"

(probably) "Of whose kingdom there shall be no end",

"Lord, who proceedeth from the Father, who with the Father
and the Son together is worshipped and glorified",

---

1 A very late writer (A.D. 1333) who, however, says that he collected most
of his material from the Library of S. Sophia.

2 Cp. the language of the letter of the Council of 382: Ἡμᾶς πιστεύειν εἰς τὸ
ὄνομα τοῦ Π. καὶ τοῦ Υ. καὶ τοῦ ʽΑ. Π., δηλαδὴ θεότητος καὶ δυνάμεως καὶ
οὐσίας μιᾶς τοῦ Π. καὶ τοῦ Υ. καὶ τοῦ ʽΑ. Π. πιστευομένης, ὁμοτίμου τε τῇ
ἀξίας καὶ συναϊδίου τῆς βασιλείας.

but coupled with this we have the assertion that they also added "God" in relation to the Holy Spirit.

This assertion would be damaging but for the fact that Gregory Nazianzen makes it clear in his Theological Orations that he himself was in favour of this addition, but that there was a strong "scripturalist" party in Constantinople who were opposed to it, and in some rather enigmatic verses he shows that he wrestled hard for its insertion at the Council, but was overruled.[1]

But if against the Macedonians the Council added "Lord" which, while it had a high significance, could also be used in a much lower sense, and abstained from saying "God", then they would have required some other title to imply, if not to assert, the deity of the Holy Spirit, and this could hardly be other than "Giver of Life", which was both scriptural,[2] had already a place in baptismal Creeds, would be allowed to denote a characteristically divine function, and is frequent in the works of Gregory of Nyssa.[3] It would seem highly probable, therefore, that they added to N "Lord, and Giver of Life, who proceedeth from the Father, who with the Father and the Son together is worshipped and glorified".

Here the Council might have stopped, for on questions not raised at the Council of Nicaea they had added the needed safeguards against heresy.

(2) The Baptism of Nectarius

But a new situation was created by the withdrawal of Gregory Nazianzen, and the election of Nectarius, who was not yet baptized. Nectarius would necessarily be required to assent to the Nicene Creed as thus enlarged against heresies which were rife in the immediate neighbourhood of Constantinople. But he had also to be instructed in and to profess the faith as set forth in his baptismal Creed. This would no doubt be the Creed of the

1 The relevant texts are quoted at the end of this chapter.

2 J. v. 21; vi. 63; Rom. iv. 17.

3 E.g. c. Eunom. (Migne, P.G. XLV. 349 B); ad Sebast. (XLVI. 1032 B); ad Herac. (XLVI. 1093 A).

diocese as it stood before the Council took place. Accordingly there were two possible alternatives: (1) that he should make his baptismal profession and then assent to the Nicene Creed as enlarged by the Council, or (2) that they should be combined together and that he should be instructed in this conflate Creed. For this combination there was abundance of precedents, that is, baptismal Creeds had been in many places combined with N, and it was also far the simpler alternative.

Now if we take C and abstract from it N plus these conciliar enlargements, every single phrase except "who with the Father and the Son together is worshipped and glorified" can be found in Creeds connected with Antioch, and therefore may well have existed in the local Creed of Constantinople. But further. The two phrases "of the substance of the Father" and "God of God", which were in N but are omitted in C, were both also omitted in the Creed of Antioch when it was enlarged from N.

An analysis of C making this point clear is given at the end of this chapter.

(3) THE LETTER OF THE COUNCIL OF 382

The likelihood of this reconstruction of history is strongly confirmed by what would appear far the most probable meaning of a passage in Theodoret (*H.E.* v. 9). Theodoret here quotes the letter sent by the Council of 382 to Pope Damasus and others. After recounting various persecutions which they had suffered, it continues: "For we...have undergone all for the sake of the evangelical faith ratified by the 318 fathers at Nicaea in Bithynia." It then describes what the Nicene Creed teaches and how it is sufficient against all sorts of heretics, Sabellians, Eunomians, Arians, and Macedonians. Then comes this statement:

Let this suffice for a summary of the doctrine which is fearlessly and frankly preached by us, and about which you will be able to be still further satisfied if you will deign to read the report of the synod of Antioch (ὁ ἐν Ἀντιοχείᾳ τόμος), and also that issued last year by the ecumenical council held at Constantinople in which we set forth our confession of faith at greater length (ἐν οἷς πλατύτερον τὴν πίστιν ὡμολογήσαμεν) and appended a written anathema against the heresies which have been recently innovated.

The "Tome of the Antiochenes" was the synodical letter of the hundred and fifty-three Eastern bishops presided over by Meletius—who signed first and called himself Bishop of Antioch —sent to Pope Damasus in 379, accompanying the documents sent by Councils held in Rome in 371, 374 and 376 or 377, to all the dogmatic requirements of which these Eastern bishops signified their assent.

The last phrase seems to refer to the first canon of Constantinople. "This canon is part of a 'Tome' or doctrinal formulary which...had been drawn up by the Council of Constantinople, properly so-called, in 381." It

begins by ordering that "the πίστις of the 318 fathers who assembled at Nicaea in Bithynia shall not be set aside, but remain in force (κυρίαν)". By πίστις is here meant belief as formulated in a document; in other words a confession of faith, or a creed....But here a question arises. The Council of Chalcedon ascribes to this Council of Constantinople, under the name of "the 150 fathers" (Mansi, VII. 109), that recension of the Nicene Creed which has practically superseded the original form....We may suppose that the members of the Council of A.D. 381 would not consider themselves to be invalidating, but rather confirming and perpetuating the formula of A.D. 325, if they adopted, with hardly any change, a development of it.[1]

The point to be decided is whether πίστις in the phrase πλατύτερον τὴν πίστιν ὡμολογήσαμεν means a Creed, as it does in the canon Μὴ ἀθετεῖσθαι τὴν πίστιν τῶν πατέρων τῶν τριακοσίων δεκαοκτὼ τῶν ἐν Νικαίᾳ τῆς Βιθυνίας συνελθόντων.

If it does (and this seems more natural than to suppose that it means some other doctrinal exposition similar to that made at the Council of Chalcedon), it is absolutely fatal to Dr Hort's hypothesis. The Council could not have told Damasus that he would find their orthodoxy clearly set forth in a Creed made by Cyril of Jerusalem, whom Rome regarded as both personally tainted by Arianism and as having been invalidly consecrated by heretics, a Creed moreover which omitted two anti-Arian phrases "of the substance of the Father" and "God from God".

---

1 Bright, *Canons of the First Four General Councils*, pp. 90, 91; and in canon 46 of the Council of Laodicea between 343 and 381: ὅτι δεῖ τοὺς φωτιζομένους τὴν πίστιν ἐκμανθάνειν. See also the Introduction to the Shorter Creed of Epiphanius.

Nor would the mere fact, if it were a fact, that Cyril had been the instructor of Nectarius justify the Council in saying "*we* have confessed the faith at greater length". But it is perfectly consonant with our hypothesis that the Council first added certain anti-heretical phrases to the Creed of Nicaea; that under its sanction this enlarged Creed was combined with the local Creed of Constantinople for the baptism of Nectarius; and that in the course of this amalgamation, following the precedent set by Meletius at Antioch, three phrases were dropped, the first as being merely explanatory of "of one substance with the Father", the second as already contained in "true God from true God", while the third phrase "visible and invisible" was abandoned as having been employed by the Macedonians to show that the Holy Spirit was "made through the Son".

(4) THE NON-RECOGNITION OF C

Supposing C to have had the weight of authority attributed to it by the Council of Chalcedon, how are we to account for the almost complete ignoring of it in the interval between 381 and 451? In part this was due to the failure to recognize the work of the Council as a whole, which in the West was regarded merely as a local synod of minor importance, except so far as its canons might interfere with the ecclesiastical arrangements approved by Rome, when non-recognition was deepened into opposition. The Creed would of course obtain a similar disfavour.

Much the same would also be the attitude of the Patriarchate of Alexandria. The condemnation of the Alexandrian nominee, Maximus the Cynic, by the Council of 381 was a heavy blow to its prestige. "Alexandria, as the chief see of the Eastern world, from the first asserted a jurisdiction which she has never formally relinquished over the see of Constantinople, more particularly in a vacancy in the episcopate" (Neale, *Patriarchate of Alexandria*, I. 206).

"The conduct of Peter, the successor of Athanasius, first in instituting Gregory of Nazianzus bishop of Constantinople by his letters, and sending a formal recognition of his appointment,

and then in substituting Maximus...furnishes unmistakable
indications of the desire to erect an Oriental papacy, by establishing the primacy of Alexandria over Constantinople and so
over the East, which was still further illustrated a few years later
by the high-handed behaviour of Theophilus towards Chrysostom."[1]

In addition, Alexandria inherited the Athanasian tradition as
to the danger of altering the Nicene Creed. The Council of
Alexandria in 362, though it dealt with the Apollinarian and
Macedonian heresies, yet kept the Nicene Creed intact, and
condemned these heresies only in its canons; and its letter sent
to Antioch, the *Tomus ad Antiochenos*, repudiated with emphatic
warmth the idea that the Nicene Creed had been revised at the
Council of Serdica.

Accordingly, wherever the Church of Alexandria could exercise any influence, the work of the Council of Constantinople
would be ignored or opposed, and in consequence we should not
expect to find C recognized at the Council of Ephesus in 431,
or at the Latrocinium in 449. But this may not be the whole
truth. The discovery of "The Bazaar" or "The Treatise of
Heracleides", while it may not be sufficient to clear Nestorius,
throws an ugly light on the character of Cyril, and strengthens
the suggestion which his conduct at the Council might seem to
warrant, that he was instigated not only by zeal for orthodoxy,
but also by personal ambition and local jealousy, and in consequence the ὅρος, not strictly a canon but a decision, as
Dioscurus said at Chalcedon, which was passed on the occasion
of the petition of Charisius of Philadelphia, that "no one should
be allowed to present, or write, or compose ἑτέραν πίστιν than
that which was definitely framed by the holy fathers at Nicaea",
might well be intended as a repudiation of C; for, as Dr Bright
shows,[2] ἑτέρα πίστις means any other Creed than the Nicene
and not merely a Creed inconsistent with it.

It is true that this interpretation of the meaning of the ὅρος
was repudiated at Chalcedon by Diogenes and Eusebius; nevertheless, it may well be that this was its original intention, as was

1 Venables, *D.C.B.* iii. 878.   2 *Councils*, p. 133.

asserted by Dioscurus, and suggested by the Egyptian archimandrites in the fourth session.

The work of the Council as a whole would also be disregarded by all the heretical communities with which it was concerned— by Arians, Apollinarians, including Eutychians, Macedonians and Marcellians. And in the face of the well-known letter of Gregory Nazianzen to Procopius (*Ep.* 130), a letter written after the Council of 381, when he was still smarting under the treatment he had then received, we cannot expect that the Council would be held in honour in any place to which his influence extended.

Lastly, as regards the silence of the Church historians, the whole work of the Council in relation to Creeds and canons is summed up by Socrates (*H.E.* v. vii) in a few lines, and though Sozomen's account (VIII. ix) is rather longer, it is not unfair to apply to both the words used by Dr Hort (*Two Dissertations*, pp. 105, 106) to cover the absence of any notice of the action of Cyril: "The records of the Council are too slight to cause surprise at their silence on this point", while, as we have seen, Nicephorus Callistus says quite definitely that the Nicene Creed was enlarged by the Council, and attributes the bulk of the added words on the Holy Spirit to Gregory of Nyssa.

Thus the "argument from silence" is too weak to be stressed; rather we should ask how it came about that the Church of Alexandria ever consented to the arrangements made at the Council of Constantinople. And this question admits of an easy answer. Alexandria was represented at the Council by only two delegates, Timothy the Patriarch and Dorotheus of Oxyrhynchus, and if they ventured to voice their disapprobation it could be disregarded, or, if necessary, the sixth canon of the Council of Nicaea could be invoked to support the Council in neglecting it as factious.

(5) THE TOME OF LEO

Leo's Tome was written in 448 and was intended to be read at the Council of Ephesus, the Latrocinium. It did not then get a hearing, but was first read in the second session of the

Council of Chalcedon in 451. It contains two passages with regard to the Creed:

Nesciens igitur [Eutyches] quid deberet de Verbi Dei incarnatione sentire, nec volens ad promerendum intelligentiae lumen in sanctarum scripturarum latitudine laborare, illam saltem communem et indiscretam confessionem[1] sollicite recepisset auditu, qua fidelium universitas profitetur, Credere se in Deum Patrem omnipotentem, et in Jesum Christum, Filium Ejus unicum, Dominum nostrum, qui natus est de Spiritu Sancto et Maria virgine (ch. ii).

Unde unigenitum Filium Dei crucifixum et sepultum omnes etiam in symbolo confitemur (ch. v).

We are not here primarily concerned with the question as to what Creed it was from which Leo was quoting, but with the impression produced; i.e. with the question, from what Creed he would have been thought by the assembled fathers to be quoting.

Leo's first statement is that Eutyches ought to have acknowledged the authority of scripture, "propheticae voces, apostolicae litterae, evangelicae auctoritates". But a knowledge of scripture could not be expected from one who did not comprehend the beginning of the Creed, "Et quod per totum mundum omnium regenerandorum voce depromitur, istius adhuc senis corde non capitur" (ch. i).

The appeal to scripture is clear and does not now concern us, but the question arises, What form of Creed would the fathers of Chalcedon think Eutyches ought to have acknowledged as authoritative?

The question admits of a double answer. The Egyptians asserted that among Creeds N was the sole text of orthodoxy, and it was as judged by this standard that Eutyches had claimed, and by the Latrocinium had been allowed, to be orthodox.

But it is equally clear that Leo was not quoting from N, and in demanding that Eutyches should acknowledge as authoritative *Qui natus est de Spiritu Sancto et Maria virgine*, he was endeavouring to enforce on a member of the Church of

---

1 Cp. "Et merito nos cognoscimus Fratribus et Coepiscopis nostris intimasse quod...una esset omnium nostrum et indiscreta confessio", Leo, *Ep. ad Episc. Gall.* lxxxvii. 2.

Constantinople a Creed which the Egyptian bishops did not accept.

The question we are discussing is not settled by saying that these words were in the Roman baptismal Creed. That was purely Western, and did not run, in the sense of being an authorized form, in the East.

But if the Eastern Church had authorized a Creed including these words which Egypt had accepted under pressure at the time, but afterwards ignored in deference to a strong sentiment and tradition, the whole situation is explained. Let us grant that Leo was quoting from R, still the words would at once suggest to Easterns the more familiar formula. Nor to Eastern ears would any other interpretation appear possible of "illam saltem communem et indiscretam confessionem, qua fidelium universitas profitetur..." and "omnes...confitemur". Such language, if it had reference not solely to the common faith but to its expression in words, could not to them mean a Western baptismal Creed; it must mean N, either in its original or in its enlarged form. Nor would they admit that Eutyches should be judged by a Western symbol.

Thus the Constantinopolitans would rejoice in Leo's apparent acceptance of the dogmatic work of the Council of 381—Leo had acknowledged C as authoritative; while on the other hand the Egyptians would be confounded—Rome, Constantinople, Antioch, were all against them.

Such a blow could not have been without effect on the proceedings of the Egyptian party. Nor was it. The opposition to the sentiment of the majority, which they had manifested in the earlier stages of the Council, died down, killed, as it appears, by Leo's Tome, and in the end N and C were accepted as authoritative with no dissentient voice.

(6) SUMMARY

The dialogue of pseudo-Athanasius shows that before the time of Nestorius there was a common consent both of the orthodox and the Macedonians that additions had been made by the Council of 381; and by repeated allusions, notably at the

Council of Chalcedon, we see that this was the Constantino-politan tradition. If, as seems more probable, we should trans-late $\pi i \sigma \tau \iota s$ as meaning "Creed" in the letter of the Council of 382, $\dot{\epsilon} \nu$ $o \hat{\iota} s$—that is, in the Tome of the Antiochenes taken with the Tome of the Council of 381—$\pi \lambda \alpha \tau \acute{\upsilon} \tau \epsilon \rho o \nu$ $\tau \dot{\eta} \nu$ $\pi i \sigma \tau \iota \nu$ $\dot{\omega} \mu o \lambda o \gamma \acute{\eta} \sigma \alpha \mu \epsilon \nu$, then we have a definite, early, and authoritative declaration that the Council expressed its faith in a Creed some-what longer than that of Nicaea, to which reference had already been made. Besides Arianism, which was now on the wane in Asia Minor, the Council had to deal with Apollinarianism, Macedonianism, and Marcellianism. As regards the last, if they added new clauses to N, as they seem to have done, and as Damasus did at Rome with regard to the Holy Spirit, the addi-tion could only have been "of whose kingdom there shall be no end". Against Apollinarianism we have the repeated assertion that they added "of the Holy Ghost and Mary the virgin", while, as regards Macedonianism, we are told that they added "Lord", and "proceedeth from the Father", and Nicephorus Callistus states that the new matter in this article was composed by Gregory of Nyssa to assert the equality of honour and unity of glory of the Holy Spirit with the Father and the Son. These phrases would collectively cover all, or nearly all, the dogmatic additions in which C differs from N, and here the work of the Council might have stopped had the Emperor's nominee, Nec-tarius, been already baptized. He would naturally have been instructed on the basis of the Creed of the church which he was to govern, but he would also have to subscribe to the Nicene Creed as recently enlarged. Accordingly, what seems to have been done was to combine these two Creeds together. The analysis of C shows that apart from these clauses, it is wholly Nicene or Antiochene, and the local Creed of Constantinople was doubtless derived from Antioch.

Against this theory is the occurrence of C in the *Ancoratus* of Epiphanius. But first, these later chapters may have been added after 381, and secondly, the evidence is simply overwhelming that the text of Epiphanius originally read not C but N, the Creed of the Council of Nicaea. Alternative is the hypothesis of

Dr Hort. But this fails to account for the reported attribution of C to the Council of Constantinople; it is incredible that the Council of 382 should have referred Damasus of Rome to the Creed of Cyril of Jerusalem as a demonstration of their own orthodoxy; and the analysis of C shows that in that case Cyril must have done more than Dr Hort supposes; he must have entirely re-written the concluding portion of his Creed, with no apparent motive, and in violation of the feelings of his flock, at a time when his own position was not secure. Moreover, the one strong point that Dr Hort appears to have, namely, that the first six clauses of C are identical with the corresponding clauses in Cyril's Creed, is balanced by the long Nicene insertion, and can be accounted for equally well if, as is not improbable, the local Creed of Constantinople contained the two clauses "Maker of heaven and earth" and "before all ages", both of which occur in Creeds of Antiochene affinities.

Finally, we have to deal with the quotations read at the Council of Chalcedon from Leo's Tome. There can be no doubt that Leo was actually citing the baptismal Creed of Rome, but it is at least highly probable that he was understood by the Egyptian party to be quoting from C. The words used, "in God the Father Almighty, and in Jesus Christ His only Son our Lord, who was born of the Holy Spirit and Mary the virgin", and "crucified and buried", are sufficiently close to those of C to be assumed to be an allusion to it; "that general and uniform confession in which the whole body of the Church expresses its belief" would naturally be taken as referring to the Nicene Creed, either in its original or in its enlarged form; and it would not occur to them that Leo was putting forth a claim that Eutyches should be judged by the standard of a Western symbol. The collapse of the Egyptian opposition after the acceptance of the Tome by the Council shows that this was the interpretation they put upon it. Constantinople, Antioch and Rome seemed all agreed against them in the acceptance of C as an authoritative enlargement of N made by the Council of Constantinople in 381.

NOTES

A. *The Statements of Nestorius*

The language of Nestorius is in any event remarkable, but it implies that C was regarded as simply an enlarged form of N, and therefore based on it and not on the Creed of Jerusalem. The comparison of the longer Creed of Epiphanius, the Creed of Jerome, and C, with N has already been made[1] and is instructive. But this language has a curious parallel.

According to Palladius's *Dialogus de vita S. Joannis Chrysostomi*, Theophilus wrote to Chrysostom that he supposed he "was not ignorant of the ordinance of the Nicene canons decreeing that a bishop should not act as a judge beyond his jurisdiction" (ὑπερόριον μὴ κρίνειν δίκην); while at a later point the bishops who supported Chrysostom retorted the same canon on Theophilus and the Synod of the Oak, "you are violating the canon of the 318 bishops at Nicaea and judging a case beyond your jurisdiction" (ὑπερόριον δικάζεις δίκην). On this Professor Turner writes:[2] "In each case the technical word ὑπερόριος is employed, and it is difficult to resist the conviction that it is derived from the canon to which allusion is being made. Now not only does the word not appear in the canons of Nicaea, but even the underlying thought can only by rather forced inference be found in them.... Where then did Theophilus and Chrysostom find the prohibition of the ὑπερόριος δίκη to which they both refer? The answer can, I think, only be, from the second canon of Constantinople in 381."

Here, then, we seem to have a parallel to (1) the confusion of the Canons of Serdica with those of Nicaea by the successive Popes of Rome, and (2) the misnaming of the Constantinopolitan Creed as Nicene by Nestorius.

B. *Analysis of the Longer Creed of Epiphanius*
(L. p. 27; H. pp. 16–18)

In the parallels Ant. = Creed of Antioch (L. p. 18); 1, 2, 3, 4, Synods of Antioch (L. pp. 22–26); *A.C.* = *Apostolic Constitutions* (L. p. 19; H. pp. 10, 11); Arm. = Armenian (Hort, pp. 146, 147); Aux. = Auxentius; Bas. = Basil; Nest. = Nestorian (L. pp. 19, 20); Phil. = Philadelphia (Hort, p. 153).

N Πιστεύομεν...πάντων ἀοράτων τε καὶ ὁρατῶν	variant of N ὁρατῶν τε κ. ἀ.
N ποιητήν...ἐν τῇ γῇ ὁρατά τε καὶ ἀόρατα,	(Cypriote addition, cp. *A.C.*; 1, 4; Arm.; Aux.; Bas.; Nest.)
N τὸν δι' ἡμᾶς...σαρκωθέντα,	τουτέστι γεννηθέντα τελείως ἐκ τῆς ἁγίας Μαρίας τῆς ἀειπαρθένου διὰ Πνεύματος Ἁγίου (catechetical expansion not intended to be recited)

1 Pp. 119–121.   2 *J.T.S.* III. p. 395.

N ἐνανθρωπήσαντα, τουτέστι...βασιλεύς, cat. expansion
N παθόντα, δὲ τὸν αὐτὸν ἐν σαρκί, cat. expansion
N καὶ ἀναστάντα,
N καὶ ἀνελθόντα εἰς τοὺς οὐρανούς, ἐν αὐτῷ τῷ σώματι, cat. expansion
  (ἐνδόξως)[1] καθίσαντα ἐν δεξιᾷ τοῦ Π. (Cypriote addition, cp. A.C.; 1, 2,
     3, 4; Arm.; Aux.; Bas.; Nest.)

N ἐρχόμενον...νεκρούς, ἐν αὐτῷ τῷ σώματι ἐν δόξῃ, cat. exp.
  οὗ τῆς βασιλείας οὐκ ἔσται τέλος, (Cypriote addition, cp. A.C.; Arm.;
     1, 3, 4)

N καὶ εἰς τὸ Ἅγιον Πνεῦμα πιστεύομεν, τὸ λαλῆσαν...πιστευό-
     μενον, catechetical expansion

Cypriote additions:

(Πιστεύομεν) εἰς μίαν καθολικὴν καὶ (cp. A.C.; Nest.)
  ἀποστολικὴν ἐκκλησίαν·
καὶ εἰς ἓν βάπτισμα μετανοίας· (cp. Arm.)
καὶ εἰς ἀνάστασιν νεκρῶν· (cp. Ant.; Phil.)
καὶ κρίσιν δικαίων ψυχῶν καὶ σω- (cp. Arm.)
  μάτων·
καὶ εἰς βασιλείαν οὐρανῶν· (cp. A.C.; Arm. and the Creed of
     Arius)
καὶ εἰς ζωὴν αἰώνιον. (cp. Ant.; 1; Arm.; Nest.; Phil.)

What Epiphanius has done is clear; he has started with N and its anathemas before him; he has added to N (a) certain catechetical enlargements—the clauses beginning τουτέστι are obviously of this kind, and this explanation will cover all the minor additions—and (b) certain clauses in which he considered N insufficient, at any rate for baptismal purposes. These clauses can all be paralleled from Antiochene sources, and we may therefore assume that they were drawn from the baptismal Creed of his own diocese.

Having ended the Creed he comes to the Nicene anathemas, and these he expands by adding two clauses dealing with the Holy Spirit (L. p. 18). "The Son or the Holy Spirit", and "or the Holy Spirit", and, at the end, "our mother and yours. And again we anathematize those who do not confess the resurrection of the dead, and all the heresies which are not of this right faith." We need not suppose that these Cypriote anathemas any more than the previous expansions were to be recited by the catechumens. This is, then, the Salaminian Creed to be learnt by all candidates for baptism, and "delivered" to their bishop (L. p. 17 top).

Two points in it at once impress themselves upon our notice: (1) that Epiphanius is so devotedly a Nicene that he has not contented himself with expanding his own Creed with clauses taken from N, but has substituted N wherever there was a difference in wording, that is, he has taken N as his basis for the enlarged Creed; and (2) that either he did not know C, the Constantinopolitan Creed, at all, or that he held it in so little esteem that he has made no use of it. The only clause in

1 Ἐνδόξως may be part of the Creed or a catechetical expansion; possibly it should be read with the previous clause, cf. Pan. III. ii. 17.

his Creed that might have been taken from C is, "of whose kingdom
there shall be no end", and this might very well have been already in
the Creed of Salamis, since it is in the Creeds of the *Apostolic Constitutions* and Armenia. On the other hand, where C might have served his
purpose equally well, he has taken no account of it, even in the catechetical expansions.

C	Epiphanius
ἐκ Πνεύματος Ἁγίου καὶ Μαρίας τῆς παρθένου	ἐκ τῆς ἁγίας Μαρίας τῆς ἀειπαρθένου διὰ Πνεύματος Ἁγίου
καὶ καθεζόμενον ἐκ δεξιῶν τοῦ Πατρός,	(ἐνδόξως) καθίσαντα ἐν δεξιᾷ τ. Π.
καὶ πάλιν ἐρχόμενον μετὰ δόξης	ἐρχόμενον ἐν αὐτῷ τῷ σώματι ἐν δόξῃ
τὸ λαλῆσαν διὰ τῶν προφητῶν.	τὸ λ. ἐν νόμῳ καὶ κηρῦξαν ἐν τοῖς π.
Εἰς μίαν ἁγίαν καθ. καὶ ἀπ. ἐκκλησίαν.	Πιστεύομεν εἰς μ. καθ. καὶ ἀπ. ἐκ. (omitting ἁγίαν)
Ὁμολογοῦμεν ἕν βαπτ. εἰς ἀφ. ἁμ.	καὶ εἰς ἕν βάπτισμα μετανοίας
Προσδοκῶμεν ἀνάστασιν νεκρῶν,	καὶ εἰς ἀνάστασιν νεκρῶν
καὶ ζωὴν τοῦ μέλλοντος αἰῶνος.	καὶ εἰς ζωὴν αἰώνιον.

C. *Analysis of C*

C.A. = Council of Antioch, 324. C.C. = Council of Constantinople.
Brackets indicate similarity; absence of brackets identity. Phrases quoted
as inserted are underlined.

N Πιστεύομεν εἰς ἕνα Θεόν, Πατέρα παντοκράτορα,	
ποιητὴν οὐρανοῦ καὶ γῆς,	Gen. 1. 1. C.A.; Arm.; Niceta; Mai.
(N) ὁρατῶν τε πάντων καὶ ἀοράτων.	(Ant.); (Arm.); (Nest.); (Phil.)
N Καὶ εἰς ἕνα Κύριον Ἰησοῦν Χριστόν,	
N τὸν Υἱὸν τοῦ Θεοῦ,	(C.A.); Nest.; (Ancyra); (Ant.); (Phil.)
(N) τὸν μονογενῆ,	
(N) τὸν ἐκ τοῦ Πατρὸς γεννηθέντα πρὸ πάντων τῶν αἰώνων,	A.C.; Arm.; Nest.; Phil.
N φῶς ἐκ φωτός, Θεὸν ἀληθινὸν ἐκ Θεοῦ ἀληθινοῦ,	
N γεννηθέντα οὐ ποιηθέντα, ὁμοού-σιον τῷ Πατρί, δι᾿ οὗ τὰ πάντα ἐγένετο,	
N τὸν δι᾿ ἡμᾶς τοὺς ἀνθρώπους καὶ διὰ τὴν ἡμετέραν σωτηρίαν κατελ-θόντα	
ἐκ τῶν οὐρανῶν,	A.C.; Arm.; Nest.; Phil.
N καὶ σαρκωθέντα	
ἐκ Πνεύματος Ἁγίου καὶ Μαρίας τῆς παρθένου,	C.C.; Ancyra { (Arm.); (Nest.); (A.C.); (Ant.); (Phil.)
N καὶ ἐνανθρωπήσαντα,	
σταυρωθέντα τε	A.C.; Ancyra; Ant.; Arm.; Nest.; Phil.
ὑπὲρ ἡμῶν	(A.C.)
ἐπὶ Ποντίου Πιλάτου,	A.C.; Ancyra; Ant.; Arm.; Nest.

N καὶ παθόντα,	
καὶ ταφέντα,	Ancyra; Ant.; Arm.; Nest.
N καὶ ἀναστάντα τῇ τρίτῃ ἡμέρᾳ	
κατὰ τὰς γραφάς,	Ant.; Nest.
N καὶ ἀνελθόντα εἰς τοὺς οὐρανούς,	
καὶ καθεζόμενον ἐκ δεξιῶν τοῦ	(C.A.); (A.C.); (Ancyra); (Arm.);
Πατρός,	(Nest.)
(N?) καὶ πάλιν	} C.C.; Ant.; Nest.; Phil.
N ἐρχόμενον	
μετὰ δόξης	A.C.; (Arm.)
N κρῖναι ζῶντας καὶ νεκρούς,	
οὗ τῆς βασιλείας οὐκ ἔσται τέλος·	A.C.; Arm.; Epiph.
(N) Καὶ εἰς τὸ Πνεῦμα τὸ Ἅγιον,	A.C.; Arm.; (Ancyra)
τὸ Κύριον,	C.C.
καὶ τὸ ζωοποιόν,	Nest.
τὸ ἐκ τοῦ Πατρὸς ἐκπορευόμενον,	C.C.; Nest.
τὸ σὺν Πατρὶ καὶ Υἱῷ συμπροσ-	
κυνούμενον καὶ συνδοξαζόμενον,	Gregory of Nyssa (?)
τὸ λαλῆσαν	Arm.; Epiph.
διὰ τῶν προφητῶν.	(Arm.); (Epiph.)
Καὶ εἰς μίαν ἁγίαν, καθολικήν, καὶ	(C.A.); (A.C.); (Arm.); (Epiph.);
ἀποστολικὴν ἐκκλησίαν·	(Nest.)
Ὁμολογοῦμεν ἓν βάπτισμα	Nest.
εἰς ἄφεσιν ἁμαρτιῶν.	Nest.; A.C.; Arm.
Προσδοκῶμεν	
ἀνάστασιν νεκρῶν,	} (C.A.); Arm.; Nest.; Phil.; (Ant.);
	(A.C.)
καὶ ζωὴν τοῦ μέλλοντος αἰῶνος.	A.C.

Πρὸ πάντων τῶν αἰώνων, ἐκ τῶν οὐρανῶν, ἐκ Πνεύματος Ἁγίου καὶ Μαρίας τῆς παρθένου, σταυρωθέντα, ταφέντα are quoted in the sermons of Nestorius; ἐκ Πνεύματος Ἁγίου καὶ Μαρίας τῆς παρθένου, Κύριον, ἐκ τοῦ Πατρὸς πορευόμενον are said in the Council of Chalcedon to have been inserted at the Council of Constantinople; καὶ πάλιν is quoted as part of N in the second session of the Council of Chalcedon; ἐκ τῆς οὐσίας τοῦ Πατρός, Θεὸν ἐκ Θεοῦ were in N, but were not adopted in the enlarged Creed of Antioch; ὁρατὰ καὶ ἀόρατα after δι᾽ οὗ τὰ πάντα ἐγένετο may well have been omitted, since the Macedonians may have misused the phrase as showing that the Holy Spirit was created through the Son; τὸ ζωοποιόν is in the Nestorian as well as other Creeds, and may well have been added to Κύριον to imply the deity of the Holy Spirit (cp. Rom. iv. 17), and τὸ...συνδοξαζόμενον is hinted at by Nicephorus Callistus as part of the addition made by Gregory of Nyssa. But the strange feature is that, but for this last phrase and the unimportant word προσδοκῶμεν, which cannot be traced earlier, though it is probably taken over from some baptismal Creed, every word of the additions can be found in Creeds connected with Antioch, and may therefore have already existed in the baptismal Creed of Constantinople.

This conclusion is supported by the fact that in 381, before the Council of Constantinople, Gregory Nazianzen preached a sermon

(*Orat.* XL *de Baptismo*) at the conclusion of which he quotes what appear to be phrases from the local baptismal Creed of Constantinople, in some cases resembling C and in others the Creed of Antioch and that of the *Apostolic Constitutions*.

Gregory	Parallel
Πίστευε τὸν σύμπαντα κόσμον,	Πιστεύομεν εἰς... ποιητὴν
ὅσος τε ὁρατὸς καὶ ὅσος ἀόρατος,	οὐρανοῦ καὶ γῆς,
...παρὰ Θεοῦ γενόμενον.	ὁρατῶν τε πάντων καὶ ἀοράτων. [C
Πίστευε...τὸν προαιώνιον Λόγον,	Τὸν ἐκ τοῦ Πατρὸς γεννηθέντα
τὸν γεννηθέντα ἐκ τοῦ Πατρὸς...	πρὸ πάντων τῶν αἰώνων [C
ἐπ' ἐσχάτων τῶν ἡμερῶν	ἐπ' ἐσχάτων τῶν ἡμερῶν [*Ap. Const.*
γεγενῆσθαι διὰ σὲ	τὸν δι' ἡμᾶς τοὺς ἀνθρώπους...
ἐκ τῆς παρθένου προελθόντα Μαρίας...	ἐκ...Μαρίας τῆς παρθένου [C
σταυρωθέντα καὶ ταφέντα...	crucifixus...et sepultus [Ant.
ἥξειν δὲ πάλιν μετὰ	καὶ πάλιν ἐρχόμενον μετὰ δόξης. [C
τῆς ἐνδόξου Αὐτοῦ παρουσίας....	
Δέχου πρὸς τούτοις ἀνάστασιν...	Προσδοκῶμεν ἀνάστασιν νεκρῶν. [C
ὃ δὴ βασιλείαν οὐρανῶν ὀνομάζομεν.	Καὶ εἰς βασιλείαν οὐρανῶν. [*Ap. Const.*

D. *The Statements of Gregory Nazianzen*

Theological Oration V, delivered in Constantinople in one of the three years 379–381 and probably in 380:

Ch. 3. They, then, who are angry with us on the ground that we are bringing in a strange and interpolated God, namely the Holy Spirit, and who fight so hard for the letter, should know that they are afraid where no fear is; and I would have them clearly understand that their love for the letter is but a cloak for impiety....But we have so much confidence in the Deity of the Spirit, whom we revere, that we will begin our teaching concerning His Godhead by applying to Him the names which belong to the Trinity, even though some persons think it over bold.

Ch. 5. But of the clever men among ourselves, some have conceived of It as an Activity, some as a Creature, some as God, and some have not known which, out of reverence for Scripture, as they say, as though Scripture did not make the matter clear either way. And so they neither worship nor dishonour Him, but take up a sort of mid-way position about Him or rather an altogether miserable one.

Ch. 6. The Holy Spirit...will be conceived of either as a creature or as God. For anything mid-way between these two, whether as having nothing in common with either, or as a compound of both, not even those who invented the goat-stag could imagine.

Ch. 10. What then? Is the Spirit God? Most certainly. Well then, is He consubstantial? Yes, if He is God.

Ch. 28. This, then, is my view with regard to these things, and may it ever be so, and that of anyone who is my friend, to worship the

Father as God, the Son as God, the Holy Spirit as God, three Persons,
one Godhead undivided in glory, honour, substance, and kingdom.

Carmina, bk. II. xi. 1703:

And what again of this? That sweet and fair fount of the ancient
faith that drew into one the august nature of the Trinity, of which
Nicaea was once the school, this I beheld miserably befouled by the
salt backwashes of the men of double minds who hold the opinions
favoured by the State, the "mid-way" men forsooth, lucky if so they
were, and not most plainly of the opposite name.

1750. And some there were who hardly and constrained yet did
agree, men who still retained some shred of freedom, to whom their
ignorance of ill was spokesman, captured by the duplicity of the
teaching and by the reverence of the "mid-way" creed, a child that
favoured ill its parentage.

xiv. 25. If I abdicated my see, what worse than this? But if un-
willingly I was thrust out, what do those deserve who dared so far?
To-day I am installed, the next deposed. What plea, false though it be,
can one find in excuse? O Christ, I am bold to utter somewhat of the
thoughts of my heart. It is my strivings that they envy me, and the
stones hurled at me. Perchance it is the Spirit that is stoned! Plainly
I speak, the Spirit, hear ye, as being God, I say. To me Thou art God,
thrice I shout it, God. There, that is it. Hurl your stones and aim them
well; unshaken stands the target of the truth. The Father, we believe,
is root and fount of good: of Him is the begotten Light, the Son and
Word, the Seal of Him the unoriginate, and the Spirit, a timeless nature;
God, my God, and God, a triple monad.

The Letter to Cledonius, Ep. 102:

I write, what you knew before,...that I never have and never can
prefer anything above the Nicene Faith, that of the Holy Fathers who
met there to destroy the Arian heresy, but am, and by God's help ever
will be, of that faith; completing in detail that which was incompletely
said by them concerning the Holy Spirit (for that question had not then
been mooted), namely that we are to believe that the Father, Son, and
Holy Spirit are of one Godhead, thus confessing the Spirit to be God.

The Letter to Procopius:

I am disposed to avoid all assemblies of bishops. For I never saw
any good end to a Council nor any remedy for evils, but rather an
addition of more evil, as its result. There are always contentions and
strivings for domination beyond what words can describe.

Chapter XIV

THE LATER HISTORY OF THE NICENE CREED AND THE ENGLISH VERSION

I. The Later History. II. The English Version.

I. The Later History

AFTER the adoption of C as the baptismal Creed of Nectarius it gradually superseded other baptismal Creeds, first in the patriarchate of Constantinople,[1] and then, after the Council of Chalcedon, throughout the East. The introduction of the Creed into the Eucharist was first made by Peter the Fuller, monophysite patriarch of Antioch (476–488). The example of Antioch appears to have been followed shortly afterwards by Alexandria; and between 511 and 518 Timothy, patriarch of Constantinople, another monophysite, ordered the regular use of the Creed in his church, where hitherto it was the custom to recite it only at the catechetical instructions on Good Friday.

In 536 in the *Acta* of a Council of Constantinople under Mennas we find a *libellus* giving an account of the events of July 15 and 16, 518, in the course of which we find: "After the reading of the Gospel and when the holy Creed ($\mu\acute{a}\theta\eta\mu a$) had been said according to the custom".

In 568 the Emperor Justin II ordered that in every catholic church the faith should be sung before the Lord's Prayer, and this was the fuller form C; but it would seem probable that the particular position which he assigned to it in the liturgy was not observed, for in Eastern rites it either precedes the kiss of peace, as in the Syrian, Egyptian and Nestorian liturgies, or follows it as in the liturgies of Constantinople and of the Greek Churches generally.

The first mention of the introduction of the Creed into the liturgy in the West is in a canon of the Council of Toledo in 589.

1 See Turner, *History and Use of Creeds*, pp. 50, 51.

The Council was summoned by Reccared king of the Visigoths, and was attended by John, Abbot of Biclaro, who had recently returned from Constantinople, where he had resided for seventeen years. The canon orders that "for reverence of the most holy faith, and for the strengthening of the weak minds of men ...through all the Churches of Spain and Galicia, following the form of the Oriental churches, the symbol of the faith of the Council of Constantinople...should be recited; so that before the Lord's Prayer be said [i.e. at the Fraction before the Communion] the Creed be chanted with a clear voice by the people"; this has remained the position given to the Creed in the Mozarabic liturgy. The text used reintroduced "God from God" from the Creed of the Council of Nicaea, and omitted the word "holy" as an epithet of the Church, this omission being common to nearly all the Latin versions of C, except that sent by Pope Leo II to the Spanish churches after the Sixth Council (681).[1] It would seem, however, that it did not contain the clause "and the Son", these words being a later insertion of some copyist influenced by the anathema of the Council, "Whoever does not believe or has not believed that the Holy Spirit proceeds from the Father and the Son, let him be anathema."[2]

As regards the double procession, the Council of Toledo of 447 had adopted the canon: "The Father is unbegotten, the Son begotten, the Paraclete not begotten but proceeding from the Father and the Son." In this canon they appear to have followed the teaching of Augustine (*de Trin.* iv. 29), and Augustine followed the teaching of Ambrose in the *Quicumque Vult*.

The addition was accepted by the Council of Hatfield presided over by Theodore in 680, but did not begin to attract notice until the end of the eighth century, when it was ventilated at the Council of Gentilly in 767, and some ambassadors of the Eastern Emperor Constantine Copronymus remonstrated against it. When the proceedings of the Second Council of Nicaea in 787 were communicated to the West, exception was taken by Charle-

---

1 On the Latin versions of N and C see Schwartz, *Z.N.W.* Bd. 25, pp. 33–88, 1926.

2 See Burn, *J.T.S.* IX. pp. 301–303, Jan. 1908.

magne to the phrase used by Tarasius, patriarch of Constantinople, "I believe in the Holy Ghost, the Lord and Giver of Life, who proceedeth from the Father through the Son", as not being in agreement with "the Nicene Creed", that is with the fuller form C with which alone he was probably acquainted, since C had superseded N. About the same time, and under his influence, the use of the Creed in the Liturgy was generally adopted by the Frankish Church. In 796 the clause was defended by Paulinus, Bishop of Aquileia, who presided at the Council of Friuli. Early in the ninth century some Latin monks, who had founded a convent on the Mount of Olives, were charged with heresy, chiefly on the ground that they said the interpolated Creed on Christmas Day. They appealed to Pope Leo III, stating that they were using the Creed as they had received it and as they had heard it sung in the Emperor's chapel, and urged that the clause was contained in "the Faith of St Athanasius". Leo communicated with the Emperor who summoned a Council at Aix in 809. The Council was unanimous in upholding the doctrine, but they felt that the interpolation of the Creed needed delicate handling, so they sent a deputation to the Pope, who was at one with them on the doctrinal question, but having received the Creed uninterpolated he objected to the addition. The delegation pointed out that to excise the term would suggest that the doctrine was condemned. Leo advised the disuse of the practice of singing the Creed, which was not used in the Mass but only in the instructions of catechumens at Rome, and he caused two silver shields to be inscribed with the true text in Greek and Latin, which he set up in St Peter's. But the Frankish Church continued to sing the Creed with the interpolations. The custom of singing the Creed was only adopted at Rome in 1014 by Benedict VIII, under pressure from the Emperor Henry II, and then it was sung in its interpolated form.

In the orthodox East the Constantinopolitan Creed is the only Creed used, and from the Liturgy it has been introduced into the Hours Offices. In the Jacobite and Maronite Churches in Syria, and among the Nestorians, Armenians, and Abyssinians there still linger local Creeds combined with N.

In the Celtic Church the Stowe Missal, one of the earliest remaining service books, probably written in the ninth century, gives the Creed in Latin almost exactly in the form used at the Council of Chalcedon, but the word *Filioque* has been added by a later hand.

II. THE ENGLISH VERSION

The English version differs from the original text: (1) in the use of the singular number "I believe" in place of the plural, in agreement with the general liturgical custom; (2) in the reintroduction of the clause "God of God" from N; (3) in the presence of the clause "and the Son", which, as we have seen, was uniform throughout the West; (4) in the repetition of "I believe in" before "the Holy Ghost" instead of "and"; (5) in the reading "I believe one...Church" without "in", instead of "in one... Church". This appears to have been a deliberate alteration on the part of Cranmer who made the translation. Rufinus and other Latin writers often drew this distinction between believing *in* Three Persons and believing about their work, and, in his *Annotation* upon the King's Book, Cranmer writes, "I believe in the Holy Ghost, and that there is a Holy Catholic Church." (6) The omission of the word "holy" as an epithet of the Church appears no less deliberate.[1] The Latin Creed ordered to be recited by the Council of Toledo had, as we have seen, *In unam catholicam apostolicam ecclesiam*, omitting *sanctam*, and this form is general in the Latin MSS. of the proceedings at Chalcedon. The collections of Councils used by Cranmer and his colleagues were probably those of Merlin first published in 1524 and republished in 1530 and 1535, which quote the Creed three times and always without *sanctam*; of Peter Crabbe, 1538, which gives C according to different translations, one with *sanctam* but not *lumen de lumine* and the other without *sanctam* but with *lumen de lumine*; and of Carranza, 1546, which professes to have consulted the Greek copies and Leo, and omits *sanctam*. And if the reformers referred to Greek Liturgies, they would probably have found no more than the opening words, "I believe in one God."

1 The texts of C and of the English version are given at the end of this chapter where all the differences are noted.

The First Prayer Book of Edward VI omitted the clause "of whose kingdom there shall be no end", but this was restored in the Book of 1552.

In general the reformers appear to have followed the most ancient Latin version known to the West, that of the Council of Toledo. Thus whereas we say, "And I believe in the Holy Ghost", the Toletan version ran: *Credimus et in Spiritum Sanctum*, but the Roman Missal does not here repeat the word *Credo*; and similarly the Toletan version ran: *Filium Dei unigenitum ex Patre natum*, where the Roman Missal inserts *et* before *ex Patre natum*.

The Roman Church is exceptional in allowing the omission of the Creed from the Eucharist except on Sundays and festivals. This was permitted by the First Prayer Book, but subsequent editions have reverted to the more catholic custom of regarding it as a regular part of the rite on the principle enunciated by St Thomas Aquinas (*Summa*, P. III, q. 83, art. 4): "When the Gospel has been read, the Creed is sung in which the people show that they give the assent of faith to the doctrine of Christ." Among Anglican revisions, the English Alternative Rite of 1928, the Scottish Liturgy of 1929, and the South African Alternative Liturgy allow its omission on weekdays not being Red Letter Days.

One further note should be added. The regular baptismal Creed in Rome from the end of the fourth century onwards was the Apostles' Creed, nor did the Roman missionaries who spread the Roman rite over Northern Europe ever take with them any other baptismal Creed. But before the extinction of the Byzantine power, the priest in Rome asked the acolyte who presented the candidates: "In what language do they confess our Lord Jesus Christ?" and if the answer was "In Greek" the acolyte recited the "Nicene" Creed, that is, the Constantinopolitan Creed without the *Filioque* clause, in Greek, and later on in Latin; if the reply was "In Latin" the Apostles' Creed continued to be used. The dates of the beginning and ending of this practice are somewhat uncertain, but it does not appear to have been of long duration.

The Text of the Constantinopolitan Creed and of the English Version

Πιστεύομεν εἰς ἕνα Θεὸν
Πατέρα παντοκράτορα,
Ποιητὴν οὐρανοῦ καὶ γῆς,
ὁρατῶν τε πάντων καὶ ἀοράτων·

I believe in one God
the Father Almighty,
Maker of heaven and earth,
And of all things visible and invisible:

Καὶ εἰς ἕνα Κύριον, Ἰησοῦν Χριστόν,
τὸν Υἱὸν τοῦ Θεοῦ τὸν μονογενῆ,
τὸν ἐκ τοῦ Πατρὸς γεννηθέντα
πρὸ πάντων τῶν αἰώνων,

And in one Lord Jesus Christ,
the only-begotten Son of God,
Begotten of his Father
before all worlds,

Φῶς ἐκ Φωτός,
Θεὸν ἀληθινὸν ἐκ Θεοῦ ἀληθινοῦ,
γεννηθέντα οὐ ποιηθέντα,
ὁμοούσιον τῷ Πατρί,

God of God,
Light of Light,
Very God of very God,
Begotten, not made,
Being of one substance with the Father,

δι᾽ οὗ τὰ πάντα ἐγένετο,
τὸν δι᾽ ἡμᾶς τοὺς ἀνθρώπους
καὶ διὰ τὴν ἡμετέραν σωτηρίαν
κατελθόντα ἐκ τῶν οὐρανῶν,

By whom all things were made:
Who for us men,
and for our salvation
came down from heaven (Gk. the heavens),

καὶ σαρκωθέντα
ἐκ Πνεύματος Ἁγίου
καὶ Μαρίας τῆς παρθένου,
καὶ ἐνανθρωπήσαντα,
σταυρωθέντα τε ὑπὲρ ἡμῶν
ἐπὶ Ποντίου Πιλάτου,
καὶ παθόντα,
καὶ ταφέντα,
καὶ ἀναστάντα τῇ τρίτῃ ἡμέρᾳ
κατὰ τὰς γραφάς,
καὶ ἀνελθόντα εἰς τοὺς οὐρανούς,

And was incarnate
by (Gk. of) the Holy Ghost
of (Gk. and) the Virgin Mary,
And was made man,
And was crucified also for us
under Pontius Pilate.
He (no and) suffered
and was buried,
And the third day he rose again
according to the Scriptures,
And ascended into heaven (Gk. the heavens)

καὶ καθεζόμενον
ἐκ δεξιῶν τοῦ Πατρός,
καὶ πάλιν ἐρχόμενον μετὰ δόξης

And sitteth
on the right hand of the Father.
And he shall come (Gk. cometh) again with glory

κρῖναι ζῶντας καὶ νεκρούς·

to judge both the quick and the dead:

οὗ τῆς βασιλείας οὐκ ἔσται τέλος.

Whose kingdom shall have (Gk. of whose kingdom there shall be) no end.

Καὶ εἰς τὸ Πνεῦμα τὸ Ἅγιον,
τὸ Κύριον, καὶ τὸ ζωοποιόν,

And I believe in the Holy Ghost,
the Lord and (Gk. the) giver of life,

| TEXT | TRANSLATION |

The Divine Tri-unity

3. Fides autem catholica haec est: ut unum Deum in trinitate et Trinitatem in unitáte venerémur (4),

And the Catholic Faith is this, that we worship (the) one God in trinity, and the Trinity in unity,

4. neque confundentes personas: neque substántiam separántes (*v*);

neither confusing the Persons, nor dividing the Substance;

5. alia est enim persona Patris, alia Filii: alia Spíritus Sáncti (*p*);[1]

for there is one Person of the Father, another of the Son, another of the Holy Ghost;

6. sed Patris et Filii et Spiritus Sancti una est divinitas: aequalis gloria, coaetérna majéstas (*p*).

but the Godhead of the Father and of the Son and of the Holy Ghost is one, the glory equal, the majesty coeternal.

Attributes of the Three Persons

7. Qualis Pater, talis Filius: et talis Spíritus Sánctus (*p*);

Such as the Father is, such is the Son, and such is the Holy Ghost;

8. increatus Pater, increatus Filius: increatus Spíritus Sánctus (*p*);

The Father uncreate, the Son uncreate, the Holy Ghost uncreate;

9. immensus Pater, immensus Filius: immensus Spíritus Sánctus (*p*);

the Father immeasurable, the Son immeasurable, the Holy Ghost immeasurable;

10. aeternus Pater, aeternus Filius: aeternus Spíritus Sánctus (*p*);

the Father eternal, the Son eternal, the Holy Ghost eternal;

11. et tamen non tres aeterni: sed únus aetérnus (*p*);

and yet there are not three eternals, but one eternal;

12. sicut non tres increati, nec tres immensi: sed unus immensus et únus increátus (4).

as also there are not three uncreated nor three immeasurables, but one immeasurable and one uncreated.

13. Similiter omnipotens Pater, omnipotens Filius: omnipotens Spíritus Sánctus (*p*);

So, likewise, the Father is almighty, the Son almighty, the Holy Ghost almighty;

14. et tamen non tres omnipotentes: sed únus omnípotens (*t*).

and yet there are not three almighties, but one almighty.

---

1 Alia persona Filii, alia persona Spiritus Sancti, Bobbio MS. (Milan, Amb. O. 212 Sup.).

TEXT	TRANSLATION

The Acknowledgement of the Trinity

15. Ita Deus Pater, Deus Filius: Deus Spíritus Sánctus (*p*);

So the Father is God, the Son is God, the Holy Ghost is God;

16. et tamen non tres dii: sed unus Deus;[1]

and yet there are not three gods, but one God.

17. Ita Dominus Pater, Dominus Filius: Dominus Spíritus Sánctus (*p*);

So the Father is Lord, the Son Lord, the Holy Ghost Lord;

18. et tamen non tres domini: sed unus Dominus.[1]

and yet there are not three lords, but one Lord.

19. Quia sicut singillatim unamquamque Personam et Deum et Dominum confiteri: christiana veritáte compéllimur (*v*),

For like as we are compelled by the Christian truth to confess severally each Person to be both God and Lord,

20. ita tres deos aut tres dominos dicere: catholica religióne prohibémur (4).

so are we forbidden by the Catholic Religion to speak of three gods or three lords.

Divine Relationships

21. Pater a nullo est factus: nec creátus nec génitus (*t*);

The Father is made by none nor created nor begotten;

22. Filius a Patre solo est: non factus nec creátus, sed génitus (*t*);

the Son is from the Father alone, not made nor created, but begotten;

23. Spiritus Sanctus a Patre et Filio: non factus nec creatus nec génitus, sed procédens (*v*).

the Holy Ghost is from the Father and the Son, not made nor created nor begotten, but proceeding.

24. Unus ergo Pater, non tres patres; unus Filius, non tres filii: unus Spiritus Sanctus, non tres spíritus sáncti (*p*).

So there is one Father, not three fathers, one Son, not three sons, one Holy Ghost, not three holy ghosts.

25. In hac Trinitate nihil prius aut posterius: nihil majus aut minus,

In this Trinity there is no before or after, no greater or less,

26. sed totae tres Personae coaeternae sibi sunt: ét coaequáles (*p*).

but all the three Persons are coeternal with each other and coequal.

27. Ita ut per omnia, sicut jam supra dictum est: et Trinitas in Unitate et Unitas in Trinitate veneranda sit.

So that every way, as is aforesaid, both a Trinity is to be worshipped in the Unity, and an Unity in the Trinity.

28. Qui vult ergo salvus esse: ita de Trinitate sentiat.

He therefore that would be in a state of salvation, let him thus think of the Trinity.

---

1 Burn reads, "únus est Déus" (*p*) in 16, and "únus est Dóminus" (*t*) in 18, giving a better rhythm.

TEXT	TRANSLATION

The Incarnation

29. Sed necessarium est ad aeternam salutem: ut incarnationem quoque Domini nostri Jesu Christi fidéliter crédat (*p*).

But it is necessary to eternal salvation that he believe faithfully also the incarnation of our Lord Jesus Christ.

30. Est ergo fides recta ut credamus et confiteamur: quia Dominus noster Jesus Christus, Dei Filius, et Deus páriter et hómo est (4);

So then the right faith is that we believe and confess that our Lord Jesus Christ, the Son of God, is at once God and man.

Christ in Two Natures

31. Deus est, ex substantia Patris ante saecula genitus: et homo ex substantia matris in saéculo nátus (*p*);

He is God, of the Substance of the Father, begotten before the worlds, and man, of the substance of His mother, born in the world;

32. perfectus Deus: perfectus homo ex anima rationabili et humana cárne subsístens (*p*);

completely God; completely man consisting of rational soul and human flesh;

33. aequalis Patri secundum deitatem: minor Patre secúndum humanitátem (*v*);

equal to the Father in respect of His Godhead; less than the Father in respect of His manhood.

Christ one Person

34. Qui licet Deus sit et homo: non duo tamen sed únus est Chrístus (*p*);

Who, although He be God and man, yet is not two, but one Christ;

35. unus autem non conversione divinitatis in carne: sed adsumptione humanitátis in Déo (*p*);

one, however, not by the conversion of Godhead into flesh, but by the taking of manhood into God;

36. unus omnino, non confusione substantiae: sed unitáte persónae (*p*);

one, in short, not by confusion of substance, but by unity of person;

37. nam sicut anima rationabilis et caro unus est homo: ita Deus et homo únus est Chrístus (*p*);

for as the rational soul and the flesh is one man, so God and man is one Christ;

The Redeemer and Judge

38. Qui passus est pro salute nostra: descendit ad inferos, resurréxit a mórtuis (*t*),

Who suffered for our salvation, descended into hell, rose again from the dead,

39. ascendit ad caelos, sedit ad dexteram Patris: inde venturus judicare vívos et mórtuos (*t*).

ascended into heaven, sat at the right hand of the Father, thence shall come to judge the quick and the dead.

TEXT	TRANSLATION
40. Ad cujus adventum omnes homines resurgere habent cum[1] corporibus suis: et reddituri sunt de factis própriis ratiónem (v);	At whose coming all men will rise again with their bodies and give account of their own deeds;
41. et qui bona egerunt ibunt in vitam aeternam: qui mala in ígnem aetérnum (p).	and they that have done good will go into life eternal, they that have done evil into eternal fire.

Conclusion

42. Haec est fides catholica: quam nisi quis fideliter firmiterque crediderit, salvus ésse non póterit (t).	This is the Catholic Faith, which unless a man faithfully and steadfastly believe, he will not be able to be in a state of salvation.

II. Its Composition

Of the so-called Athanasian Creed two things may be said with confidence at the outset: that it was originally written in Latin, and cannot therefore be Athanasian, and that it is not a Creed. All the early commentaries and allusions or quotations are in Latin, and the various Greek texts show undoubted signs of being translations, nor do the Greek MSS. go back earlier than the fifteenth century. And that it is not technically a Creed is shown by its form and purpose; it is a hymn, or rhythmical prose composition, intended to be memorized and sung or recited, to prevent the lapse of the orthodox into heresy, and to warn the heretics of the seriousness of their errors.[2] Though not strictly polemical, and in no way argumentative, it obviously owes its origin to some orthodox champion in times of controversy, and the very phrase "catholica fides", occurring at the beginning and the end, has the same anti-heretical ring as "catholica ecclesia" in contrast with unorthodox sects. The fact that the *Quicumque Vult* obviously has this character is some indication of its probable date. The heretical views against which

1 Agreeing with Dom Morin, *J.T.S.* xii. p. 171 n., against Turner.

2 "A mon avis le Quicumque est tout simplement une sorte de catéchisme élémentaire, destiné à mettre à la portée des esprits même les moins cultivés les formules dogmatiques...touchant la Trinité et l'Incarnation: le tout avec un certain sens pratique, qui ne s'accuse pas au même degré dans la plupart des anciennes professions de foi." Dom Morin, *Revue Bénéd.* 1901, p. 339.

its warnings are uttered are concerned with the doctrines of the Trinity and of the Incarnation, but in regard to the latter the heretical teachings are Arian and Apollinarian; there is no suggestion of Nestorianism or Eutychianism, and the parallel "as the rational soul and the flesh is one man, so God and man is one Christ" was not likely to be used when Eutychianism was prevalent.

The *Quicumque Vult* cannot, then, be earlier than the latter half of the fourth century, and there is some probability that it is not later than the end of the fifth; we can say almost with certainty that it is not later than the sixth.

(1) *Quotations and References*

(*a*) There are undoubted quotations from the *Quicumque Vult* in a canon of the Fourth Council of Toledo in 633:

Nec personas confundimus nec substantiam separamus. Patrem a nullo factum vel genitum dicimus; Filium a Patre non factum sed genitum asserimus; Spiritum vero Sanctum nec creatum nec genitum, sed procedentem ex Patre et Filio profitemur. Ipsum autem Dominum nostrum Jesum Christum Dei Filium et Creatorem omnium, ex substantia Patris ante saecula genitum.... Aequalis Patri secundum divinitatem, minor Patre secundum humanitatem.... Haec est catholicae ecclesiae fides; hanc confessionem conservamus atque tenemus; quam quisquis firmissime custodierit perpetuam salutem habebit.

(*b*) It is highly probable also that it is the *Quicumque* which is referred to in a canon of the Council of Autun, *c.* 670:

Si quis presbyter, aut diaconus, subdiaconus, clericus symbolum quod Sancto inspirante Spiritu Apostoli tradiderunt, et fidem sancti Athanasii presulis irreprehensibiliter non recensuerit, ab episcopo condemnetur.

(*c*) Columban, *Instructio* 1 (*c.* 543–616):

Credat itaque primum omnis qui vult salvus esse in primum et in novissimum Deum unum ac trinum, unum substantia, trinum subsistentia, unum potentia, trinum persona....Ubi habes in veritate Trinitatem in unitate et unitatem in Trinitate.

(*d*) Caesarius of Arles (bishop 502–542): *Excarpsum de Fide Catholica* (Append. August. *S.* 244):

Rogo et ammoneo vos, fratres carissimi, ut quicumque vult salvus esse, fidem rectam ac catholicam discat, firmiter teneat, inviolatamque conservet. Ita ergo oportet unicuique observare, ut credat Patrem, credat Filium, credat Spiritum Sanctum. Deus Pater, Deus Filius, Deus et Spiritus Sanctus; sed tamen non tres dii, sed unus Deus. Qualis Pater, talis Filius, talis et Spiritus Sanctus. Attamen credat unusquisque fidelis, quod Filius aequalis est Patri secundum divinitatem, et minor est Patri secundum humanitatem carnis...; Spiritus vero Sanctus ab utroque procedens.

Pater Deus, et Filius Deus, et Spiritus Sanctus Deus et hi tres unus Deus: nam et singillatim singulae quaeque Personae plenus Deus, et totae tres simul unus Deus (*S.* LXXXIII. 5).

(*e*) Avitus of Vienne (490–523), *de Divinitate Spiritus Sancti*:

Quem nec factum legimus nec genitum nec creatum....Sicut est proprium Spiritui Sancto a Patre Filioque procedere, istud Fides Catholica etiamsi renuentibus non persuaserit, in suae tamen disciplinae regula non excedit.

Avitus is definitely quoting from some written work, and *Fides Catholica* is one of the earliest titles given to the *Quicumque Vult*.

(*f*)   Vincent of Lérins, *Commonitorium*, c. xiii (A.D. 434):

Ecclesia vero catholica...et unam Divinitatem in Trinitatis plenitudine, et Trinitatem aequalitatem in una atque eadem majestate veneratur; et unum Christum Jesum, non duos, eundemque Deum pariter atque hominem confitetur....Alia est persona Patris, alia Filii, alia Spiritus Sancti....Altera substantia Divinitatis, altera humanitatis; sed tamen Deitas et humanitas non alter et alter, sed unus idemque Christus, unus idemque Filius Dei, et unius ejusdemque Christi et Filii Dei una eademque persona; sicut in homine aliud caro, et aliud anima; sed unus idemque homo, anima et caro...unus idemque Christus Deus et homo...idem Patri aequalis et minor; idem ex Patre ante saecula genitus idem in saeculo ex matre generatus; perfectus Deus, perfectus homo; in Deo summa Divinitas, in homine plena humanitas....Unus autem non corruptibili nescio qua Divinitatis et humanitatis confusione, sed integra et singulari quadam unitate personae.

(*g*) Phoebadius of Agen (Mai, t. III. p. 236, *Frag.* XVII):

Pater Deus, et Filius Deus, Spiritus Sanctus Deus et haec omnia unus Deus.

The last of these parallels is so slight as to be of little value, but the whole group from Caesarius onwards belong to the same school, and this shows that the *Quicumque Vult* was known at Lérins at latest from the middle of the fifth century.

(*h*) Finally it would appear either that the *Quicumque Vult* was known to Augustine, or that it is in part based upon his writings. A long list of parallels is given in Appendix A of Burn's *Introduction to the Creeds*; I quote some of the most outstanding:

4. *de Trin.* vii. 6. Ut neque personarum sit confusio, nec talis distinctio qua sit impar aliquid.

10. *Serm.* 105. Aeternus Pater, coaeternus Filius, coaeternus Spiritus Sanctus.

13. *de Trin.* v. 8. Itaque omnipotens Pater, omnipotens Filius, omnipotens Spiritus Sanctus.

14. *de Trin.* v. 8. Nec tamen tres omnipotentes sed unus omnipotens.

42. *de Trin.* i. 4. Haec est catholica fides;

15. *de Trin.* i. 5. sed in ea nonnulli perturbantur cum audiunt Deum Patrem
16. et Deum Filium et Deum Spiritum Sanctum, et tamen hanc Trinitatem non tres deos sed unum Deum.

17. *c. Maxim.* ii. 23. Sic et Dominum si quaeras, singulum quemque re-
18. spondeo; sed simul omnes non tres dominos deos, sed unum Dominum Deum.

19. *de Civ. Dei*, ix. 24. Cum de singulis quaeritur, unusquisque Eorum et Deus et omnipotens esse respondeatur; cum vero de omnibus simul, non tres dii, vel tres omnipotentes, sed unus Deus omnipotens.

20. *de Trin.* v. 14. Nam et singillatim si interrogemur de Spiritu Sancto.

21. *Serm.* 140. Dicimus Patrem Deum de nullo.

24. *c. Maxim.* ii. 23. Unus est Pater, non duo vel tres; et unus Filius, non duo vel tres; et unus amborum Spiritus, non duo vel tres.

25. *Serm.* 214. In hac Trinitate non est aliud alio majus aut minus.

30. *Enchir.* 35. Proinde Christus Jesus Dei Filius est et Deus et homo.
31. Deus ante omnia saecula, homo in nostro saeculo.

32. *Serm.* 238. Adversus Arium, veram et perfectam Verbi divinitatem, adversus Apollinarem, perfectam hominis in Christo defendimus veritatem.

33. *Ep.* 137. Aequalem Patri secundum divinitatem, minorem autem Patre secundum carnem, hoc est secundum hominem.

34. *in Joh. Tract.* 78. Agnoscamus geminam substantiam Christi, divinam scilicet qua aequalis est Patri, humanam qua major est Pater. Utrumque autem simul non duo sed unus est Christus.

35. *Enchir.* 34. Verbum caro factum est, a divinitate carne suscepta, non in carnem divinitate mutata.

36. *Serm.* 186. Idem Deus qui homo, et qui Deus idem homo, non confusione naturae sed unitate personae.

37. *in Joh. Tract.* 78. Sicut enim unus est homo anima rationalis et caro, sic unus est Christus Deus et homo.

Of these extracts the fifth and sixth, *de Trin.* i. 4 and 5 (the two passages are consecutive), are the most striking, and at once remind us of the quotation from Avitus. The words "cum audiunt" look as though Augustine also was referring to a formula familiar to his audience, which he too named *Fides Catholica*.

Dr Headlam writes: "The evidence in favour of the *Quicunque* belonging to a period earlier than the rise of Nestorianism, *i.e.* the year 429, is very strong.... The attribution to Caesarius of Arles has the authority of Dom Morin upon its side.... It seems to us...that the reasons for an earlier date are too strong to enable us to accept this suggestion.... Up till now [1909] he has adduced nothing which would not be equally well explained supposing that Caesarius were well acquainted with the language of the *Quicunque* and had learnt it by heart."[1]

Kattenbusch thought it to be earlier than the writings of Augustine. "The formula can be fitly regarded as a forerunner of the speculations of Augustine. In fact it seems to me that Augustine was already acquainted with it.... I think it more probable that some of its expressions or clauses had fixed themselves in Augustine's memory, than that the author of the formula should have created out of the references adduced by Burn his strikingly similar or completely parallel terms of speech."[2]

In support of this claim is the use of the word *substantia* as a translation of the Greek οὐσία. Augustine's regular equivalent is *essentia*, and though he admits *substantia* in some of his later writings (e.g. *cont. Max.* II. 1), in *de Trin.* VII. v. 10 he says: "Manifestum est abusive Deum substantiam vocari, ut nomine usitatiore intelligatur essentia, quae vere ac proprie dicitur." His practice is well illustrated by a single-sentence from S. LXXI. xi. 18 in which he employs both words, but in different senses: "Et hanc Trinitatem, quamis servata proprietate et *substantia* personarum; tamen propter ipsam individuam et inseparabilem aeternitatis, veritatis, bonitatis *essentiam* vel naturam, non esse tres deos, sed unum Deum."

Moreover, if once we grant that the *Quicumque Vult* was known to members of the school of Lérins, their revolt against his teaching on grace and free will would make it more probable that they would use a work from which Augustine also might quote, than one based on his writings, particularly if the author had a wide influence in Gaul. And if the *Quicumque Vult* was

1 *History, Authority and Theology*, pp. 127, 128.
2 *Theologische Literaturzeitung*, 1897, p. 144.

known to Augustine we can think of no author of it more probable than Ambrose.

(2) The Letter of the Council of 382

The *Quicumque Vult* is obviously directed against Sabellianism, Arianism, Apollinarianism, and Macedonianism. We may therefore confidently date it later than the Council of Constantinople in 381. This puts us on another track. If we turn to the letter sent by the Council of 382 (Theod. *H.E.* v. 9) we seem to find the source of some of the wording of the *Quicumque*:

(The faith of the Council of Nicaea) teaches us to believe in the name

τοῦ Πατρὸς καὶ τοῦ Υἱοῦ καὶ τοῦ Ἁγίου Πνεύματος, δηλαδὴ θεότητος καὶ δυνάμεως καὶ οὐσίας μιᾶς τοῦ Π. καὶ τοῦ Υ. καὶ τοῦ Ἁ. Π. πιστευομένης, ὁμοτίμου τε τῆς ἀξίας καὶ συναϊδίου τῆς βασιλείας.	6 Patris et Filii et Spiritus Sancti una est divinitas, aequalis gloria, coaeterna majestas.

Thus there is neither room for the heresy of the Sabellians

συγχεομένων τῶν ὑποστάσεων,	4 Neque confundentes personas

thus also the blasphemy of the Eunomians, of the Arians and of the Pneumatomachi is nullified

τῆς οὐσίας...τεμνομένης...	neque substantiam separantes.
καὶ τὸν τῆς ἐνανθρωπήσεως δὲ τοῦ Κυρίου λόγον ἀδιάστροφον σώζομεν, οὔτε ἄψυχον, οὔτε ἄνουν, ἢ ἀτελῆ τὴν τῆς σαρκὸς οἰκονομίαν παραδεχόμενοι, ὅλον δὲ εἰδότες	29 Incarnationem quoque Domini nostri Jesu Christi fideliter credat.
	32 Ex anima rationabili et humana carne subsistens.
τέλειον μὲν ὄντα πρὸ αἰώνων Θεὸν	31 ante saecula genitus...
Λόγον, τέλειον δὲ ἄνθρωπον ἐπ᾽	32 perfectus Deus,
ἐσχάτων τῶν ἡμερῶν διὰ τὴν	perfectus homo...
ἡμετέραν σωτηρίαν γενόμενον.	38 pro salute nostra.

Here the parallelism is too exact to allow us to doubt that the *Quicumque Vult* is based on the letter. This letter was sent to Damasus, Ambrose and others, and was a reply to the Roman Synod of 380 at which Ambrose was present, and which sent to Paulinus of Antioch a Creed with twenty-four anathemas, some of which have points of contact with the *Quicumque Vult*, e.g.:

vv. 3, 28. Haec ergo est salus Christianorum, ut credentes Trinitati id est, Patri et Filio et Spiritui Sancto (et baptizati, Greek translation, Theod. *H.E.* v. 11) in eam veram, solam, unam divinitatem et potentiam Ejusdem, haec sine dubio credamus (anath. 24).

v. 6.   Si quis non dixerit Patris et Filii et Spiritus Sancti unam divinitatem, potestatem, majestatem, potentiam, unam gloriam, dominationem, unum regnum atque unam voluntatem ac veritatem etc. (anath. 20).

v. 8.   Anathematizamus Arium atque Eunomium qui Filium et Spiritum Sanctum asserunt esse creaturas (anath. 3).

vv. 13, 26.   Si quis non dixerit tres Personas veras Patris et Filii et Spiritus Sancti aequales...omnia potentes etc. (anath. 21).

v. 16.   Quod siquis partiatur Deum Patrem dicens et Deum Filium Ejus et Deum Spiritum deos dici et non Deum etc. (anath. 24).

v. 23.   Si quis dixerit Spiritum Sanctum facturam esse etc. (anath. 18).

v. 31.   Si quis non dixerit Filium natum de Patre, id est, de substantia Ipsius divina etc. (anath. 11).
dicunt Dei Verbum in humana carne versatum...(anath. 7).

v. 32.   Anathematizamus eos, qui pro hominis anima rationabili et intelligibili....

To these possible sources we may add Gregory Nazianzen:

3 and 27 *Orat.* xxv. 17.   Νῦν δὲ δίδασκε τοσοῦτον εἰδέναι μόνον μονάδα ἐν τριάδι, καὶ τριάδα ἐν μονάδι προσκυνουμένην.

19 *Orat.* xl. 41.   Ταύτην δίδωμι...τὴν μίαν θεότητα καὶ δύναμιν ἐν τοῖς τρισὶν εὑρισκομένην ἑνικῶς, καὶ τὰ τρία συλλαμβάνουσαν μεριστῶς· οὔτε ἀνώμαλον οὐσίαις ἢ φύσεσιν, οὔτε αὐξομένην ἢ μειουμένην ὑπερβολαῖς καὶ ὑφέσεσι, πάντοθεν ἴσην, τὴν αὐτὴν πάντοθεν....Θεὸν ἕκαστον καθ' ἑαυτὸ θεωρούμενον, ὡς Πατέρα καὶ Υἱόν, ὡς Υἱὸν καὶ τὸ Ἅγιον Πνεῦμα....Θεὸν τὰ τρία σὺν· ἀλλήλοις νοούμενα, ἐκεῖνο διὰ τὴν ὁμοουσιότητα, τοῦτο διὰ τὴν μοναρχίαν.

25 *Orat.* xxxi. 14.   Ἡμῖν εἷς Θεός, ὅτι μία θεότης· καὶ πρὸς ἕν τὰ ἐξ Αὐτοῦ τὴν ἀναφορὰν ἔχει, κἂν τρία πιστεύηται· οὐ γάρ, τὸ μὲν μᾶλλον, τὸ δὲ ἧττον Θεός· οὐδὲ τὸ μὲν πρότερον, τὸ δὲ ὕστερον· οὐδὲ βουλήσει τέμνεται, οὐδὲ δυνάμει μερίζεται...ἀλλὰ ἀμέριστος ἐν μεμερισμένοις, εἰ δεῖ συντόμως εἰπεῖν, ἡ θεότης...ὅταν μὲν οὖν πρὸς τὴν θεότητα βλέψωμεν, καὶ τὴν πρώτην αἰτίαν, καὶ τὴν μοναρχίαν, ἐν ἡμῖν τὸ φανταζόμενον, ὅταν δὲ πρὸς τὰ ἐν οἷς ἡ θεότης, καὶ τὰ ἐκ τῆς πρώτης αἰτίας ἀχρόνως ἐκεῖθεν ὄντα καὶ ὁμοδόξως, τρία τὰ προσκυνούμενα.

29 and 30 *Orat.* xl. 45.   Πίστευε, τὸν Υἱὸν τοῦ Θεοῦ...τὸν γεννηθέντα ἐκ τοῦ Πατρὸς ἀχρόνως...τοῦτον ἐπ' ἐσχάτων τῶν ἡμερῶν γεγενῆσθαι διὰ σὲ... ἐκ τῆς παρθένου προελθόντα Μαρίας...ὅλον ἄνθρωπον, τὸν αὐτὸν καὶ Θεόν.

Of these orations xxv and xxxi were published in 380 and used by Ambrose in his work *de Spiritu Sancto* in the following year, while Oration xl, on Baptism, was delivered on 6 January 381. In the first and third extracts the parallelism with the *Quicumque Vult* is marked, while the second seems to give us the original of the adverb *singillatim*.

This derivation gives an obvious reason why there are no clauses in the *Quicumque Vult* directed against Nestorianism and Eutychianism; the "Fides Catholica" is a right faith in the

Trinity and the Incarnation as contrasted with these earlier heresies.

(3) *Theodosius and Ambrose*

Now let us adduce certain parallels to clauses 1, 2, 28 and 42 which bear on this point:

1 and 42. Catholicam fidem omni favore veneramur, sine qua salvi esse non possumus...ut cultores omnipotentis Dei non aliud nisi catholicos esse credamus. Rescript of the Emperor Theodosius, A.D. 384, *Corp. Script. Eccl. Lat.* xxxv. p. 46.
2. Nemo potest resurrectionis gloriam videre, nisi qui integrum mysterium Trinitatis incorrupta fidei sinceritate servaverit. Ambrose *in Luc.* vii. 9.
28. Audivimus hodie dicentes eos (obsessos) quibus manus imponebantur, neminem posse esse salvum...qui Trinitatis omnipotentem virtutem non crederet. Ambrose, *Ep.* xxii. 21, A.D. 386.

The rescript of Theodosius would seem to be based on the *Quicumque Vult*, and in that case we can date the latter between 382 and 384, and with high probability ascribe its authorship to Ambrose.

(4) *Parallels in Ambrose*

But if so the writings of Ambrose ought to furnish many parallels. Out of the much fuller list given by Brewer, *Das sogenannte Athanasianische Glaubensbekenntnis*, 1909, I select the following:

(a) *Phrases*

2. *in Luc.* vii. 9. Already quoted.
   de Fide, iv. 14. Non quicumque vult, nisi qui fideliter credit (caelum) ingredietur.
3. *de Fide*, i. 6. Adsertio autem nostrae fidei est, ut unum Deum esse dicamus,
4. neque...Filium separemus...neque Patrem confundamus et Verbum.
5. *in Luc.* ii. 12. Alius Pater, alius Filius, alius Spiritus Sanctus.
6. *Ep.* xlviii. 4. Hanc Trinitatem unius esse substantiae, majestatis, divinitatis. A direct reference to the letter of the Council of 382.
7. *Hexaem.* i. 19. Filius est imago Dei invisibilis; qualis ergo Deus est, talis imago.
8. *de Inc.* 112. Unde quia increatus Pater, increatus et Filius.
9. *de Fide*, v. 228. Immensum Te Filiumque Tuum et Spiritum Sanctum legi frequenter, credo libenter.
10. *de Inc.* 17. Non possum de Patris aeternitate dubitare, cujus aeternus est Filius.
    de Spir. S. i. 8. Ergo si mutationem non habet, aeternitatem habet, et ideo Spiritus Sanctus sempiternus est.
13. *de Inc.* 112. Following on 8: omnipotens Pater, omnipotens Filius.

14. *de Fide*, ii. 36. Ergo et Patris et Filii omnipotentia; sed tamen Deus unus omnipotens.
15. *in Luc*. x. 4. Et Pater Deus et Filius Deus, sed unus Deus.
16. *de Fide*, v. 46. Pater autem et Filius...non duo dii, sed unus Deus.
17, 18 *in Luc*. x. 4. Et Pater Dominus et Filius Dominus...et non duo domini, sed unus Dominus.
19. *de Fide*, 1. Singularitas ad personam pertinet, unitas ad naturam.
20. *de Spir. S*. iii. 107. Sacrilegium est tres deos aut dominos dicere.
22. *Ep.* lxiii. 49. (Filius) ex Patre solo natus.
de Fide, ii. 1. Genitus, non creatus.
23. *de Spir. S*. i. 120. Spiritus quoque Sanctus cum procedit a Patre et Filio.
25. *de Fide*, iv. 146. Increata...Trinitas, quae unius est aeternitatis et gloriae, nec tempus nec gradum vel posterioris recipit vel prioris.
28. *Ep.* xxii. 21. Already quoted.
29. *de Fide*, v. 106. Incarnationis Dei mysterium universae salus est creaturae.
30. *in Luc*. x. 3. Ergo et Deum Christum et hominem credamus: unum in utroque.
31. *de Spir. S*. iii. 168. Ante saecula ex Patre ut Dei Filius natus, et in saeculo ut homo carnis assumptione generatus.
32. *in Luc*. iv. 45. Jesum Deum hominemque, in utroque perfectum.
33. *in Gestis Aquileiens*. 37. Secundum carnem Filius minor est Patre, secundum divinitatem aequalis est Patri.
34. *in Luc*. vii. 120. Unus et Deus et homo Christus.
35. *de Inc*. 56. Non est Verbi natura in carnis conversa naturam.
36. *de Fide*, i. 9. Non confusione personae, sed unitate naturae.
37. *de Inc*. 11. Homo ex anima rationali constat et corpore.
40. *in Ps*. 1, n. 51. Actuum suorum in die judicii rationem reddituri sunt.

(b) *Points of Style*

1. Vult salvus esse.	*de Fuga Saec*. 4. qui salvus esse vult.
	Hymnus, iii. 28. qui credidit, salvus erit.
Ante omnia	*de Cain*, ii. 8. ante omnia fides nos commendare Deo debet.
Fidem tenere	*de Exc. Fratr*. i. 47. etsi fidem erga Deum tenerent.
	in Inc. i. 13. qui autem de Deo sunt, fidem tenent.
Catholica fides	*de Fide*, ii. 139. fidei catholicae in te vigentis habituri simus auxilium.
2. (Fides) integra	*Explan. Sym*. (M. 17, 1157 B). fides integra adversus Sabellianos....Ubi fides integra est.
Integra inviolataque	*Explan. Sym*. (M. 17, 1155 B). integra et inviolabilis conservatur.
(Fidem) servare	*in Ps*. 37, n. 8. si servaveris fidem.
	in Luc. vii. 9. Already quoted.
Absque = sine	*de Parad*. 59. absque caeteris.
In aeternum perire	*in Ps*. 118, xiv. 30. hujus anima non perit in aeternum.
3. Fides autem catholica haec est	*de Fide*, i. 6. Already quoted.
Deum venerari = adorare	*Ep*. xlviii. 4. ut Patrem Deum et Filium Ejus unigenitum et S. S. veneremur.
11, 14, 16, 18. Et tamen	*de Fide*, v. 200. et tamen eligant.

13. Similiter	*de Spir. S.* iii. 85. similiter itaque et Spiritus.
19. Confiteri...compelli- mur.	*in Ps.* 118, xx. 21. (athleta) certare compellitur.
26. Totae	*de Fide*, ii. 130. hoc enim totis scripturarum exponitur libris. Cp. Niceta, *de Lapsu Virginis*, 41, in totis quinque civitatibus; Avitus, *Ep.* 57, totis tribus personis; and Rönsch, *Itala und Vulgata*, p. 338.
27. Per omnia	*in Ps.* 118, vi. 30. διὰ παντός non solum significat quod semper sed etiam id quod per omnia, quia ille per omnia legem custodit.
28. De Trinitate sentire	*in Ps.* i. n. 40. ne forte sit grave nobis hoc sentire de Christo.
29. Fideliter credere	*de Fide*, iv. 14. nisi qui fideliter credit.
30. Pariter	*de Offic.* i. 248. mente pariter et corpore.
34. Licet...non duo tamen	*in Luc.* v. 69. licet...multa sint lenocinia verborum pleraque tamen.
36. Unus omnino	*in Luc.* i. 17. nunquam omnino.
40. Ad cujus adventum	*de Virg.* 60. bonum est ut ad adventum Domini interiora turbentur. Si ad angeli adventum Maria turbata est, quanto majus ad Christi nos turbamur adventum.
Omnes homines	*de Poen.* i. 13. nam omnes homines sub peccato nascimur.
Resurgere habent	*de Elia*, 7. per escam culpa haberet intrare. *de Cain*, ii. 26. ubi enim frater habebat occidi. *de Abr.* ii. 91. qui incipere habet.
Corporibus suis... propriis	*in Luc.* vi. 87. (natura) nec suos agnoscit ortus, usu tamen proprio recognoscit.
Facta = actus, opera	*Apol. David.* 24. similiter et facta bona manifesta sunt. *in Ps.* 43. nequis glorietur in suis factis.
Repetition	*de Spir. S.* i. 112. donat solus Pater, solus Filius, solus Spiritus Sanctus.
Antithesis	*de Spir. S.* iii. 109. ergo sanctus Pater sanctus et Filius sanctus et Spiritus: sed non tres sancti, quia unus est Deus sanctus.

(5) *Faustinus, Philaster, Honorius of Autun, Sicardus of Cremona, Rufinus*

On the other hand it is possible to trace a dependence on the *Quicumque Vult* not only in the rescript of Theodosius but also in the *de Trinitate sive de Fide contra Arianos* written by Faustinus about the year 384:

6. vii. 1. Una est ergo divinitas Patris et Filii et Spiritus Sancti;
7. iv. 1. Qualis enim Pater Deus est, talis et Filius Deus est;
13, 14. iii. 2. Sed ne duos omnipotentes intellegas praecavendum est; licet enim et Pater omnipotens sit et Filius, tamen unus est omnipotens sicut et unus Deus;

where the third quotation seems conclusive.

Similarly in chapter 93 of the *Liber de Haeresibus* by Philaster[1] of Brescia written at about the same date at the request of the Empress Flaccilla:

5.   Ergo est vera persona Patris, quae misit Filium, et est vera persona Filii, quae advenit de Patre, et est vera persona Spiritus, quae a Patre et Filio missa est. Trium itaque harum personarum una est veritas, majestas, et substantiae aequalitas, et divinitas
7, 9.   sempiterna. Qualis est enim immensa et inenarranda Patris persona, talis est et Filii, talis est et Spiritus Sancti.

And at the conclusion of the same chapter:

Sed ut Patris veram personam, et Filii talem qualem Patris, et Spiritus Sancti sicut Filii veram credamus personam: harumque personarum unam qualitatis substantiam, majestatem, et potentiam cognoscamus...haec ita (Christus) dignatus est operari et loqui pro salute nostra.

The connexion of the *Quicumque Vult* with Theodosius and his court is brought out in two curious documents of the middle ages, where nevertheless it is attributed to Athanasius, who died in 373, while Theodosius became Emperor in 379.

Honorius of Autun (*c.* 1090–1125), *Gemma Animae*, II. 59 (Migne, *P.L.* CLXXII. 634), enumerates four Creeds, the Apostles', Nicene, Constantinopolitan, and the *Quicumque Vult*, and writes: "Quartam fidem Quicumque Vult [ecclesia catholica] quotidie ad Primam iterat quam Athanasius, Alexandrinus episcopus, *rogatu Theodosii Imperatoris* edidit." And Sicardus of Cremona (1185–1215), *Mitrale*, IV. 6 (Migne, *P.L.* CCXIII. 170), speaking of Prime says: "Subditur symbolum fidei, scilicet Quicumque Vult, quod Athanasius, Alexandrinus episcopus, *rogatu Theodosii Imperatoris* ad eradicandam invalescentem haereticorum perfidiam et divulgandam fidem catholicam edidit."

If Ambrose is the author of the *Explanatio* and one of the writers referred to by Rufinus[2], we may be disposed to attach some importance to what appears to be a reference to the *Quicumque* in the latter's *Ecclesiastical History*, x. 29: "ut

---

1 Philaster was probably commended to the Church of Brescia by Ambrose who would have known of his opposition to Auxentius at Milan. He took part in the Council of Aquileia in Sept. 381, which was presided over by Valerian and Ambrose. He was at Milan some time between 384–387 and died before 397.

2 "Nonnulli illustrium tractatorum", *in Symb.* 1.

ejusdem substantiae ac deitatis, cujus Pater et Filius, etiam
Spiritus Sanctus crederetur, nec quicquam prorsus in Trinitate
aut creatum aut inferius posteriusve diceretur".[1] Cf. also
"Trinitas in personarum distinctione, unitas in veritate substantiae...Filius Dei...carne et anima humana suscepta...
passus est pro salute nostra...resurrexit a mortuis...ascendit
ad caelos". *Apol.* i. 4.

(6) *The Letter of Ambrose to Valentinian*

The early use of the *Quicumque Vult* at Milan cannot be
absolutely proved, but is rendered highly probable by different
lines of evidence. In his letter to Valentinian (*Ep.* xxi) written
in 386 Ambrose encloses a discourse against Auxentius, near the
end of which occurs the following passage:

Hymnorum quoque meorum carminibus deceptum populum ferunt.
Plane nec hoc abnuo. Grande carmen istud est, quo nihil potentius.
Quid enim potentius quam confessio Trinitatis, quae quotidie totius
populi ore celebratur? Certatim omnes student fidem fateri; Patrem
et Filium et Spiritum Sanctum norunt versibus praedicare; facti sunt
igitur omnes magistri, qui vix poterant esse discipuli.

On the meaning of "hymnus" see *de Off.* i. 220: "Sed
possumus et hominem...honorare: hymnus specialiter Deo
dicitur"; and compare *de Spir. S.* iii. 112 where the *Sanctus*
is called a hymn. "Carmen" is a liturgical formula and the
Psalms are repeatedly called "hymni" and "carmina" by
Ambrose, and "versus" could be similarly applied. There is,
therefore, nothing in this language which would render it inappropriate to the *Quicumque Vult*, and the description as a
whole fits it admirably.

That the *Quicumque Vult* may be rightly called a "hymn"
or "canticle" is shown not only by its form, but also by the
fact that from the close of the eighth century it is found in a
large number of Psalters, together with a series of canticles
which always includes the *Te Deum*; and concurrently there

---

[1] Cf. Rufinus's translation of Origen, *de Princ.* i. 63 (ed. Koetschau, p. 60):
"Porro autem nihil in Trinitate majus minusve dicendum est." This is
generally regarded as Rufinus's own interpolation; see Koetschau's note.

is a nearly continuous testimony in episcopal charges and admonitions and conciliar decrees enjoining its use.

The Liturgy of Milan is independent in origin from that of Rome, whether secular or monastic (Benedictine), and spread westward, and where it differs from the Roman it often seems to reflect the mind of Ambrose. Thus, in the *Oratio ad consecrandam Ecclesiam* (Mercati, *Antiche Reliquie Liturgiche*, p. 23), the Milanese rite has "Omnesque homines venientes adorare in hoc loco propitius dignare respicere ut...constanter in sanctae Trinitatis unitate et fide catholica perseverent"; where the corresponding prayer in the Gelasian Sacramentary (ed. Wilson, p. 133) omits "unitate et", a characteristically Ambrosian phrase, which appears in the *Quicumque Vult* in almost identical form.

The evidence for the use of the *Quicumque Vult* at Milan is as follows: *Epistola Canonica*, published by the Ballerini and assigned by them to the sixth century, but by Dom Morin (*J.T.S.* xii. p. 178) to the seventh or eighth, is an episcopal charge directing that all the clergy should learn the Catholic Faith by heart. It belongs to North Italy and was adopted by Atto, Bishop of Vercellae, in the tenth century. Ratherius of Verona in Lent 966 directed that they should learn the three Creeds, ascribing the *Quicumque* to Athanasius.

A Synod held at Siponto at the end of the ninth century directed all the clergy to sing the Creed every Lord's day.

Then the anonymity of the *Quicumque Vult* tells in favour of its Ambrosian authorship. Nearly all the hymns assigned to Ambrose are anonymous, and they are attributed to him: (1) because they correspond in style and matter with writings known to be his; (2) because they appear to have been in early use in Milan; (3) in a few instances because they are attributed to writers approximately contemporary to whom they clearly do not belong. The *Quicumque Vult* fulfils all these conditions. It resembles the known works of Ambrose in style and phraseology; it deals with precisely the heresies which he combated; its use at Milan is probably at least as early as, and independent of, its use in Gaul; it is ascribed in the Canon of Autun to Athanasius. Finally it is a hymn intended for antiphonal singing, and the practice of antiphonal singing was introduced at Milan by Ambrose from the East, the list of canticles sung at Milan closely resembling that of Remesiana and Constantinople; the *Cursus Leoninus* in which the *Quicumque Vult* is written was probably an Eastern importation; and certain phrases seem to go back to the letter of the Council of Constantinople in 382, which was addressed, among others, to Ambrose.

These considerations, drawn for the most part from the work of Brewer to which reference has been already made, if they do not prove the Ambrosian authorship of the *Quicumque Vult*, an impossible task, at any rate far outweigh the evidence for the claim of any other author, and have the support of Seeberg in modern Germany, and before his death convinced Dr Burn in England.[1]

If we allow on the one hand that the *Quicumque Vult* is dependent on the letter of the bishops at Constantinople in 382, and on the other hand that the rescript of Theodosius in 384 is dependent on it, we obtain narrow limits for the date of its composition.

III. Its Name and Use

The earliest and only proper title of the *Quicumque Vult* is *Fides Catholica*. It is so called by writers in the ninth century who describe it as a *sermo* or instruction. In this period it is also called a Hymn concerning Faith of the Trinity, and in the constitutions of English bishops of the thirteenth century a Psalm. The name *symbolum* was first attached to it by Regino of Prum (*c.* 892).

At the beginning of the ninth century it was used at Prime at the Benedictine Abbey of Fleury, and in 922 was adopted in the monastic church of St Martin at Tours, while at the end of the tenth century it was sung antiphonally both in England and France. The canon of Autun was probably passed to ensure that the clergy should know it for this purpose. It is incorporated in Psalters of the eighth century, and the frequency of quotations from it in sermons is probably due to its regular recitation. As

1 See *J.T.S.* XXVII. 105, pp. 19–28.

regards Rome the evidence would tend to show that it was not in use there before the eleventh century. At Milan and Tours it was sung daily, but at Rome only on Sundays, and owing to the frequent "occurrence" of festivals its use has become almost limited to the Sundays in Advent, and from Septuagesima to the end of Lent. The English use was to recite it daily between the Psalms and the prayers at Prime. The "symbolic" authority of the *Quicumque Vult* was mainly the work of the Reformation. Orthodox reformers were anxious to make their position clear on the great questions of the faith and dreaded being accused of Socinianism; so they accepted the popular terminology of "the three Creeds". In the Prayer Book of 1549 it was to be said after the *Benedictus* at Mattins on six great festivals, seven saints' days being added in 1552; in both books it was to be followed by the Apostles' Creed, but in the Prayer Book of 1662 the Apostles' Creed was dropped on these occasions, and so the *Quicumque Vult* appeared to be a substitute for it.[1]

It is never recited in the East, though from the latter part of the eighteenth century it has been printed in the Appendix of the Greek Horologium, of course without the *Filioque* clause, probably because all editions of that book used to be printed at Venice and so were accessible to Western influences.

In the Russian service books it appears at the beginning of the Psalter, and seems to have been introduced in the middle of the seventeenth century. The translation has been made from a Greek version and of course omits the *Filioque* clause.

How it first obtained the name of "Athanasian" is unknown, but another document, the *Fides Romanorum*, was occasionally ascribed to him, and as the *Quicumque Vult* was specially directed against Sabellianism, Arianism, and Apollinarianism, the attribution would not be unnatural; in the great controversy

---

1 "On peut dire que le Quicumque est vraiment de facture classique...; et pourtant, cette concision s'y trouve alliée à une telle clarté, que la plupart des simples fidèles devaient être à même de le comprendre et d'en retenir la texte, du moins à l'époque où il fut composé. On pourrait même dire jusqu'à l'époque moderne, le *Quicumque* ou sa traduction ayant trouvé place dans presque tous les Livres d'Heures à l'usage des laïques. Cranmer n'a donc tant innové en l'admittant dans le Prayer Book à l'usage de l'Église Anglicane." Morin, *J.T.S.* XII. 169.

between the East and the West on the doctrine of the Double Procession, the Latin Monks on Mount Olivet quoted a document which they described as the Faith of Athanasius, and henceforth the use of the *Quicumque Vult* in the West became intensified.

IV. The English Translation

An English translation of the *Quicumque Vult* was first included in the various editions of *The Manuall of Prayers, or the Prymer in Englysshe set out at lengthe...set forth by John* [Hilsey] *late Bishop of Rochester*, 1530, and there entitled *The symbole or crede of the great Doctour Athanasius*. That made for the Prayer Book of 1549 was corrected by the Greek version in "῞Ωραι τῆς ἀειπαρθένου Μαρίας κατ᾽ ἔθος τῆς ῥωμαϊκῆς ἐκκλησίας", Aldus, Venice, 1497, and possibly by a Greek Psalter published by Cephaleus at Strasburg in 1524, and at Antwerp in 1533. The Reformers deemed it right to follow the most authentic source, and could not think that a document whose Western origin was not then imagined, and which bore the name of a Greek doctor, was written in any other language than Greek. A parallel error may be found in Jewel's argument that writings in Greek could not be by Clement of Rome; "Were the Bishop of Rome's books ...written in Greek?" he asks (*Works*, 1. p. iii, Parker Soc.).

I give specimens of variations:[1]

2.	inviolatum	undefiled ἀμώμητον
4.	substantiam separantes	dividing μερίζοντες
9.	immensus	incomprehensible ἀκατάληπτος
12.	non tres increati, nec tres immensi	not three incomprehensibles, nor three uncreated οὐδὲ τρεῖς ἀκατάληπτοι οὐδὲ τρεῖς ἄκτιστοι
19.	singillatim...confiteri	acknowledge...by himself ἰδίᾳ ἕκαστον
29.	fideliter credat	believe rightly ὀρθῶς πιστεύσῃ
42.	fideliter firmiterque	faithfully πιστῶς

1 A fuller list is given by Swainson, *Nicene and Apostles' Creeds*, pp. 492, 493.

Note proposed to be added to the rubric by the Royal Commission in 1689, first made public in 1854.

The Articles of which ought to be received and believed as agreeable to the Holy Scriptures, and the condemning clauses are to be understood as relating only to those who obstinately deny the substance of the Christian Faith.

SYNODICAL DECLARATION

Made by the Convocation of the Province
of Canterbury in 1873, and re-affirmed in 1879.

"For the removal of doubts, and to prevent disquietude in the use of the Creed commonly called the Creed of St Athanasius, this Synod doth solemnly declare:

1. "That the Confession of our Christian faith, commonly called the Creed of St Athanasius, doth not make any addition to the faith as contained in Holy Scripture, but warneth against errors which from time to time have arisen in the Church of Christ.

2. "That as Holy Scripture in divers places doth promise life to them that believe, and declare the condemnation of them that believe not, so doth the Church in this Confession declare the necessity for all who would be in a state of salvation of holding fast the Catholic faith, and the great peril of rejecting the same. Wherefore the warnings in this Confession of faith are to be understood no otherwise than the like warnings in Holy Scripture, for we must receive God's threatenings even as His promises, in such wise as they are generally set forth in Holy Writ. Moreover the Church doth not herein pronounce judgment on any particular person or persons, God alone being the Judge of all."

PART IV

THE "COMMUNION OF SAINTS" AS AN ARTICLE OF THE CREED

CHAPTER XVI

THE "COMMUNION OF SAINTS" AS AN ARTICLE OF THE CREED

I. Introduction. II. Theological Considerations. III. *Sanctorum Communio* not equivalent to "The Church". IV. Date and Language. V. Grammatical Construction. VI. The Early Interpretation: (1) Council of Nîmes, (2) *Simbolum graeca lingua est*, (3) Basil and Chrysostom, (4) Augustine, (5) Niceta of Remesiana. VII. Later Interpretations: Faustus of Riez and others. VIII. Conclusion.

I. INTRODUCTION

THE subject of our enquiry is historical rather than dogmatic or apologetic; it is not directly concerned with modern interpretations of this phrase, but rather with its meaning during the period in which the Apostles' Creed was in process of formation, that is, from the middle of the second to the middle of the seventh century. Our present Apostles' Creed appears in its entirety, but for a minute variation, in the works of Priminius about A.D. 750, and it is not improbable that the particular phrase occurred in a Christian Creed in Asia Minor as early as the time of Irenaeus; but though our main enquiry will be confined within these boundaries, the use of the word "communion" in the New Testament may help to throw light on the meaning of the phrase at the beginning of the period, and certain later arrangements may perform a similar office at its close; so we shall allow ourselves to trespass in both directions beyond the limits we have assigned.

By thus narrowing our scope we shall avoid being entangled in highly controversial questions. We shall not ask whether or no the modern mind has a particular tendency, what views are congenial to it and what repugnant, what help or hindrance is supplied by modern psychology or modern physical or biological science, questions which raise a cloud of controversy in regard to another article of the Creed, "the resurrection of the body"; nor shall we contend that the meaning attached to any phrase in ancient times is the only meaning legitimate in our day. We cannot indeed avoid theological considerations, but they will be such considerations as would limit the possibilities of the meaning attached to the phrase in the ancient Church, without urging that the modern mind ought or ought not to view theological questions from the same standpoint; and these theological presuppositions are for the most part to be deduced from the dogmatic formulas in which they are embodied.

Within our period there are, in fact, three different though interlacing strands guiding us to our conclusion; they are: (1) theological, what sort of statements were considered fitting to be made matters of dogmatic requirement; (2) grammatical, what would be the natural interpretation of *sanctorum communio* or κοινωνία τῶν ἁγίων as determined by grammatical usage; and (3) what direct evidence we have of the actual meaning attached to the phrase by ancient authors. The task proposed will be satisfactorily accomplished if these three lines of enquiry all lead to the same solution of our problem.

II. THEOLOGICAL CONSIDERATIONS

Rightly or wrongly the ancient Church was subject to none of our modern scruples and hesitations with regard to the need of dogma. It did not regard the Christian faith as a speculation but as a revelation. It does not seem to have felt dogmatic statements as burdens on the conscience or fetters on the intellect, but rather as instruments for the removal of errors, and as welcome truths giving to the intellect a sure basis for advance. And in consequence it had no hesitation in expelling refractory members from its own body, not merely for moral or disciplinary offences, but for holding views opposed, in its judgement, to that faith which it was its office and privilege to proclaim. And in fact it went beyond mere expulsion, and held that the heretic was not only cut off from its communion on earth, but that his eternal salvation was also thereby imperilled. It might perhaps have hesitated to say *"Extra ecclesiam nulla salus est"*; it would not have scrupled to say with every confidence *"Extra ecclesiam nulla salus revelata est."*

The teaching of the Church no doubt ran beyond its Creeds, but the Creed represented the bare minimum of dogmatic requirement; it was that on which the Church claimed to have fully and finally made up its mind. But the Church did not believe in the stability of its own faith considered subjectively; it believed in the inalterability of the objective facts; and it was this which was implied when it spoke of the inalterability of the faith. The faith, it asserted, was the same from age to age, because the facts could not change; they partook of a double immutability, in the changelessness of God who wrought them, and in the changelessness of past history which not even God Himself can alter.

Thus, even if it asserted a belief in the Church, it was not a belief in itself as a merely human society, or in its own goodness or merit or power; God was its founder, His Spirit illumined and sanctified it. Irenaeus might be extravagant in saying *Ubi Spiritus Dei, illic ecclesia* but the whole Church was convinced that *Ubi ecclesia, ibi est Spiritus Dei*.[1]

Similarly in the Nicene Creed "We confess one baptism" is not a statement of the duty of being baptized or of bringing infants to baptism, it is a profession of faith in the benefits God gives in the ordinance. Nor in the teaching of the Church would the two great sacraments of the Gospel be separated. The Church of England may or may not be right in asserting that these two are "generally necessary to salvation"; it is at any rate in the most complete agreement with the teaching of the Church in

---

1 *Adv. Haer.* III. xxxviii. 1. Cp. Tert. *de Bapt.* 6, "Ubi tres, id est Pater et Filius et Spiritus Sanctus, ibi ecclesia"; *de Pudic.* 21, "Ecclesia proprie et principaliter Ipse est Spiritus"; Clem. Alex. *Paed.* i. p. 114, οὕτω τὸ πιστεῦσαι μόνον καὶ ἀναγεννηθῆναι τελείωσίς ἐστιν ἐν ζωῇ· οὐ γάρ ποτε ἀσθενεῖ ὁ Θεός. Ὡς γὰρ τὸ θέλημα Αὐτοῦ ἔργον ἐστί, καὶ τοῦτο κόσμος ὀνομάζεται· οὕτως καὶ τὸ βούλημα Αὐτοῦ ἀνθρώπων ἐστὶ σωτηρία, καὶ τοῦτο ἐκκλησία κέκληται.

earlier ages, to which expulsion from the society and excommunication were the same thing. However difficult it might be to secure regularity of communicating, the Church did not hesitate to say that by the one sacrament the supernatural life of Christians was initiated, and by the other it was sustained.

So also, if the Creed proclaimed the resurrection of the dead, that event was thought of not as a stage in a natural evolution, but as the action of God's power; the dead were not simply to arise but to be raised. And so in the last article of the Creed, eternal life, or the life of the coming age, existed already as an objective fact, over against the believer, in Jesus.

In short, if we examine the actual forms taken by the Creed, we find that the subjective element is confined to the introductory words "I" or "we believe"; all the rest is a statement of what the Church held to be objective facts, which neither belief nor unbelief could alter. But more than that, the particular facts selected for commemoration were facts on which salvation was held to rest. Unless God had become incarnate, unless Jesus had died, and risen, and ascended, and been seated at the right hand of the Father; unless the Spirit had been sent; unless the Church had been founded; unless sins were remitted; then salvation would not have been received. In short, to the mind of the early Church the Creed stated, and stated only, the necessary objective conditions of salvation. Salvation had for the individual subjective conditions also; he must orientate his life by this Creed and in accordance with these facts; and for the accomplishment of that purpose he must first of all accept the facts in accordance with which his manner of life was to be regulated. Thus the insistence on a right faith was but the assertion from another point of view of the value and truth of the facts to be believed; the subjective need and the objective truth involved each other.

This characteristic at once states for us certain limits as to what the phrase "communion of saints" might mean at the time when it was inserted into the Creed. It must not merely state a truth, it must state an objective ground or necessary condition of salvation; and this ground or condition must not be alterable; in the sense of "the things to be believed" the "faith" had been the same ever since Pentecost.

Clearly, therefore, "the communion of saints" could not mean the intercourse of living and dead Christians as such; temporal life and death have no relevance; at Pentecost there were no dead Christians. This, of course, does not exclude the meaning "the mutual intercourse of Christians to which death makes no difference"; it merely insists that "the communion of saints" could not at its first insertion into the Creed have meant the mutual intercourse of two distinct classes of Christians, the living and the dead.

Nor could the phrase intend to assert any spiritual activity on the part of believers whether living or departed. The Church laid emphasis on the duty of mutual love and on its expression in mutual prayer, but the spiritual effect of such activity on its recipient was to intensify the atmosphere or medium across which the action of God could pass; men might be placed by it in a state more favourable to salvation, but the salvation which they became more fitted to welcome and to receive was God's work. The Pelagianism which imputed a saving value to a man's own efforts and the Donatism to those of his fellows were alike reckoned heresies; they detracted from the completeness of the objective work wrought in Christ. Consequently, as an article of the Creed, "the communion of saints" could not mean "that spiritual atmosphere of mutual charity or holiness which believers foster by the use of grace"; it must express some divine act or gift. The Church held, no doubt, a high opinion of the duty and value of intercession, but neglect of this duty, while it might imperil the salvation of the man himself, did not threaten the salvation of those for whom he failed to intercede: it was the intercession of Christ, and not of Christians, that possessed saving efficacy. The Christian could assert as an article of his faith that his salvation depended on the oblation of Himself made by Christ; he could not assert that his salvation depended on the oblation of himself made by anyone else, however exalted. Intercession, to the mind of the early Church, was not a power which saves; it could at the utmost be a condition of salvation but never a cause of it. The phrase, therefore, could not, in the Creed, mean "I believe in the mutual love, intercourse, assistance, or prayer of saints, or of any class of saints"; that would appear to be imputing to Christians as a source the power which belonged to them only as a gift; it was on the verge of idolatry; it would certainly be thought to be Pelagian or Donatist.

This kind of explanation of the phrase is to-day widespread; it is certainly not primitive. The modern mind tends to become absorbed in interest in its own activities; the mind of the early Church had a far more objective outlook, it was considering the work of God.

The other explanation now commonly given is that the "communion of saints" means not the "intercommunion" but the "community" of Christians; that is, the phrase is a synonym of "the holy catholic Church". Clearly this meaning is admissible on theological grounds; if it is to be excluded at all it must be either because *communio* or κοινωνία will not bear this concrete sense; because the words "Church" and "communion of saints" are found separated from one another; or from direct testimony that as a matter of fact this phrase was not so regarded.

III. *SANCTORUM COMMUNIO* NOT EQUIVALENT TO "THE CHURCH"

Each of the terms of this phrase is individually ambiguous. *Communio* can be used in a concrete sense to mean a body of persons, and *sanctorum* can be either masculine or neuter. Supposing *communio* to be concrete, then *sanctorum*, if it be masculine, will be a possessive genitive. Grammatically this is quite possible both in Latin and in Greek, though apparently it is more common in the former than in the latter. Supposing this to be the meaning of both words, then *sanctorum* must include all Christians; the restriction to the "departed", or "the specially holy" is not earlier than the fifth century, and then appears only in the West, while dead Christians and specially holy Christians, "saints" in the popular sense, form no separate community of their own, but are members of a single society which embraces the living as well as the dead, and sinners as well as saints. It is perfectly true that the Donatists, like other puritans in other ages, claimed that the title "saints" belonged to them exclusively, but they did so because "holy" was the epithet most regularly applied to the Church from very early times, and they asserted that they themselves formed the entire Church.

This meaning, however, would seem to be definitely excluded from the phrase as used in the Creed by the fact that the "communion of saints" and "the Church" are often found separated from each other, whereas if they were regarded as equivalents they must have been always closely connected. Starting from the West, the order of clauses in the Bangor Antiphonary is *Sanctam ecclesiam catholicam, Abremissa peccatorum, Sanctorum communionem*. In *Miss. Gall.* 1. the interpunctuation assigns *Spiritum Sanctum, Sanctam ecclesiam catholicam* to Article 9, and places *Sanctorum communionem, Remissionem peccatorum* in Article 10. Similarly, when separate articles are assigned to individual Apostles, Priminius gives *Sanctorum communionem* to Jude as Article 11; pseudo-Augustine, Sermon 241 to Simon Zelotes as Article 10; the *Book of Deer* joins *Sanctam ecclesiam* by *que* to *Spiritum Sanctum*; a Gallican Creed of the tenth or eleventh century[1] joins *Sanctorum communionem* with *Remissionem peccatorum* by *et* where *Miss. Gall.* 2 has *ac*, unless this be a mistake for *abremissionem*. Coming further East the Creed of Jerome obviously draws a distinction between the Church and the communion of saints, since it runs: *Credo remissionem peccatorum in sancta ecclesia, Sanctorum communionem*; and the distinction is no less marked in the sermon of Niceta of Remesiana who writes: *Ergo in hac una ecclesia credis te communionem consecuturum esse sanctorum*. Finally, in Armenia we have a Creed[2] with a similar arrangement to that of the Bangor Antiphonary: "We believe in the forgiveness of sins in the holy Church, and in the communion of saints." A distinction between the Church and the communion of saints so widely

1 Hahn³, p. 82.

2 Cartegian, *de Fidei Symbolo quo Armenii utuntur*, Venice, 1893, p. 39.

distributed is decisive against holding that the second phrase is a mere equivalent of the first.

It is noticeable that the phrase "communion of saints" is exclusively liturgical. It is found in a canon of the Council of Nîmes in 394, and in Basil of Caesarea, *Regulae brevius tractatae*, Interrog. cccix, and in Sermon 52 of Augustine, but beyond these three examples seems to be limited either to the Creed itself or to expositions of it. Thus the number of possible occurrences is narrowly limited, and this makes the wide extension of the authorities noticed the more remarkable, and definitely shuts out the concrete meaning of "the Christian body or society". And by the same reasoning we must exclude also that mutual membership of Christians in each other which follows from their common membership in Christ and in the Church. Theologically this is not a ground of salvation but an effect of participation in Christ, and would thus not have been, in the mind of the early Church, a fit object for dogmatic assent; historically it obviously was not so asserted in fact.

IV. DATE AND LANGUAGE

Besides the authorities already cited the phrase occurs in the Creed of Faustus of Riez (bp. 449–482) who came from Lérins; in a Gallican sermon attributed to Augustine (Serm. 242); in a second Gallican sermon, *Simbolum graeca lingua est*, and in others of a later date; in the Missal of Bobbio—a monastery founded by Columban the Irishman after leaving Bregenz—and in the Mozarabic Liturgy. It does not occur in the Creed of Africa, either in the time of Augustine or in that of Fulgentius of Ruspe at the beginning of the sixth century, nor in the Creed of Rome until the adoption of the *Textus Receptus*. It would seem, therefore, to be employed in liturgical formulas solely in places which lie on the great road from Asia Minor, across the Bosphorus, through Pannonia, Aquileia, the plain of Northern Italy and Southern France, to Spain; and in its northern fork, over the Brenner, by the Lake of Constance, to Northern France, Britain and Ireland.

Thus all our earliest authorities point back to Asia Minor and the Greek language. The Lower Rhône valley was largely dominated by Greek influence. Nîmes was probably trilingual, speaking Greek, Latin, and Celtic. The presbyters and deacons who came thither *de ultimis partibus Orientis* doubtless spoke Greek and may have brought the phrase with them along this road. The Mozarabic Liturgy has many Eastern affinities. The Creed of Jerome cannot be dissociated from that of Niceta; this latter was of Eastern origin and Niceta is either himself translating from a Greek original or using a translation already made. Basil of Cappadocia of course wrote and spoke in Greek, and Armenia was evangelized from Cappadocia. Thus the origin of the phrase is Greek and must be looked for in Asia Minor not later than the fourth century. Not later—but possibly two centuries earlier.

We have already drawn attention to the Creed of the Marcosians given by Irenaeus,[1] and there is good reason for supposing that it is a parody of a Christian Creed of six clauses, which, by comparison with other early Creeds, we should judge to be a probable length for this date; we saw that the fourth and fifth clauses might well represent in the Christian original:

> In one (holy) church
> And forgiveness of sins.

We are then left in the parody with καὶ κοινωνίαν τῶν δυνάμεων and this would seem to represent καὶ κοινωνίαν τῶν ἁγίων. The separation of "the communion of saints" from "the Church" has many parallels, and in the Armenian Creed Cartegian reads "Holy Church; Forgiveness of sins; Communion of saints", and Caspari, "Forgiveness of sins in holy Church; Communion of saints". But independently of the Marcosian Creed we can assert that the language of the phrase "communion of saints" was Greek, its home Asia Minor, and its date not later than the fourth century.

1 See pp. 24, 28, 29, 35.

V. Grammatical Construction

Having settled the question of language, we need only attach a subordinate importance to Latin translations, and confine ourselves in the main to the phrase in Greek.

The New Testament

In the New Testament wherever κοινωνία is followed by a noun in the genitive case, the genitive is either (*a*) possessive, (*b*) descriptive, or (*c*) partitive, and the last is by far the most common; "communion with" is always expressed by the use of the preposition μετά, πρός or εἰς.

Absolute:

Gal. ii. 9, "The right hands of fellowship".

Heb. xiii. 16, "Forget not well-doing and fellowship" or "hospitality".

With dependent genitive:

(*a*) Possessive: Phil. i. 5, ἐπὶ τῇ κ. ὑμῶν εἰς τὸ εὐαγγέλιον.

(*b*) Descriptive: Phil. ii. 1, εἴ τι παραμύθιον ἀγάπης, εἴ τις κ. πνεύματος (possibly partitive, see below).

Philem. 6, ἡ κ. τῆς πίστεώς σου.

(*c*) Partitive: 1 Cor. i. 9, ἐκλήθητε εἰς κ. τοῦ υἱοῦ αὐτοῦ.

(Cp. Heb. iii. 14, μέτοχοι τοῦ Χριστοῦ γεγόναμεν.)

1 Cor. x. 16, κ. τοῦ αἵματος τοῦ Χριστοῦ...κ. τοῦ σώματος τοῦ Χριστοῦ.

2 Cor. viii. 4, τὴν κ. τῆς διακονίας τῆς εἰς τοὺς ἁγίους.

(Cp. Rom. xii. 13, ταῖς χρείαις τῶν ἁγίων κοινωνοῦντες.)

Phil. iv. 14–16, συνκοινωνήσαντές μου τῇ θλίψει....οὐδεμία μοι ἐκκλησία ἐκοινώνησεν εἰς λόγον δόσεως καὶ λήμψεως...εἰς τὴν χρείαν μοι ἐπέμψατε.

1 Tim. vi. 18, εὐμεταδότους εἶναι, κοινωνικούς.

Rom. xv. 27, τοῖς πνευματικοῖς αὐτῶν ἐκοινώνησαν τὰ ἔθνη.)

2 Cor. xiii. 13, ἡ κ. τοῦ ἁγίου πνεύματος. (Possibly descriptive, but cp. Heb. vi. 4, μετόχους γενηθέντας πνεύματος ἁγίου; 2 Pet. i. 4, γένησθε θείας κοινωνοὶ φύσεως.)

Phil. iii. 10, κ. τῶν παθημάτων αὐτοῦ.

With a preposition = "fellowship with":

μετά:

1 John i. 3, 6, 7, ἵνα καὶ ὑμεῖς κ. ἔχητε μεθ᾽ ἡμῶν· καὶ ἡ κ. δὲ ἡ ἡμετέρα μετὰ τοῦ πατρὸς καὶ μετὰ τοῦ υἱοῦ αὐτοῦ....Ἐὰν εἴπωμεν ὅτι κ. ἔχομεν μετ᾽ αὐτοῦ...κ. ἔχομεν μετ᾽ ἀλλήλων.

πρός:

2 Cor. vi. 14, τίς κ. φωτὶ πρὸς σκότος; (= contribution towards).

εἰς:

Rom. xv. 26, κ. τινὰ ποιήσασθαι εἰς τοὺς πτωχοὺς τῶν ἁγίων.
2 Cor. ix. 13, δοξάζοντες τὸν Θεὸν ἐπὶ τῇ...ἁπλότητι τῆς κ. εἰς αὐτούς.

There remains Acts ii. 42, which, as it has been so persistently misinterpreted, claims fuller treatment:

ἦσαν προσκαρτεροῦντες τῇ διδαχῇ τῶν ἀποστόλων καὶ τῇ κοινωνίᾳ
τῇ κλάσει τοῦ ἄρτου   καὶ ταῖς προσευχαῖς.

Here κοινωνία is used absolutely, for

(1) According to N.T. usage "communion with" the Apostles would be expressed by μετά or πρός or εἰς.

(2) And if κ. were to be taken with τῶν ἀπ. the Greek would run
τῇ διδαχῇ καὶ τῇ κοινωνίᾳ τῶν ἀποστόλων or τῇ τῶν ἀπ. δ. καὶ κ.

(3) Moreover the rhythm is against this conjunction.

(4) In the succeeding clause it is impossible to take ταῖς προσευχαῖς with τοῦ ἄρτου, as the parallelism would require.

(5) Each part of the phrase would seem to be used technically, as is certainly true of τῇ κλάσει τοῦ ἄρτου, and technically κοινωνία means not "communion with" but "contribution to" or "community of goods".

(6) The succeeding verses are a comment on this. The δ. τῶν ἀπ. was enforced by signs and wonders, v. 43; the κλ. τοῦ ἄ. was κατ᾽ οἶκον, v. 46; the προσευχαί included the θυσία αἰνέσεως, v. 47; and ἡ κ. is explained to mean οἱ πιστεύσαντες εἶχον ἅπαντα κοινά, καὶ τὰ κτήματα καὶ τὰς ὑπάρξεις ἐπίπρασκον καὶ διεμέριζον αὐτὰ πᾶσιν καθότι ἄν τις χρείαν εἶχεν, vv. 44, 45.

(7) The Vulgate translates: perseverantes in doctrina apostolorum et communicatione fractionis panis et orationibus.

Subapostolic Writers

There are few traces of the use of the word in the next age; none in Clement; Ignatius has κοινὴ ἐλπίς three times, κοινὸν ὄνομα once, κοινῇ three times adverbially of common or public action in the Church, εἰς τὸ κοινόν once of ministering to the Church, ἀπὸ τοῦ κοινοῦ once (Polyc. 4. 3) of a common Church fund. Nothing more. The Epistle to Diognetus, 5, says τράπεζαν κοινὴν παρατίθενται, ἀλλ᾽ οὐ κοινήν, with a play on the double sense of the word "in common" or "unclean".

Justin Martyr uses κοινωνία with a descriptive genitive in Ap. II. viii. 5: καὶ ὅτι ἀληθῆ λέγω εἰ μὴ ἀνηνέχθησαν ὑμῖν αἱ κ. τῶν λόγων, ἕτοιμος καὶ ἐφ᾽ ὑμῖν κοινωνεῖν τῶν ἐρωτήσεων.

In the Dialogue with Trypho he has κοινωνεῖν ἀπάντων of Christian liberality in contrast with Jewish exclusiveness. In a disparaging sense he has οὐ γὰρ ὡς κοινὸν ἄρτον οὐδὲ κοινὸν πόμα ταῦτα λαμβάνομεν, in his description of the Eucharist, and desires that Christians abstain from certain kinds of food as κοινά.

In Irenaeus we have κ. followed by a descriptive genitive: πρὸς τῆς συζυγίας κοινωνίαν (adv. H. i. i. 18); and by a partitive: ὅσα τὴν πρὸς Θεὸν τηρεῖ φιλίαν, τούτοις τὴν ἰδίαν παρέχει κοινωνίαν. κοινωνία δὲ Θεοῦ, ζωή, καὶ φῶς, καὶ ἀπέλαυσις τῶν παρ᾽ Αὐτοῦ ἀγαθῶν, an obvious parallel to 2 Pet. i. 4.

And similarly τὴν κοινωνίαν τῶν δυνάμεων in the Marcosian Creed is clearly partitive. Cp. i. vii. 2: ὅσας ἀξίας ἡγεῖται μετόχους τῆς χάριτος αὐτοῦ.

The construction with a preposition is given in the Latin version of IV. xxxi. 2: si quis...non recte dividat eam quae est ad proximum communionem, representing the Greek ἐὰν μὴ ὀρθῶς διέλῃ τὴν πρὸς τὸν πλησίον κοινωνίαν.

And Irenaeus, when describing the agreement of Anicetus and Polycarp to differ about the date of Easter, says: ἐκοινώνησαν ἑαυτοῖς (Euseb. H.E. v. 24), meaning that Anicetus allowed Polycarp to celebrate the Eucharist.

Athenagoras, *Leg.* xii.

With πρός:

τίς ἡ τοῦ Παιδὸς πρὸς τὸν Πατέρα ἑνότης, τίς ἡ τοῦ Πατρὸς πρὸς τὸν Υἱὸν κ.;

Third Century

Origen:

With πρός:

ἵνα ἡ ἀνθρωπίνη τῇ πρὸς τὸ θειότερον κοινωνίᾳ γένηται θεία (c. Cels. iii. 28).

φήσομεν πρὸς αὐτὸν ἐγκαλοῦντα τῷ περὶ τῆς μακαρίας ζωῆς λόγῳ καὶ τῷ περὶ τῆς πρὸς τὸ θεῖον κοινωνίας (ib. iii. 80).

Dionysius of Alexandria:

With πρός:

μὴ τοῦτο εἶναι μηδὲ ὅλως ἔχειν πρὸς ταῦτα κοινωνίαν (ap. Euseb. H.E. vii. 9).

τοῖς μέλεσι πᾶσι τήν τε πρὸς ἄλληλα κοινωνίαν περιέβαλε (Praep. Ev. xiv. 26).

With partitive genitive:

τὴν τοῦ θανάτου διάδοσιν καὶ κοινωνίαν ἐκτρεπόμενοι (H.E. vii. 22).

Liturgies

St Mark: εἰς κ. μακαριότητος ζωῆς αἰωνίου καὶ ἀφθαρσίας.
St Basil: εἰς ἑνὸς Πνεύματος τοῦ Ἁγίου κ.
St Chrysostom: εἰς κ. τοῦ Ἁγίου Σου Πνεύματος.

Fourth Century

Basil:

Partitive:

ὁ μέντοι ἁγιασμὸς...τὴν τελείωσιν αὐτοῖς ἐπάγει διὰ τῆς κ. τοῦ Πνεύματος (de S. S. xvi. 38).

Descriptive:

ἱκανῶς παραδηλοῦν τὴν κ. τῆς φύσεως τοῦ τικτομένου πρὸς τὴν γεννήσασαν (ib. v. 12).

ἐν τῇ κοινωνίᾳ τῆς θεότητός ἐστιν ἡ ἔνωσις (ib. xviii. 45).

With πρός:

ἡ δὲ 'σὺν' τὴν πρὸς Θεὸν κοινωνίαν τοῦ Πνεύματος ἐξαγγέλλει (ib. xxvii. 68).

Gregory of Nyssa:

Partitive:

ὁ ὀφθαλμὸς...ἐν κ. τοῦ φωτὸς γίνεται (Or. Catech. 5).

τῷ αὐτεξουσίῳ κινήματι τοῦ κακοῦ τὴν κ. ἐπεσπασάμεθα (ib. 8).

κοινωνία τῶν κατὰ ἁμαρτίαν παθημάτων γίνεται τῇ τε ψυχῇ καὶ τῷ σώματι (ib. 8).

εἴπερ τὸν ἀπαθῆ κατὰ τὴν φύσιν πρὸς κ. πάθους ἐλθεῖν διορίζονται (ib. 16).

With πρός:

ἡ δὲ τοῦ νοῦ πρὸς τὸ σωματικὸν κ. (de Hom. Opif. 15).

Cyril of Jerusalem:

Partitive:

τούτου τοῦ Ἁγίου Πνεύματος τὴν κ. ἐχαρίσατο (Cat. xvii. 12).

τὸ οὖν ἐπιορκιστὸν ἔλαιον σύμβολον ἦν τῆς κ. τῆς πιότητος τοῦ Χριστοῦ (ib. xix. 3).

κἀμοὶ...διὰ τῆς τοῦ ἄλγους κ. χαρίζεται σωτηρίαν (ib. xx. 3).

ἐκείνη γὰρ κοινωνίαν ἔσχε δαιμόνων, αὕτη δὲ κοινωνίαν Θεοῦ (ib. xx. 6; cp. 1 Cor. x. 16).

With πρός:

τίς σοι πρὸς τοὺς ἀνελπίστους κοινωνία; (ib. xvi. 6).

The rule in Greek theological writers is therefore the same as that in the New Testament, namely, that when a genitive follows κοινωνία it is either possessive, partitive, or descriptive, and that "communion with" is expressed by the use of a preposition. This rule is commonly also maintained by Latin writers, but the exceptions are rather less infrequent.

Partitive:

> Niceta, *de Symbolo*, 10. Ut communionem vitae perpetuae impertiret.
>
> Aug. *c. Ep. Parmenian.* ii. 8. Communione sacramentorum, sicut dicitis, contaminantur.
>
> *de Civ. Dei*, i. 35. Connexos communione sacramentorum nec secum futuros aeterna sorte sanctorum (where "sacramentorum" is a partitive and "sanctorum" a possessive genitive).
>
> *Serm.* 214. Malos... tolerat in communione sacramentorum.

With *cum* or *inter*:

> Aug. *Serm.* 71. xii. 18. Nos voluerunt habere communionem et inter nos et Secum.
>
> *Passio Perpet.* i. Ut... communionem habeatis cum sanctis martyribus et per illos cum Domino Jesu Christo.
>
> Cp. Aug. *Ep.* XLIII. vii. 9. Sed postquam... experti sunt cum Caeciliano permanere communionem orbis terrarum, et ad eum... communicatorias litteras mitti... cur se ipsi ab innocentis orbis terrarum communione praeciderent, cum... sinerent episcopo quem... ordinassent a toto orbe non communicari... totus orbis non eis communicat.

Thus Zahn's statement that ἡ κοινωνία τῶν ἁγίων "could only be interpreted as 'participation in the holy things'"[1] may be too strong; the genitive might conceivably be possessive, but it would undoubtedly be a strain on the Greek to make it mean "communion with holy persons", and though no number of instances could prove that this translation was absolutely impossible, they do illustrate what was the prevailing usage. And the stylistic or grammatical argument is reinforced by the theological. If, as would seem to be the case, the early Church inserted into the Creed only statements of those objective facts on which it held that salvation depended; and if, as was undoubtedly true, the Greek theological mind of the first four centuries was occupied all but exclusively with the consideration of such facts, then κοινωνία τῶν ἁγίων could not be a statement of what Christians did. The early Church emphasized, as we see by the instances quoted, the need of participation in Christ or in the Holy Spirit, but the intercommunion of Christians was a by-product of this common participation.

1 *Articles of the Apostles' Creed*, p. 197.

VI. The Early Interpretation

Having thus excluded certain impossible, or at least improbable, interpretations, we come to one which in the fourth century we may regard as established, even though some later Latin writers departed from it.

(1) *The Council of Nîmes* 394

The Canon of the Council of Nîmes runs:

In primis quia multi, de ultimis Orientis partibus venientes [*sc.* Manichaeans] presbyteros et diaconos se esse confingunt...(qui) sanctorum communione speciae (speciem?) simulatae religionis (*add* sibi) impraemunt (imprimunt): placuit nobis (*add* ut) si qui fuerint ejusmodi ...ad ministerium altarii (altaris) non admittantur.

Here there can be no doubt that what the presbyters and deacons were trying to obtain was the *ministerium altaris*. The action of these Manichaeans could claim in its favour the Canons of the Council of Serdica (343). A bishop if deposed might, except in special cases, enjoy λαϊκῶν κοινωνία, Can. 1.[1] To a legitimate bishop on travel συγχωρητέον εἶναι κρίνω...συνέρχεσθαι καὶ λειτουργεῖν, Can. 12; this was the ἐπισκόπων κοινωνία, cp. Julius's letter (340) τί...ἔδει ποιεῖν ἡμᾶς, ἢ ἔχειν αὐτὸν [Marcellus], ὥσπερ καὶ εἴχομεν ἐπίσκοπον, καὶ μὴ ἀποβάλλειν τῆς κοινωνίας; and the letter of Irenaeus to Victor, καὶ τούτων οὕτως ἐχόντων, ἐκοινώνησαν ἑαυτοῖς, καὶ ἐν τῇ ἐκκλησίᾳ παρεχώρησεν ὁ 'Ανίκητος τὴν εὐχαριστίαν Πολυκάρπῳ. So Charisius at the Council of Ephesus (431) complains of some presbyters of Constantinople that ὡς αἱρετικὸν τῆς κοινωνίας καὶ λειτουργίας ἐκώλυσαν, "refused to communicate him and forbade him to minister".[2]

Compare with the action of the Councils of Serdica and Nîmes the following passages:

Quapropter facere te oportet plenissimas litteras ad coepiscopos nostros...ne ultra Marcianum...insultare patiantur...qui jam pridem

---

1 Cp. 'Εκρίναμεν μὴ μόνον αὐτοὺς ἐπισκόπους μὴ εἶναι, ἀλλὰ μηδὲ κοινωνίας μετὰ τῶν πιστῶν αὐτοὺς καταξιοῦσθαι. Letter of the Council quoted Ath. *Ap.* 49.

2 Mansi, IV. 1343.

jactat...quod...*a communicatione se nostra segregaverit*, cum Novati-
anus...ad nos...legatos misisset optans *ad communicationem nostram
admitti*, hinc...sententiam retulerit, se foris esse coepisse *nec posse a
quoquam nostrum sibi communicari*, qui...*profanum altare erigere* et...
sacrilega contra verum sacerdotem sacrificia offerre tentaverit....Sufficiat
multos illic ex fratribus nostris...*excessisse sine pace* (Cyprian to Pope
Stephen, *Ep.* lxviii).

Addimus...ut etiam *si qui presbyteri aut diaconi*...*contra altare
unum atque divinum sacrificia falsa ac sacrilega offerre conati sint*, eos
quoque hac conditione suscipi, cum revertuntur, ut *communicent laici*
et satis habeant *quod admittuntur ad pacem* (Cyprian and his Council
to Stephen, *Ep.* lxxii).

Qui sic magna et caelestia ecclesiae munera haereticis concedit...
quid aliud agit quam *communicat eis*...? Et frustra jam dubitat in
caeteris quoque consentire eis...ut et simul cum eis conveniat et
orationes pariter cum eisdem misceat et *altare ac sacrificium commune
constituat* (Firmilian, of Pope Stephen, Cypr. *Ep.* lxxv. 17).

Quid enim humilius...ut venientibus non solum *pax et communio*,
sed et tectum et hospitium negaretur? (*ib.* 25).

Council of Antioch, 341, canon 11. If a bishop, priest, or any
other ecclesiastic presumes to go to the Emperor without the
consent of and letters from the bishops of the eparchy, and
especially from the metropolitan, ἀπόβλητον γίνεσθαι, οὐ μόνον
τῆς κοινωνίας, ἀλλὰ καὶ τῆς ἀξίας, ἧς μετέχων τυγχάνει.

So Basil orders in Canon 16 of his letter to Amphilochius:

Διάκονος ἐν χείλεσι μιανθεὶς καὶ μέχρι τούτου μόνου ἡμαρτηκέναι
ὁμολογήσας, τῆς λειτουργίας ἐπισχεθήσεται, τοῦ δὲ μετέχειν τῶν ἁγιασμάτων μετὰ τῶν διακόνων ἀξιωθήσεται· τὸ αὐτὸ καὶ πρεσβύτερος. εἰ δέ τι
τούτου πλεῖον φωραθείη τις ἡμαρτηκώς, ἐν ᾧ ἂν εἴη βαθμῷ καθαιρεθήσεται.

If a bishop or presbyter held that a layman was a heretic, the
public act by which he signified the fact was by refusing to give
him communion; if he were a deacon or presbyter, by refusing
to admit him *ad ministerium altaris*; if a bishop, by refusing to
allow him to celebrate the mysteries; and *per contra*, the public
act by which testimony was given to their orthodoxy was by
admission to the privileges of their respective ranks. To "excommunicate" was quite literally to cut off from participation
in the eucharist.

(2) The Sermon "Simbolum graeca lingua est"

This sermon probably belongs to the first quarter of the seventh century and the neighbourhood of the Lake of Constance, near which was the monastery of St Gallen, whence, through Bâle and Belfort, there would be an easy connexion with Vésoul. The explanation which it gives of *sanctorum communionem* is "Ibi est communicatio sancta (per invocationem) Patris et Filii et Spiritus Sancti, ubi omnes fideles diebus dominicis communicare debent".

(3) Basil and Chrysostom

The words occur in Basil (*Regulae brevius tractatae*, Interrog. cccix) in the phrase τολμᾶν εἰς κοινωνίαν τῶν ἁγίων προσέρχεσθαι, meaning "to dare to make one's communion", and a similar usage is found in a set of canons attributed to the Council of Constantinople,[1] most of which are paralleled in the third Canonical Epistle of Basil to Amphilochius:

Basil, *Ep.* CLXXXVIII, Canon 3. Διάκονος...ἀπόβλητος μὲν τῆς διακονίας ἔσται· εἰς δὲ τὸν τῶν λαϊκῶν ἀπωσθεὶς τόπον, τῆς κοινωνίας οὐκ εἰρχθήσεται.

Canon 1. ἀκοινώνητος ἔσται τῶν ἁγιασμάτων...τότε μεθέξει τῶν ἁγιασμάτων. (=Basil, Canon 56.)

Canon 2. ἀκοινώνητος ἔσται τῶν ἁγιασμάτων...τῷ ἑξῆς εἰς τὸ ἁγίασμα δεχθήσεται. (=Basil, Canon 57, εἰς τὰ ἅγια.)

Canon 6. κωλυθήσεται τῆς τῶν ἁγιασμάτων κοινωνίας. (=Basil, Canon 61.)

Canon 21. εἰ μὲν λαϊκοὶ εἶεν...ἔδοξεν ἐξοδεύουσι μὲν αὐτοῖς τῶν μυστηρίων μεταδίδοσθαι.

Chrys. *In I Ep. ad Cor. Hom.* XXVII. 1. τῆς συνάξεως ἀπαρτισθείσης μετὰ τὴν τῶν μυστηρίων κοινωνίαν ἐπὶ κοινὴν πάντες ᾔεσαν εὐωχίαν.

Here τὰ ἅγια, τὰ ἁγιάσματα, and τὰ μυστήρια are treated as synonyms, as they are in the Liturgies.

Thus in the Liturgy of St James the deacon says: ὅπως γένηται ἡμῖν ἡ μετάληψις τῶν ἁγιασμάτων Αὐτοῦ; while the priest says, ἐπὶ τῇ μεταλήψει τῶν ἀχράντων μυστηρίων. The Liturgy of St Basil has ἀποδεχόμενοι τὴν μερίδα τῶν ἁγιασμάτων Σου, the Apostolic Constitutions μεταλαβεῖν τῶν ἁγίων Σου μυστηρίων, and along with these we must take the regular phrase τὰ ἅγια τοῖς ἁγίοις which Cyril of Jerusalem, his name-

---

1 *J.T.S.* xv. pp. 164–167.

sake of Alexandria, and Chrysostom explain to mean that the consecrated elements are for holy persons.

And as τὰ ἅγια is used liturgically by itself, so also is κοινωνία; thus Eusebius says of the Montanists (H.E. v. 16. 11): οὕτω δὴ τῆς τε ἐκκλησίας ἐξεώθησαν καὶ τῆς κοινωνίας εἴρχθησαν, and, quoting Hippolytus (ib. 28. 4): Victor Θεόδοτον...ἀπεκήρυξε τῆς κοινωνίας; cp. Isidore of Pelusium (5th cent.): κοινωνία κέκληται ἡ τῶν θείων μυστηρίων μετάληψις διὰ τὸ τὴν πρὸς Χριστὸν ἡμῖν χαρίζεσθαι ἕνωσιν καὶ κοινωνοὺς ἡμᾶς τῆς Αὐτοῦ ποιεῖν βασιλείας (Ep. 1. 228).

Indeed this use of κοινωνία, κοινωνεῖν, κοινωνικὰ γράμματα, ἀκοινώνητος, ἀκοινωνησία is too common to need illustration.

(4) Augustine

In Latin κοινωνία in this sense is translated according to the taste of the particular author either by communio or communicatio (cp. communicatio sacra in the sermon Simbolum graeca lingua est), the other words being communicare, excommunicare, excommunicatio.

In place of sanctorum Augustine generally prefers sacramentorum which he seems to use in the plural both of the eucharist: "sicut etiam in hoc paradiso, id est ecclesiae, solent a sacramentis altaris visibilibus homines disciplina ecclesiastica removeri" (de Gen. ad litt. xi. xl. 54) and of more than one sacrament: "Utrum in unitate et eorundem communione sacramentorum mali contaminent bonos" (Retract. ii. 17), and sometimes he adds an epithet: "quamvis...Dei sacramenta communicet cum eis cum quibus in communione divinorum sacramentorum manebat" (cont. Crescon. iii. xxxvi. 40).

On the other hand he can use communio by itself: "Et illud non est tacendum, etiam cognitos malos bonis non obesse in ecclesia, si eos a communione prohibendi aut potestas desit aut..." (Ep. 87).

He only once appears to use communio sanctorum, and then it is in this liturgical sense: "Et removit istos [the Patripassians] ecclesia catholica a communione sanctorum, ne aliquem deciperent, ut separati litigarent" (Serm. lii. 6), "excommunicated them"; cp. the quotation just given from Eusebius about the Montanists. The conclusion that *sanctorum* is here neuter is rendered all but certain by comparing other passages:

> Multi tales sunt in *sacramentorum communione* cum ecclesia et tamen non sunt in ecclesia.... Sicut ergo jam denuo *communicans* nondum insertus est: sic et antequam visibiliter *excommunicetur*, quisquis contra veritatem... inimicum gerens animum, jam praecisus est (*cont. Donat. Ep.* 74).

> Si ad te quisquam catechizandus venerit... difficillimum omnino est ut non multa nostrarum scripturarum litterarumque cognoverit, quibus jam instructus ad *sacramentorum participationem* tantummodo venerit (*de Catech. Rud.* viii. 12).

> Sanctam quoque ecclesiam... honorate...: quae malos in fine separandos, a quibus interim discedit disparilitate morum, tolerat *in communione sacramentorum* (*Serm.* ccxiv. 11).

> Natalis... dixit:... quod haeretici *communicationem* habere nobiscum non possunt, nisi ecclesiastico baptismo baptizati fuerint.

> *Communicationem*, credo, eam dicit, quae pertinet ad columbae societatem: nam *in participatione sacramentorum* procul dubio *communicabant* eis, neminem judicantes, nec a jure *communionis* aliquem, si diversum sentiret, amoventes....Certe enim non *communicet* haereticus, nisi ecclesiastico baptismo baptizatus (*de Bapt. cont. Donat.* vii. xlvii. 92, 93).

No one reading these passages together can doubt that *communio, communicatio, participatio sanctorum* or *sacramentorum* means the same thing as the Greeks called κοινωνία τῶν ἁγίων, ἁγιασμάτων, or μυστηρίων.

(5) *Niceta of Remesiana*

In the light of this evidence we approach the Sermon of Niceta of Remesiana. The whole passage runs:

> Post confessionem beatae Trinitatis iam profiteris te credere sanctae ecclesiae catholicae (*al.* sanctam ecclesiam catholicam). Ecclesia quid est aliud quam sanctorum omnium congregatio? Ab exordio enim saeculi sive patriarchae, Abraham et Isaac et Jacob, sive prophetae, sive apostoli, sive martyres, sive ceteri justi, qui fuerunt, qui sunt, qui erunt, una ecclesia sunt, quia una fide et conversatione sanctificati, uno Spiritu signati, unum corpus effecti sunt: cujus corporis caput Christus esse perhibetur et scriptum est. Adhuc amplius dico. Etiam angeli, etiam virtutes et potestates supernae, in hac una confoederantur ecclesia, apostolo nos docente, quia *in Christo reconciliata sunt omnia, non solum quae in terra sunt, verum etiam quae in caelo.* Ergo in hac una ecclesia credis te communionem consecuturum esse sanctorum. Scito unam

hanc esse ecclesiam catholicam in omni orbe terrae constitutam, cujus communionem debes firmiter retinere. Sunt quidem et aliae pseudo-ecclesiae, sed nihil tibi commune cum illis, ut puta Manichaeorum, Cataphrigarum, Marcionistarum, vel ceterorum haereticorum sive schismaticorum, quia jam desinunt esse ecclesiae istae sanctae, siquidem daemoniacis deceptae doctrinis aliter credunt, aliter agunt, quam Christus Dominus mandavit, quam apostoli tradiderunt. Credis deinde Remissionem peccatorum. Haec est enim ratio gratiae quia credentes, Deum et Christum confitentes, consequuntur per baptisma remissionem suorum omnium peccatorum. Unde et regeneratio dicitur, quia plus homo innocens et purus redditur, quam cum de matris suae utero generatur. Consequenter credis et Carnis tuae resurrectionem et Vitam aeternam. Revera enim, si hoc non credis, frustra in Deum credis. Totum enim, quod credimus, propter nostram credimus resurrectionem. Alioquin, *si in hac vita tantum speramus in Christo, sumus* vere, ut ait apostolus, *miserabiliores omnibus hominibus,* quando utique ad hoc Christus carnem suscepit humanam, ut communionem vitae perpetuae mortali nostrae substantiae impertiret.

There is a natural tendency to imagine that *communio sanctorum* near the middle of the paragraph bears the same sense as *sanctorum omnium congregatio* at the beginning. This is, however, obviously untrue of the phrase as a whole; it would amount to saying that in the *sanctorum omnium congregatio*, the Church, you will obtain the *sanctorum communio*, the Church again; Niceta clearly cannot mean this. Nor can we assume that even the word *sanctorum* by itself has the same meaning in both passages. That interpretation would be natural if the second use of it were in a phrase coined by Niceta; an author might be expected not to use a single word in two distinct senses near together, if in both cases the word were his own; but in the second case *sanctorum communio* is a phrase of the Creed which Niceta is quoting. Nor is the choice of the word *sancti* in the first instance determined by the phrase following. Niceta has interpreted *sancta ecclesia catholica* in the Creed to include the patriarchs, prophets, and angels, whom he could not denominate by the alternatives *Christiani* or *fratres*, but who would all be covered by the word *sancti*. This inference is therefore unjustified, and must not be allowed to bias our interpretation.

"In the Catholic Church alone", says Niceta, "you will obtain the *communio sanctorum*. You must hold fast to your membership in it. There are other false churches, you have *nihil commune cum illis*. Christ took human nature that He might give us *communio vitae perpetuae.*" *Communio* in the last instance means "participation in". In the first instance, it means "membership in", and is not something to be acquired, as given from outside, but something to be retained, as already possessed; between these comes *nihil commune cum*, "nothing in common with". It would seem to follow that *communio sanctorum* is like *cujus communio* and *communio vitae* and unlike *commune cum illis*; that is, the grammatical probability is in favour of *participation in*. But not conclusively so. *Sanctorum* may be a possessive genitive, that *communio* which the *sancti* possess and the heretics do not. But if we ask what it is that the orthodox have and the heretics have not, Niceta furnishes the answer; the heretics do not hold the faith which Christ taught, nor practise the *actiones* which He prescribed. Niceta is not decrying the morals of heretics; they have been deceived by the teaching of devils, so that they have no true faith and no proper *actiones*, and in both respects they differ from the Church. It is difficult not to see in Niceta's language a reference to the common reproof against them, that they imitated or parodied both the Christian Creed and the Christian sacraments. Besides a right faith, the Eastern Church and Africa, in common with the West, claimed an exclusive possession of sacraments. Tertullian, *de Bapt.* 15, says: "There is to us one and but one baptism, as well according to the Lord's gospel as according to the apostle's letters, inasmuch as (he says) 'One God, and one baptism, and one church in the heavens'. But it must be admitted that the question, 'What rules are to be observed with regard to heretics?' is worthy of being discussed. For it is to *us* [catholics] that that assertion refers. Heretics, however, have no fellowship in our discipline, whom the mere fact of their excommunication testifies to be outsiders". And it is difficult also not to think that the *actiones* prescribed by our Lord were, in Niceta's thought, baptism and the eucharist. "I received of the Lord Jesus that which I also delivered unto you", says St Paul, and the word *apostoli* in Niceta clearly means primarily St Paul, as the quotations from his epistles show.

Moreover, Niceta's Creed, which he is translating, reached him from Asia Minor, and Creeds owed their elaboration to opposition to heretics; they stated a truth dogmatically, but the facts stated were, at any rate beyond the bare skeleton, largely selected with a controversial purpose. And in Eastern Creeds *communio sanctorum* occupies for the most part the position taken in other examples by βάπτισμα, and baptism was often emphasized as "one" in the same way as Tertullian asserts.

Thus in the Council of Nîmes, in the sermon *Simbolum graeca lingua est*, and in St Basil, the meaning of the phrase is definite and unambiguous; the phrase itself would seem to go back to Asia Minor before the time of St Basil, probably to the time of Irenaeus. Is not Niceta's homily to be placed in the same group?

VII. LATER INTERPRETATIONS

In later times the phrase in the Creed received a different interpretation in the West, but the arguments employed show that this meaning was not early, and they are confronted by the considerations both theological and grammatical which we have brought forward.

Faustus of Riez

We notice already a change of meaning in the homily of Niceta. In the New Testament all Christians are ἅγιοι by virtue of an act of divine consecration; from the second century onwards ἁγία is almost a standing epithet of the Church as successor to the privileges of the "holy" people; but in Niceta it is suggested that the Church derives its holiness from its members, and not *vice versa*, and these are holy not by virtue of a divine act of consecration, but rather by virtue of their creaturely correspondence with grace. This conception is carried a stage further in Faustus, who seems to distinguish between the catholic Church and the *sancti* who belong to it, and to narrow the denotation of this latter term to martyrs.

Credamus *et* sanctorum communionem, sed sanctos non tam pro Dei parte, quam pro Dei honore veneremur...colamus in sanctis timorem et amorem Dei, non divinitatem Dei; colamus merita, non quae de proprio habent sed quae accipere pro devotione meruerunt. Digne itaque venerandi sunt, dum nobis Dei cultum et futurae vitae desiderium contemptu mortis insinuant.[1]

Here the clause is being used in favour of the growing cultus of the martyrs, which the Aquitanian priest Vigilantius had vainly sought to check.

In another Gallican sermon the defence becomes an intemperate censure of the Vigilantian party. "Illos hic sententia ista confundit qui sanctorum et amicorum Dei cineres non in honore debere esse blasphemant, qui beatorum martyrum memoriam sacrorum reverentia monumentorum colendam esse non credunt. In symbolum praevaricati sunt et Christo in fonte mentiti sunt."[2] "This extravagance was due to local and temporary causes, and disappeared with them; but wherever the new clause travelled, the tendencies of the age secured the transmission with it of the later interpretation."[3]

Another homily, falsely attributed to Augustine (App. *Serm.*242), which is worked into the *Missale Gallicanum vetus*, and seems to have been authorized in some Gallican dioceses for use at the *Traditio Symboli*, reads: "*Sanctorum communionem*: id est, cum illis sanctis qui in hac quam suscepimus fide defuncti sunt, societate et spei communione teneamur"; where we notice the two constructions, of *communio cum* and *communio* with a dependent genitive.

Sermo 240 puts the meaning entirely into the future: "*Sanctorum communionem*: quia dona Sancti Spiritus licet in hac vita diversa sint in singulis, in aeternitate tamen erunt communia in universis, ut quod quisque sanctorum minus habuit in se, hoc in aliena virtute participet".

But in Sermon 241 we seem to get back to the earlier meaning: "Credentes ergo sanctam ecclesiam catholicam, sanctorum habentes communionem, quia ubi fides sancta, ibi est sancta communio, credere vos quoque in corporum resurrectionem et remissionem peccatorum oportet. Omne sacramentum baptismi in hoc constat, ut resurrectionem corporum et remissionem

---

1 Caspari, *Anecdota*, I. p. 338.   2 Caspari, *Alte und neue Quellen*, p. 273.
3 Swete, *Apostles' Creed*, p. 85.

peccatorum nobis a Deo praestanda credamus". In this sermon both Kattenbusch and Zahn hold that *sanctorum communionem* must mean communion in holy things; and here also we have the same collocation of faith and sacraments which we find in Niceta. The sermon is generally supposed to be Gallican, but Kattenbusch thinks it was known to Priminius and may possibly be Irish.

Though overlaid, this earlier meaning persisted locally. Peter Abelard (*Expos. in Symb. Ap.* Migne, *P.L.* CLXXVIII. 630), after offering other explanations, adds: "possumus et *sanctorum* dicere neutraliter, id est, sanctificati panis et vini in sacramentum altaris". Ivo of Chartres (*ib.* CLXII. 606) combines both interpretations: "id est ecclesiasticorum sacramentorum veritatem cui communicaverunt sancti, qui in unitate fidei de hac vita migraverunt".

A trilingual MS. in Anglo-Saxon, Norman-French, and Latin in the Library of Trinity College, Cambridge (R. 17), *c.* 1125, gives:

> Halegan hiniennesse
> La communion des seintes choses
> Sanctorum communionem.

In the *Lay Folk's Mass Book* (thirteenth century) we read:

> Wel I trow in tho holi gost,
> And holi kirc that is so gode;
> And so I trow that housel es
> bothe flesshe & blode.

In *Pierce the Ploughmans Crede* (late fourteenth century):

> And in the heighe holly gost · holly y beleue,
> And generall holy chirche also · hold this in thy minde;
> And in the sacrement also · that sothfast God on is,
> Fullich his fleche & his blod · that for us dethe tholede.

The Sarum *Office for the Visitation of the Sick* comprises both meanings: "Dearest Brother, dost thou believe in...the communion of saints; that is that all men who live in charity are partakers of all the gifts of grace which are dispensed in the Church, and that all who have fellowship with the just here in the life of grace have fellowship with them in glory?"[1]

1 Maskell, *Mon. Rit.* I. 92.

Pearson[1] says κοινωνία τῶν ἁγίων may be as well understood in the neuter as the masculine, and instances

Ἐξαρεῖ Ἀαρὼν τὰ ἁμαρτήματα τῶν ἁγίων (Ex. xxviii. 34).

Καὶ ἁμάρτῃ ἀκουσίως ἀπὸ τῶν ἁγίων Κυρίου (Lev. v. 15).

Καὶ προσεχέτωσαν ἀπὸ τῶν ἁγίων τῶν υἱῶν Ἰσραήλ (Lev. xxii. 2).

Ἄρχοντες τῶν ἁγίων καὶ ἄρχοντες Κυρίου (1 Chr. xxiv. 5).

The Catechism of the Council of Trent (*P.I.* ix. p. 25) says that *sanctorum communio* is a kind of explanation ("veluti explicatio quaedam") of the article on the Church, but continues: "Hac autem sanctorum communione sacramentorum communionem intelligi debere Patres in symbolo significant illis verbis: Confiteor unum baptisma. Baptismum vero in primis eucharistia, et deinceps caetera sacramenta consequuntur".

VIII. Conclusion

All the available evidence seems to point to Asia Minor for the origin of this phrase in the Creed. The Creed of Niceta doubtless came thence to Remesiana; the Creed of Armenia was also imported from the same region. The limitation of the phrase to localities on or near the great road which ran to Spain and Northern France, and the movement of other Creed phrases along it from East to West, tell the same tale. Moreover, though the official Christian language of Nîmes was Latin, yet the inhabitants probably also understood Greek, and that was the means of communication with those coming from the far East; the Creed of Remesiana came to it in Greek and Niceta is translating it, or using a previous translation, to a Latin-speaking audience; St Basil of course wrote Greek, and in Greek Armenia was evangelized.

Nor is it difficult to understand the purpose of the incorporation of the phrase into the Creed. The Creeds of Asia Minor, like Creeds elsewhere, were positive in language, but to a large extent controversial in the motive of their enlargement. It is to this that we must almost certainly ascribe their repetition of the word "one" in its various connexions.

1 Note (c) on this Article in his *Exposition of the Creed.*

"Oneness" is insisted upon by St Paul for the most part in controversy with Judaistic teachers. Accordingly, when at a later date protest was raised against heresy, the language to be employed was already at hand. This stage was reached at least as early as the letters of Ignatius. In his epistle to the Ephesians we read:

Some are wont of malicious guile to hawk about the Name.... These men...are mad dogs, biting by stealth; against whom ye ought to be on your guard for they are hard to heal. There is one only Physician of flesh and spirit...Jesus Christ our Lord.

In the epistle to the Trallians, 6, 7:

I exhort you, therefore...take ye only Christian food, and abstain from strange herbage, which is heresy; for these men do even mingle poison with Jesus Christ.... Be ye therefore on your guard against such men.... He that is within the sanctuary (ὁ ἐντὸς θυσιαστηρίου) is clean, but he that is without the sanctuary is not clean.

And against heresy Ignatius insists on the maintenance of unity:

It is profitable for you to be in blameless unity, that ye may be partakers of God always (*Eph.* 4).

Abstain from noxious herbs, which are not the husbandry of Jesus Christ.... Not that I have found divisions among you, but infiltration. ...As many as shall repent and enter into the unity of the Church, they also shall be of God (*Philad.* 2).

Be ye careful therefore to observe one eucharist (for there is one flesh of our Lord Jesus Christ and one cup unto union in His blood; there is one altar (θυσιαστήριον) as there is one bishop together with the presbytery and the deacons my fellow-servants), that whatever ye do, ye may do it after God (*ib.* 5).

"Of all the fathers of the Church, early or late, none is more incisive or more persistent in advocating the claims of the threefold ministry to allegiance than Ignatius.... Yet with himself this subject, prominent as it is, was secondary.... The ecclesiastical order was enforced by him almost solely as a security for doctrinal purity. The unity of the body was a guarantee of the unity of the faith" (Lightfoot, *Ap. Fathers*, Pt. II, vol. I, pp. 39–40).

Mark ye those that hold strange doctrine touching the grace of Jesus Christ which came to us, how they are contrary to the mind of God.

...They abstain from eucharist and prayer because they allow not that the eucharist is the flesh of our Saviour Jesus Christ.

Let no man do ought of things pertaining to the Church apart from the bishop. Let that be held a valid eucharist which is under the bishop or one to whom he shall have committed it. Wheresoever the bishop shall appear there let the people be; even as where Jesus may be, there is the universal Church. It is not lawful apart from the bishop either to baptize or to hold a love-feast (*Smyrn.* 6 and 8).

It is therefore fairly certain that the "oneness" of the Church and the "oneness" of baptism were insisted on in the Creed as protests against heresy; and this language went back to the time of Ignatius to whom we may also trace the use of the epithet "catholic". But Ignatius did but emphasize language already familiar through the Epistles of St Paul. If we were to select from the Pauline Epistles phrases which speak of the one common heritage of the Church we could in fact construct a formula having a close resemblance to the later Christian Creed.

> There is one faith (in)
> One God the Father of all
> One Lord Jesus Christ
> One Spirit
> One Church
> One Baptism
> One Bread
> One hope of our calling, i.e. everlasting life.

It is therefore highly probable that the Marcosian Creed parodies a Christian Creed enlarged from the baptismal formula in opposition to heresies of a docetic or gnostic type; and it is noticeable also that the phrase "communion of saints" not only occupies the place taken in most Eastern Creeds by baptism, but that the three Eastern Creeds, those of Jerome, Niceta and the Armenian Creed, which contain the words "communion of saints", contrary to common Eastern usage omit the mention of baptism, while the Creed of Priscillian, which possesses other Eastern features, and is somewhat later than that of Niceta, has *In sanctam ecclesiam, Spiritum Sanctum, Baptismum salutare,* but not "communion of saints"; it would look as if baptism were already implied in the corresponding phrase, and along with baptism—including the confirmation which completed it—the eucharist. Certainly if some Eastern Creeds made belief in baptism a point of faith, there is nothing strange if others put with baptism the second great Christian sacrament under a common designation of the two. Τὰ ἅγια is a regular expression in the liturgies for the consecrated elements; the actual phrase κοινωνία τῶν ἁγίων occurs in St Basil, and its equivalent in the Canon of the Council of Nîmes, though there it is used to include not merely the *jus communicationis*, but also the *ministerium altaris*.

Throughout the sermon of Niceta the liturgical reference is unmistakable. Put together *In hac una ecclesia credis te communionem consecuturum esse sanctorum; credentes...consequuntur per baptisma remissionem peccatorum; haeretici sive schismatici ...aliter agunt quam Christus Dominus mandavit, quam apostoli tradiderunt; ad hoc Christus carnem suscepit humanam, ut communionem vitae perpetuae...mortali nostrae substantiae impertiret*, and compare with this last clause, which is almost certainly based on a phrase in the Liturgy itself, οὕτως καὶ τὰ σώματα ἡμῶν μεταλαμβάνοντα τῆς εὐχαριστίας μηκέτι εἶναι φθαρτά, τὴν ἐλπίδα τῆς εἰς αἰῶνας ἀναστάσεως ἔχοντα (Iren. *adv. Haer.* IV. xxxi. 3), and with the former: οἱ γὰρ ἀπόστολοι... οὕτως παρέδωκαν ἐντετάλθαι αὐτοῖς· τὸν Ἰησοῦν λαβόντα ἄρτον κ.τ.λ. (Justin, *Ap.* I. 66), and "Eucharistiae sacramentum et in tempore victus et omnibus mandatum a Domino sumimus" (Tert. *de Cor. Mil.* 3).

The allusions are covert and suggestive rather than explicit, but that is precisely what we should expect. Niceta's homily is more than once reminiscent of Cyril's catechetical lectures, and Cyril says: "Nor before catechumens do we discourse plainly about mysteries; but many things many times we speak in a covert manner, that the faithful who know may understand, and that those who know not may receive no harm" (vi. 29).[1] If the

---

1 Cp. Tert. *Apol.* vii; Basil, *de Spirit. S.* xxvii; Lact. *Inst.* vii, xxv; *Can. Hipp.* 29 and 30.

faithful who were familiar with "holy things to holy persons" in the Liturgy and with the meaning of "communion", "communicate", "excommunicate", heard Niceta say that only in the catholic Church could they obtain "*communionem sanctorum*" they would hardly hesitate as to what meaning was to be attached to the phrase. It is at any rate certain that the meaning "communion with the saints" was introduced later when the cult of the martyrs was coming into vogue, and that the words "the saints" meant in earlier times all Christians. Nor is it at all easy to say that *communio sanctorum* is that *communio* which Christians have as such. The possessors of the *communio* would be spoken of not distributively, but corporately, as "the Church"; the fact that the two words are used would be nearly sufficient in itself to show that a distinction of meaning was intended; the participation which the Church possesses and heretics do not is "participation in the holy things"; and this distinction is emphasized when the two phrases "the holy catholic Church" and "the communion of saints" are separated either in actual position or in distribution into sections.

For those who think that there is an inner logic which lies behind the structure of the Creeds, the mention of "baptism" or "the communion of saints" fills what would otherwise be a logical hiatus. The work of salvation is stated to be accomplished in our Lord by the end of the second paragraph; it is regarded as the possession of believers in the closing words "eternal life", or the "life of the coming world"; but without the mention of the sacraments there is nothing to state the means by which the benefits won by Christ are bestowed.

The present writer cannot help feeling that we are haunted by a sort of semi-pelagian subjectivism. Our minds are dwelling disproportionately on what we can or ought to do. Our idea of God is in danger of becoming an idea of a God who is merely there as an object to be looked at, contemplated, and admired, but not that of a God who at the cost of immeasurable self-sacrifice takes, has taken, and will take, a part in the history of the world and of the life of the individual, the power and effectiveness and importance of which it is impossible to exaggerate. It is in consequence difficult for us to throw ourselves back into the mind of the Church in earlier ages, when it was God and His mighty works which the Christian was exhorted to study, and by studying to learn the art of worship. Yet this is the entire burden of those hymns of thanksgiving, the Creeds. These facts, as at least the Church held them to be, are there stated as manifestations of God's glorious power, and the foundations of Christian hope. It is not the merits or efficiency of our fellows that the Church invites us to think about or demands that we should recognize, but certain characteristic acts of God, whom it proclaims as the Creator, the Ruler, and the Saviour of the world.

PERSONS: ANCIENT

PERSONS: MODERN

COUNCILS

CREEDS, *SEE ALSO* PERSONS, COUNCILS AND DOCUMENTS

DOCUMENTS, ETC.

PHRASES, ETC.

CAMBRIDGE: PRINTED BY W. LEWIS, M.A., AT THE UNIVERSITY PRESS